PRIVATE
AFFLUENCE
PUBLIC
AUSTERITY

PRIVATE AFFLUENCE PUBLIC AUSTERITY

Economic Crisis &
Democratic Malaise
in Canada

Stephen McBride
& Heather Whiteside

Fernwood Publishing
Halifax & Winnipeg

Editing: Mary Beth Tucker
Cover design: John van der Woude
Printed and bound in Canada by Hignell Book Printing

Published in Canada by Fernwood Publishing
32 Oceanvista Lane
Black Point, Nova Scotia, B0J 1B0
and 748 Broadway Avenue, Winnipeg, Manitoba, R3G 0X3
www.fernwoodpublishing.ca

Fernwood Publishing Company Limited gratefully acknowledges the financial support of the
Government of Canada through the Canada Book Fund, the Canada Council for the Arts, the
Nova Scotia Department of Tourism and Culture and the Province of Manitoba, through the Book
Publishing Tax Credit, for our publishing program.

Library and Archives Canada Cataloguing in Publication

McBride, Stephen
Private affluence, public austerity: Economic crisis and democratic malaise in Canada / Stephen
McBride, Heather Whiteside.

Includes bibliographical references and index.
ISBN 978-1-55266-430-8 (bound).—ISBN 978-1-55266-403-2 (pbk.)

1. Canada—Economic policy—21st century. 2. Canada—Politics
and government—21st century. 3. Neoliberalism—Canada. 4. Global
Financial Crisis, 2008-2009. 5. Canada—Economic conditions.
I. Whiteside, Heather, 1982- II. Title.

HC115.M348 2011   330.971   C2010-908049-1

CONTENTS

1. THE NEOLIBERAL CHICKENS COME HOME TO ROOST 1

Neoliberal Financial Crises and the
International Financial Architecture 2
The 2007 Financial Crisis 4
Policy Responses 5
Canada's Response 10
Conclusion 16

2. THEORIES OF CAPITALIST CRISES 18

Long Waves 20
Harvey: Overaccumulation and Spatio-Temporal Fixes 28
Policy Paradigms 31
Conclusion 33

3. THE KEYNESIAN WELFARE STATE 35

Keynes's Theory of Crisis 36
The Keynesian Welfare State — Social Base 39
The Keynesian Welfare State — Programs in Canada 40
Institutional Base 45
Crisis of the Keynesian Welfare State 47
Conclusion 50

4. THE NEOLIBERAL STATE 52

The Neoliberal Account of the Crisis of Keynesianism 52
Globalization and Neoliberalism 55
Free Trade and the Social Base of Neoliberalism 57
The Neoliberal State at Home 58
Institutions in the Neoliberal Era 72
Conclusion 78

5. A TALE OF THREE CRISES 80

Recession in the 1980s: The First Crisis of Neoliberalism in Canada 83
Recession in the 1990s: The Second Crisis of Neoliberalism in Canada 86
Global Financial Meltdown and the
Attempt to Restore "Business as Usual" 90
Conclusions 91

6. CANADA'S COMPOUNDED POLITICAL CRISIS 92

Neoliberalism and Democratic Malaise 92
The Democratic Deficit 95
Rise of Democratic Malaise 96
Erosion of Civil Liberties 98
Lack of Knowledge about the Political System 101
Inequalities Generated by Neoliberalism 106
The Relationship between Neoliberal Inequalities
and Democratic Malaise 107
International Priorities 108
Conclusion 110

CONCLUSIONS 112

The Legacy of Neoliberalism 112
The Future of Neoliberalism 113
Canada, the G-20, and the Search for Exit Strategies 120
The Conditions for Change 121

NOTES 124
BIBLIOGRAPHY 127
INDEX 147

Chapter 1

THE NEOLIBERAL CHICKENS COME HOME TO ROOST

Unlike previous financial crises in the 1990s and early 2000s, the global economic crisis that began in 2007 originated in the U.S., the heartland of global capitalism and its ideological twin, neoliberalism. The financial and banking sectors were affected first as a slumping housing market in late 2006 led in 2007 to revelations of toxic financial assets associated with subprime lending markets.[1] Within another year many significant investment banks in the U.S. had collapsed (for example, Bear Stearns in March and Lehman Brothers in September 2008), as had mortgage giants Fannie Mae and Freddie Mac. All were bailed out by the federal government through massive debt purchasing schemes. Reflecting the ideological tenor of the times these were often labeled "pre-privatization" measures rather than the partial nationalizations that they actually were. These bailouts were significant, and various U.S. government agencies have committed to or spent trillions of dollars in loans, asset purchases, guarantees, and direct spending on bailouts related to the crisis (Goldman n.d.). Financial market woes also revealed serious accumulation problems within the so-called real economy, as stock markets began to tumble: in November 2008 the S&P was down nearly 45 percent compared to its 2007 high (Altman 2009). The big three auto manufacturers also became insolvent, and again this sector was bailed out by the U.S. taxpayer, as $17.4 billion in emergency loans were extended in 2009 (MSNBC 2008). Because of the highly integrated North American auto industry these bailouts were ultimately cost-shared between the U.S. and Canadian governments.

What began as a U.S. banking and financial market crisis quickly spread around the world, particularly to countries such as the U.K., which had highly internationalized financial sectors, highly leveraged banks, and a high level of exposure to toxic assets associated with the U.S. subprime mortgage market. Bailouts and de facto nationalization of banks and financial institutions were also undertaken elsewhere around the world in order to combat the crisis. Similarly, the internationalization of financial markets quickly exposed other underlying problems within the global economy generally, such as overheated housing markets, overproduction, and credit-reliant consumption. Thus a U.S. financial crisis quickly turned into a global economic crisis.

Global recession soon followed. Core neoliberal countries with interest rates at already historical lows — so low that monetary tools were essentially exhausted — began to engage in Keynesian-style stimulus spending in order to help ease economic woes and jump-start recovery. While the experiment in fiscal stimulus may have been effective in averting a deeper recession, and while many in the mainstream media suggested that this indicated a significant policy shift was underway, upon closer examination we see that stimulus was instead relatively shallow, selective, and temporary. Despite the clear need for government intervention in order to help cushion the blow of the financial crisis and subsequent economic recession, there has been little intrusion on neoliberal ideological dominance. This is made evident by the content of the stimulus packages, and in this chapter we briefly examine those of the U.S., U.K., Germany, and Canada. Despite differences in emphasis, including the proportion of stimulus provided through spending versus tax reduction measures, they are equally timid and do not indicate a break with neoliberal rule. The Canadian government in particular appears to have taken a typical approach to crisis management — denial, minimalism, and policy harmonization with the U.S. In the face of a crisis of these dimensions, the disinclination to re-examine fundamental policy choices that had been made over previous decades is striking.

Neoliberal Financial Crises and the International Financial Architecture

The recent global financial crisis is only the latest occurrence of instability and volatility in the neoliberal era. There has been a series of spectacular and mostly unpredicted financial crises in emerging markets; for example, Mexico in 1994–95, East Asia in 1997–98, Russia 1998, Turkey 2000, and Argentina 2001–03 (Kenen 2001). A key source of trouble intrinsic to the neoliberal global governance model has been the lack of clear leadership with respect to the regulation of global financial flows. Instead, governance of the international financial architecture (IFA) consists of a web of public and private forums, institutions, and organizations which together play varied, overlapping, and/or discrete roles in the functioning of capital markets. This group includes international financial institutions, such as the International Monetary Fund (IMF), World Bank, Bank for International Settlements (BIS), and regional development banks; private regulatory and standard setting bodies, such as the International Accounting Standards Board and rating agencies; international organizations, such as United Nations agencies; and multilateral forums, such as the G-7; and the Organisation for Economic Cooperation and Development (OECD); and a host of national regulations that are not always synchronized with one another.

A recognition that recurring crises in international capital markets might become chronic began to emerge in the mid-1990s, yet suggestions for reform were largely monopolized by neoliberal technocratic interventions. Common to this line of reasoning was that enhanced standards, information, and transparency were the key to quelling instability and contagion. Further, since financial market crises have in the past been centred on emerging markets, national policy-oriented suggestions, which placed the onus on domestic reform in those countries, were also popular. For instance, initial suggestions for reform of the IFA were issued by the G-7 following the Halifax summit of 1995. It called for crisis prevention through the adoption of sound monetary and fiscal policies within each country, as well as greater surveillance of national economic policies, financial market events, and data dissemination (Pelaez and Pelaez 2005).

Over the years the belief that the policies of developing countries and other minor technical regulatory issues were to blame for episodes of financial crisis came to assume a dominant position in suggestions for reform of the IFA. It became standard for developing countries to be "urged to adopt measures such as tight national prudential regulations to manage debt, higher stocks of international reserves and contingent lines as a safeguard against speculative attacks, and tight monetary and fiscal policies to secure market confidence, while maintaining an open capital account and convertibility" (Akyuz 2000: 2). This tendency to blame the emerging market economies at the centre of financial meltdowns clearly ignored the systemic nature of instability that results from deregulated global financial markets and the wild speculative behaviours of investors operating most often from within the core neoliberal economies.

Furthermore, best practice advice offered to emerging markets was often in contradiction to activities taking place in the neoliberal heartland. Within the wider context of a neoliberal push to deregulate finance in the late 1970s and early 1980s, a series of policy and regulatory bungles were also committed by the U.S. in the early 2000s and directly contributed to the crash of 2007–2008. These should have warned of looming disaster as U.S. policies read like a laundry list of don'ts. One could even argue that it was a crisis waiting to happen. A few examples are particularly revealing:

- In 2000–01 the U.S. Federal Reserve lowered the Federal Funds rate 11 times, from 6.5 percent in May 2000 to 1.75 percent in December 2001. In 2003 Federal Reserve Chair Alan Greenspan lowered the key interest rate to 1 percent, the lowest it had been in forty-five years (Federal Reserve n.d.).
- Low interest rates combined with prior deregulation and poor oversight of financial markets created an environment of cheap credit that fueled the growth of U.S. subprime mortgages and imprudent lending generally. From 2003 to 2007 U.S. subprime mortgages increased by 292 percent, from $332 (U.S.) billion to 1.3 trillion (Bernanke 2008).
- In October 2004 the U.S. Securities and Exchange Commission effectively

suspended the net capital rule for five firms: Goldman Sachs, Merrill Lynch, Lehman Brothers, Bear Stearns, and Morgan Stanley. The net capital rule limited the amount of debt these institutions could assume, and without it they began to engage in very risky business — buying massive amounts of mortgage-backed securities, which were often leveraged 20, 30, or 40 to 1 (Labaton 2008).

- As early as January 2005 serious concerns over subprime lending practices began to surface. Federal Reserve Governor Edward Gramlich even warned that a portion of the industry was veering close to a breakdown. However, no specific policy action was recommended, or taken (Kirchhoff 2005).

The 2007 Financial Crisis

By early 2007 the U.S. subprime industry, worth at that time an estimated $1.3 trillion, was poised for collapse. It began in February when Mortgage Lenders Network U.S.A., the country's fifteenth largest subprime lender, filed for Chapter 11 bankruptcy protection. This was followed by several other lenders including New Century Financial, Accredited Home Lenders Holding, and Countrywide Financial, which announced significant losses, declared bankruptcy, or put themselves up for sale.

In August 2007 a world-wide credit crunch began to emerge, as subprime mortgage-backed securities were discovered in the portfolios of banks and hedge funds around the world. French investment bank BNP Paribas announced the first of many credit losses and write-downs due to a "complete evaporation of liquidity" in the subprime market (*New York Times* 2007). This announcement triggered the first attempt in a series of coordinated central bank efforts to re-inject liquidity into global capital markets. The European Central Bank pumped 156 billion euros ($214.6 billion U.S.) into the European banking market in August 2007; the U.S. Federal Reserve injected $43 billion (U.S.); the Bank of Japan committed 1 trillion yen ($8.4 billion U.S.); and smaller amounts came from the Australian and Canadian central banks (Moore 2007). In October a consortium of U.S. banks backed by the federal government also announced that they had created a super fund of $100 billion (U.S.) to purchase mortgage-backed securities whose value plummeted with the subprime collapse (Tett et al. 2007).

In 2008 the subprime disaster began to spread into other sectors of the economy. Global stock markets were soon affected, and in March alone the Dow Jones Industrial Average fell by more than 20 percent. Bankruptcies and collapses of key institutions also began: in March, Bears Stearns was purchased for $2 a share by JP Morgan Chase in order to avoid bankruptcy (Sorkin 2008); in July, Indymac Bank was placed in receivership, representing the fourth largest bank failure in U.S. history (Shalal-Esa 2008); and losses of $435 billion (U.S.) were reported on July 17 by major banks and financial institutions that had borrowed and invested heavily in mortgage-backed securities (Fineman and Keoun 2008). In September 2008, the troubles worsened as the federal government was forced to take over Fannie Mae and Freddie Mac (which at that point owned or guaranteed about half of the U.S. mortgage market); Merrill Lynch was sold to Bank of America; Lehman Brothers filed for bankruptcy; and Washington Mutual was seized by the Federal Deposit Insurance Corporation and its assets were sold to JP Morgan Chase for $1.9 billion (Duhigg 2008; BBC 2008; CNBC 2008).

By October 2008, stock markets had become seriously affected. During the week of October 6–11, the U.S. stock market suffered its worst week in seventy-five years (Bajaj 2008). The Dow Jones declined 22.1 percent, its worst week on record, and the S&P index lost 18.2 percent, its worst since 1933. The week concluded with the highest volatility day ever recorded for the Dow Jones in its 112-year history. From the highs experienced in early 2007, paper losses on U.S. stocks totaled $8.4 trillion (U.S.) by October 11, 2008.

Policy Responses

Despite clear warning signs that the liquidity boom, low short-term interest rates, and inflated equity prices were unsustainable and could likely precipitate a market crash once investor confidence was lost, market mechanisms were relied upon and risk-taking behaviour was continually encouraged by policy makers world-wide (Liu 2007). Although the crisis had clearly hit as early as mid- to late-2007, it took a 2008 IMF declaration that the U.S. was in the grips of "the largest financial crisis… since the Great Depression" (Stewart 2008) to spur on a concerted effort on the part of policy makers to interfere with markets and take decisive, coordinated action. Policy interventions seriously lagged behind market realities. It was not until October 11, 2008, that the G-7 met in Washington, agreeing to urgent and unprecedented coordination in an attempt to avoid a global depression, yet even then no concrete plan for dealing with the crisis was announced. One month later, on November 15, 2008, the G-20 also met in Washington to discuss policy harmonization. The principles that emerged from this meeting were consistent with earlier technocratic proposals to reform the IFA: strengthening transparency and accountability, improving regulation, promoting market integrity, and reinforcing cooperation. Some members of the G-20, notably France and Germany, desired more rigorous reform of international institutions and even the creation of a new international organization capable of managing and/or regulating global financial markets.

Thus far there has yet to be any significant reform of the IFA. This is not to say that there has been no progress, as some improvements have been made to financial market-related policies, particularly those of the IMF and Financial Stability Board (FSB), but the deep reforms that are required to resolve the inherent structural flaws of the neoliberal financial order and its propensity for crisis have yet to even be agreed upon by policy makers, let alone legislated and implemented.[2] Instead, efforts have focused on easing the credit crunch by injecting capital into financial markets and engaging in coordinated reductions to central bank interest rates, as well as shoring up faltering banks and corporations through taxpayer-funded bailouts. This was followed by fairly shallow and temporary Keynesian-style stimulus (typically lasting from only 2008–2010) in an effort to jump-start economies that had plunged into recession.

We will now briefly review the actions taken by policy makers in an effort to help thwart the crisis. It reveals just how narrow the policy reaction has been, and the degree to which neoliberal commitments remain entrenched. It is particularly interesting to note that the preferred policy instrument of the neoliberal era — monetary policy — was ruled out early on as an effective strategy given that interest rates were already at rock bottom levels, and thus proved to be utterly useless as a mechanism of economic stimulus. Instead public sector support for capital and labour took the form of bailouts and stimulus packages, the latter designed to be temporary and the former remaining consistent with private sector debt socialization as a familiar neoliberal practice.

Monetary Policy
Policy harmonization with respect to deep interest rate cuts were agreed to by central banks around the world — including the U.S., England, China, Canada, Sweden, Switzerland, and Europe — in October 2008, with rates lowered to roughly 1.5 percent by early 2009, representing historically significant lows; for example, for the Bank of Canada, 1.5 percent was the lowest it had been since 1958; and for the Bank of England, 1.5 percent was its lowest in 315 years. This effectively exhausted the ability to achieve further economic stimulus through this means.

Bailouts
A string of bailouts drawing on billions of taxpayer dollars also took place around the world (although principally in the U.S.), often resulting in the de facto nationalization of huge private sector banks and other financial institutions. Examples include the February 17, 2008, nationalization of Northern Rock by the U.K. government; the October 14, 2008, announcement by the U.S. federal government that $250 billion (U.S.) of public money would be pumped into the U.S. banking system; the November 24, 2008, U.S. government $45 billion (U.S.) rescue of the global giant Citigroup; the January 9, 2009, German government investment of 10 billion (euros) into

Commerzbank, the second largest lender in the country; the January 15, 2009, U.S. government bailout of Bank of America to the tune of $20 billion (U.S.) in capital injections and a guarantee of $118 billion (U.S.) of potential losses on toxic assets; and the Irish government nationalization of the Anglo Irish Bank, the country's third largest lender, on January 15, 2009. In total, the U.S. Troubled Asset Relief Program, set up to purchase assets and equity from financial institutions, has committed $89 billion (U.S.) of taxpayer money as of April 2010 (Bansal 2010). When financial market woes revealed trouble within the real economy, the part that actually produces goods and services as opposed to simply engaging in financial transactions, hard-hit sectors like auto manufacturing were also bailed out by the taxpayer. In the U.S., for example, the big three — GM, Ford, Chrysler — received $17.4 billion (U.S.) in emergency loans in 2009 (MSNBC 2008). In the neoliberal world-view, such offerings of public funds must, of course, be repaid through future reductions in public spending. Much political discussion at the time of writing centres on how soon this can begin with deep public sector austerity now imminent.

In the midst of these billion-dollar bailouts a scandal emerged surrounding the amounts handed out in 2009 to corporate executives as compensation and bonuses rewarding performance at a time of financial catastrophe and great economic hardship for many. AIG was at the centre of the scandal, having just received an emergency government loan of $85 billion (U.S.), yet rewarding its traders with $165 million (U.S.) in bonuses (Newman 2009). Given that these were typically the same people whose reckless behaviour precipitated the crisis to begin with, public reaction was predictably hostile. In 2010 U.S. President Obama used the public outcry as leverage to support his proposal for a bank tax as a way of recouping taxpayer dollars and even avoiding future bailouts at taxpayer expense, stating that "if these companies are in good enough shape to afford massive bonuses, they are surely in good enough shape to afford paying back every penny to taxpayers" (MSNBC 2010a). While the idea of a bank tax gained some support at the G-20, Canada refused to go along with the measure, which encouraged Australia, Japan, Brazil, and Switzerland to help scuttle the idea (*Montreal Gazette* 2010).

Stimulus Packages

United States
The serious financial and banking sector troubles experienced in the U.S. economy beginning in late 2007 were quickly compounded by recession. Real GDP declined in every quarter starting in Q3 2008, when oil prices peaked (IMF 2009a) with growth only beginning to pick up again in Q3 of 2009 (BEA 2010). However, in retrospect, economists now agree that the U.S. recession had already begun as early as December 2007. The significant economic turmoil, dubbed the Great Recession, led Congress to pass the October 2008 stimulus

package, the largest in the world — worth $700 million (U.S.). By March 2009 this had grown to $804,070 million (U.S.), or 5.9 percent of 2008 GDP (OECD 2009a). The U.S. stimulus package was split evenly between revenue measures and spending measures. On the revenue side, there were sizeable cuts made to personal income tax, as well as corporate tax cuts; on the spending side, large investments in infrastructure such as roads, public transit, and high speed rail were made (with a protectionist Buy American clause attached). Some measure of relief was provided for working- and middle-class families through a temporary expansion in unemployment insurance generosity (ibid.). Other spending measures involved funding the modernization of the health care sector (for example, through the digitization of patient records) and upgrading laboratories, classrooms, and libraries (ibid.).

Overall, the crisis response contained comparatively weak active labour market policies, and what was provided to cushion the blow of the recession came late in the U.S. compared with other advanced economies (OECD 2009b). Employment measures associated with crisis containment involved a reinforcement of the social safety net for workers through temporary extensions of unemployment benefits as well as wider coverage of benefits (ibid.). Expanded educational and training options for the unemployed were also offered. Thus the labour market policy reaction to the crisis focused mainly on income safeguards and external flexibility and as such complemented rather than contradicted the maintenance of a neoliberal policy stance overall.

United Kingdom
The British government has been congratulated by the IMF for having pursued "aggressive policy measures" to ensure that the financial sector did not break down. The policies included: injections of public capital into weak banks; provision of liquidity into the banking sector; and insuring troubled assets (Iakova 2009). Despite these aggressive measures, a deep recession set in during fall 2008. This was the first recession to hit the U.K. since the early 1990s (Guillen n.d.). Like many other countries, the U.K. also committed to a fiscal stimulus package. Total stimulus, as of March 2009, came to roughly $38 million U.S. (just under 1.9 percent of GDP), which was much smaller than that of the U.S. (OECD 2009a). It also differed from the American stimulus package in that it committed nearly all funds to tax cuts and other revenue measures, offering very little by way of spending measures. This was achieved largely through a cut in the value added tax (a levy on sales which was temporarily reduced from 17.5 percent to 15 percent) and sizable cuts made to personal income tax. The spending measures that were included involved investment in environmentally friendly technology, broadband roll-out, and an acceleration of capital and investment projects.

Compared to the U.S., U.K. labour market policies tend to offer the unemployed a higher level of security, and thus crisis measures were aimed less at increasing the generosity of benefits, and instead at extending subsidies for recruitment and further training. The U.K. stimulus package therefore implemented a new subsidized jobs program for young job seekers, improved their employment services by providing individual support and training through Jobcentre Plus,[3] and additional benefits were offered for those unemployed under the age of twenty-five who sought retraining (OECD 2009c). Unemployment in 2009 was below the OECD average (OECD 2010a). This could be the result of active labour market policies, but it has also been noted by the IMF that wage flexibility played the largest role in supporting employment levels (Balakrishnan and Berger 2009). The May 2010 election produced a Conservative-Liberal coalition which, in its first budget, announced major cuts in public spending with most department budgets to decrease by 25 percent.

Germany

Despite the German banks IKB and Sachsen LB being caught up in the fall 2007 subprime mortgage market collapse, the German economy was left relatively unscathed, and for most of 2008 it appeared as though Germany would avoid the crisis altogether (Andersen 2009). This led to a modest stimulus package in fall 2008, half of which was spent on lending to a state development bank; the other half went to funding building renovations, infrastructure spending, and the use of tax incentives to encourage home repairs and the purchasing of new cars (Reuters 2009). However, in fall 2008 exports and investment began to drop sharply due to the global recession, both of which undermined business confidence (Andersen 2009). Germany then slipped into recession in 2009. A second stimulus package was thus announced in spring 2009. The second package included more tax relief, tax incentives to buy new cars, cuts to health insurance contributions, and credit guarantees to help firms dealing with the credit crunch (Reuters 2009). Altogether the total stimulus has amounted to roughly $108 billion U.S. (3 percent of the 2008 GDP), half of which was devoted to spending measures and half to revenue measures (OECD 2009a). The main objectives have been infrastructure spending, employment retention (through income tax cuts, funding, and guarantees), training and upgrading grants, innovation and research and development (particularly in green technologies), and providing assistance to the auto sector.

Despite the relatively large stimulus, the German economy slumped in 2008 and 2009. In 2007 Germany was experiencing robust average annual growth of 3.5 percent, which contracted in the second half of 2008 (Andersen 2009). Altogether in 2009 the economy shrunk by 2.25 percent, which was its worst performance since the post-World War II era (Guillen n.d.). However, despite the decline in economic growth, unemployment in Germany has remained below the OECD average although it is higher than some countries, such as Norway (OECD 2010a). This is the result of far stronger automatic stabilizers and the use of a short-term work scheme to ease the incidence of unemployment. Short-term work schemes are being used by other continental European countries, but Germany's is by far the most generous, and more than 1.4 million workers are participating in the program (OECD 2009d). This job retention measure is designed to allow firms experiencing difficulties to reduce working hours rather than leaving workers unemployed completely, and the OECD has credited it as a leading factor contributing to the lower than average job loss experienced in Germany, despite its higher than average slump in economic growth during 2008 and 2009 (OECD 2010d). In addition, the German government added new employment service staff, temporarily lowered some social insurance contributions, and expanded subsidies for vocational training for workers threatened by unemployment, older workers in SMEs and temporary agency workers (OECD 2009d).

Canada's Response

In the face of serious economic and financial turmoil around the world, the Canadian policy response was comparatively both muted and timid. While this can in part be attributed to the country's avoidance of some of the worst effects of the crisis, it is also likely that a commitment to neoliberal ideals prompted the lack of speed and urgency displayed. This is best exemplified through the government's limited interference in the operation of market forces overall, with an important exception being the commitments made in the 2009 budget to spend $70 billion to buy up shaky mortgages from the country's largest banks (via the Canadian Mortgage and Housing Corporation), and the establishment of a $200 billion fund, called the Emergency Financing Framework, to support these banks should they need to borrow money. Aside from these commitments made to capital, the Canadian policy response to the crisis was one that seriously lagged behind market events, down-played the sense of urgency exhibited elsewhere, and aimed for harmonization with the U.S. at the expense of made-at-home initiatives. We can term these denial, business as usual, and bilateralism (McBride 2011). Together, they indicate a government that was committed to as fast a return to normality as possible, a position it pressed in international gatherings, as well as on its home base.

Denial

Despite the 2007 implosion of global subprime markets and subsequent credit crunch in 2007, and the 2008 stock market collapse, the Canadian government's initial response to the crisis was one of official denial. It is true that the Canadian banking system was in a far stronger position than elsewhere as it had been subject to more stringent regulations than those in effect in other jurisdictions. However, while there is clearly some truth to the argument that limited exposure to toxic assets and the subsequent avoidance of a meltdown in the Canadian banking sector was due to federal regulations, the persistence of stronger regulations owed much to fortune.[4] The Harper government had begun to introduce forms of deregulation just prior to the onset of the global crisis. In 2007 the federal government began allowing U.S. banking sector competition into Canada, thus prompting rule changes by the Canadian Mortgage and Housing Corporation which contributed to the exposure of Canadian banks and encouraged risk-taking behaviours — such as dropping the down payment required on a house purchase to zero and extended amortization periods to forty years (Campbell 2009). These measures directly contributed to the need for the federal government to later pump very large sums of money into supporting financial institutions, as Canadian banks have had to write down billions of dollars in bad loans. However, the deregulatory thrust was discontinued. Perhaps as a result, Canada has not had to nationalize banks, as has been the case elsewhere (Loxley 2009: 70–71). Even so, complacency is hardly warranted. It does seem that questionable lending and mortgage practices were starting to creep into the Canadian financial system just prior to the onset of the crisis (Ireland and Webb 2010).

Unsurprisingly, the prospect that the global financial sector woes would translate into an economic crisis for Canada was down-played by the ruling Conservatives during the 2008 federal election campaign. On October 4 Prime Minister Stephen Harper reinforced his earlier opinion that "if we were going to have some kind of crash or recession we would have had it by now" (Laghi and Carmichael 2009) by criticizing the U.S. Congress for "panicking" after deciding on a $700 billion bail-out package: "I think if we don't panic here, we stick on course, we keep taking additional actions, make sure everything we do is affordable, we will emerge from this as strong as ever" (CanWest News Service 2008: A2).

The election on October 14, 2008, resulted in another minority Conservative government. Perhaps more surprising than its position during the campaign, the government continued to deny the severity of the economic situation in the immediate post-election period. Indeed, when the government presented a fiscal and economic update to Parliament on November 27 it turned out to contain a series of neoliberal policies, emphasizing its business-as-usual approach in the face of the economic crisis that was unfolding around the world. Relevant examples include suspending the right for federal civil servants to strike until 2011, suspending the right of female federal employees to achieve remedies on pay-equity issues, privatization of some Crown assets, and elimination of subsidies to political parties. Most important of all, Finance Minister Jim Flaherty declined to introduce a stimulus program at that point in time and opted instead for low taxes and a small budget surplus (Valpy 2009: 9–10). These measures launched the country into a short but bitter constitutional crisis as a coalition of opposition parties representing a majority of seats in the House of Commons unsuccessfully attempted to oust the minority Conservative government (see Russell and Sossin 2009; also see this volume, chapter 6).

Minimalism

Early signs of a neoliberal business-as-usual approach on the part of the Canadian government included an emphasis on tax cuts rather than spending as a way of producing a stimulus. As late as November 29, 2008, these were defended as an adequate response to the crisis. Certainly the tax cuts were significant, amounting to 2 percent of GDP (Blackwell 2008). Moreover, they were conceived as permanent, i.e., to remain in place after any recession had ended. Finance Minister Flaherty contrasted them with any temporary spending stimulus package that, in his view, gave only a transitory economic boost (Blackwell 2008). By January 3, 2009, he was contemplating further tax cuts plus infrastructure spending.

As global economic conditions continued to deteriorate, the federal government's stance of official denial in 2008 would be replaced by a minimalist response in early 2009 when the January 27 budget admitted that the crisis had reached Canada and that the economy was in recession (albeit one that had come later and was shallower than elsewhere). In the 2009 budget the government claimed it would provide a stimulus of $30 billion or 1.9 percent of GDP (Canada 2009: 10). However, mechanisms were also put in place to dampen the stimulus spending as the announced dollar figure assumed that provinces and municipalities would step forward with matching funds for infrastructure programs. To the extent that they did not, the stimulus could fall to 1.5 percent (Canada 2009: 30). Almost 35 percent of the stimulus came in the form of broad-based and corporate tax cuts, measures with poor stimulative multipliers compared to spending programs (Macdonald 2009: 5). The Canadian Centre for Policy Alternatives (CCPA) calculated that only 4 percent of the budget tax cuts were directed to low-income Canadians, arguably the group most likely to spend any monies received and thus help stimulate the broader economy (CCPA 2009: 3). The spending component of the stimulus package was explicitly declared to be temporary in order to enable a quick return to balanced budgets (Canada 2009: 12). Thus program spending, 13 percent of GDP in 2007–08, was projected to rise to 14.7 percent in 2009–10, before falling back to 13.1 percent in 2013–14 (Canada 2009: 29).

This clearly illustrates that stimulus spending and other similar measures at the time were designed with the intention to minimize the amount of government intrusion in the economy in the long run, aiming instead to revert back to the status quo once the immediate crisis was over. Spending and tax cuts were dwarfed by the $70 billion spent on purchasing unsound mortgages and the $200 billion made available to fill gaps in credit markets through the Emergency Financing Framework. While these measures were off book (they do not appear as expenditures by the federal government, and instead appear on the books of the Bank of Canada and the Canadian Mortgage and Housing Corporation), they in effect "have increased the government's borrowing from $13.6 billion in 2007-08 to $89.5 billion in 2008-09, or double the fiscal deficit now projected for 2009" (Campbell 2009).

Just as Canada's early domestic stance on the crisis could be characterized as business as usual, so too was its reaction in international circles. Early manifestations of crisis in 2007 were met with the Bank of Canada's refusal to ease monetary conditions or resort to economic stimulus. At the IMF meeting of finance ministers and central bank governors in October 2007 the conclusion was drawn that the private sector was responsible for developing solutions to rectify the credit crisis. Reportedly, Canada was one of the strongest advocates of leaving it to the private sector (Baragar 2009: 88).

In 2008, during preparations for a G-20 meeting of finance ministers and central bankers, the *National Post* reported that Canada was opposing efforts by European states to make significant reforms in the global financial architecture — crafting financial regulations to bind all countries and having them enforced by a stronger IMF. Canada, together with the U.S. and Australia, emphasized domestic regulation, and, according to John Kirton, Canada was on "the minimalist end of the spectrum and is probably even more minimalist than the United States" (Vieira and Callan 2008: FP1). The subsequent G-20 leaders' summit adopted a compromise declaration that emphasized better international oversight of large financial institutions, greater transparency of financial products, and monitoring of executive salaries (Callan 2008), and a more detailed communiqué was issued after the London G-20 in April 2009.

By the spring of 2010, Canada would play a more active international role by championing a swift return to neoliberal-style global governance, as the Harper Conservatives were in large part responsible for scuttling an IMF-proposed global bank tax, supported by many European leaders and the U.S., which would have been dedicated to insuring the global banking system by using the profits, salaries, and bonuses of banks, not taxpayer dollars, to bail out banks in the future. Not only did Canada refuse to sign onto a global bank tax, under the auspices that "Canada will not go down the path of excessive, arbitrary or punitive regulation of its financial sector" (Scoffield 2010), but Prime Minister Harper and Finance Minister Flaherty also used their status as host country representatives at the June 2010 G-20 summit in Toronto to avoid discussing initiatives of this nature at the meeting, despite the obvious need to address the problems experienced by most other countries through significant governance reforms. Instead they urged that the G-20 should focus on previously agreed upon commitments to bolster capital requirements, strengthen liquidity, and discourage excessive leveraging (ibid.). These measures are entirely consistent with neoliberalism's minimalist financial governance style, and as a result the meeting of the world's leading twenty economies accomplished very little in terms of significant financial sector reform, despite the Great Recession that hit two years earlier.

Bilateralism and the Pursuit of Special Status
The tendency towards bilateralism can be seen at work in Canadian reactions to the buy American components of the U.S. stimulus package and in the me too-ism of the bailouts of the automobile industry. There is a partial offset to this focus on bilateralism in the attempt to negotiate a comprehensive trade agreement with the European Union. Paradoxically, however, any concessions to the E.U. could also be extended, under "most favoured nation" language, to Canada's NAFTA partners. Hence, attempted diversification could also reinforce continental integration.

Buy American
The U.S. stimulus package contained provisions barring foreign suppliers from participation in funded projects. As most of the money in question was to be spent by state and municipal governments, which are not part of either WTO or NAFTA government procurement provisions, U.S. officials considered the measures compliant with trade agreements. Initially, Canadian politicians and officials reacted by seeking a presidential veto of the legislation or for exemptions to be made for Canadian suppliers (Laghi and Carmichael 2009). These attempts were unsuccessful yet contributed to a climate of rising fear expressed by business organizations over the potential threat of protectionism and the growing risk of a trade war (Clark and McKenna 2009). It soon became apparent that threatening action under trade treaties was an empty gesture since the U.S. was correct that state and municipal procurement was excluded. The Canadian tactic then switched to calls for reciprocal procurement liberalization. Under these proposals Canadian companies would have access to procurement in the U.S., and Canadian provinces and municipalities, some of which had adopted proposals for retaliatory action against U.S. companies, would be open to bids from U.S. companies. There was broad provincial agreement and some support, too, from highly integrated companies with cross-border supply chains (CBC 2009a).

By February 2010, a deal exempting Canadian firms had been reached. The opposition Liberals dubbed this too little, too late as the majority of the U.S. stimulus money had already been allocated (CBC 2010a). In exchange, Canadian provincial and municipal governments agreed to sign onto the WTO's government procurement agreement, thereby agreeing to allow U.S. companies to now bid on public works projects at the sub-national level. As usual when Canada is the demandeur in bilateral trade negotiations with the

U.S., it seemed that Canada had made the greater concessions. Moreover, notwithstanding NAFTA rhetoric concerning the three amigos of North America, Canada's proposal entirely ignored Mexico.

Auto

The crisis of the tightly integrated North American auto industry meant that Canada had a strong interest in making sure it participated in any industry bailout lest a U.S. package privilege auto production in that country. To ensure a share of North American production, Canada pledged 20 percent of whatever the bailout would cost (Waddell 2010: 153). With 12 percent of manufacturing GDP and 150,000 direct jobs and another 340,000 in distribution and after market activities (Van Praet and Vieira 2008) the sector was a high priority for Canada. In this area Canada was a "policy-taker" in that it was the U.S. which devised the package, leaving Canadians as "ultimately passive observers, who can only cross our fingers and hope that the Obama administration's plans save Canadian autoworkers' jobs" (Ibbitson 2009: A19).

The negotiations between the U.S. government and the auto industry were protracted. Over the course of 2008–09 a pattern gradually emerged. It was clear that Canada's contribution would be proportionate to the package established by the U.S. Similarly, conditions attached to the deal in the U.S. would resonate north of the border — reduced labour costs, amounting to $10 per hour, and changes in work organization, were a prominent part of the U.S. deal. Because of the integration of the industry and the North American auto market it could be argued that Canada would have little choice but to follow suit (Van Praet and Vieira 2008). In this respect the governments of Canada and Ontario were far from passive, and applied significant pressure on the CAW to make concessions (Waddell 2010). When the U.S. had determined the size of the bailout for GM, the Canadian contribution was deemed to be $10.5 billion, one third of which would be paid by Ontario. The deal was described by Prime Minister Harper as a "regrettable but necessary step." He went on to say: "I wish there were an alternative but the alternative to what we are doing today would be vastly more costly and more risky" (*Toronto Star* 2009). As a result of its participation in the bailout Canada acquired 18 percent of the restructured GM.

In April 2010, GM announced that it had completed the repayment of its bailout loans from the Canadian and U.S. governments (Kim and Lawder 2010), totaling $8.1 billion (U.S.). While this repayment does come much earlier than scheduled, the government bailout package also took the form of equity purchases, and thus the U.S. government came to own a 61 percent stake in GM, and Canada to own 18 percent. Taxpayers will only get their money back if public offerings of stocks are able to recoup the investment. Whether taxpayers do get their money back depends, of course, on the price of the shares that governments sell, and that is partly a question of the timing of sales. However, their flexibility in this regard is limited by the terms of the agreement. It requires them to sell 5 percent of the shares annually, 30 percent within three years, and 65 percent within six years (Van Alphen and Ferguson 2010). By committing to sell fixed proportions in set periods the governments have reduced their ability to maximize returns for taxpayers. The bailouts did save some jobs in the auto sector but the overall pattern of job losses in the industry continued notwithstanding returning profitability (Macaluso 2010).

Conclusion

The global financial and economic crisis that emerged in 2007 is a salient indicator of the deep and long standing economic malaise that has been induced by the adoption of neoliberalism world-wide. In contrast to earlier crises, this one first hit the neoliberal centre, with initial warning signs emerging in the U.S. as early as 2006. By late 2007 toxic assets associated with subprime lending markets led to a serious credit crunch, the exhaustion of monetary tools by central banks around the world, and a series of spectacular financial institution collapses in 2008. Beginning in late 2008 and early 2009, trillions of taxpayer dollars were summarily apportioned by governments around the world in order to bail out the financial sector and selected corporations. However, as significant as this latest crisis episode has been, the pattern of risk taking, volatility, collapse, and subsequent socialization of debt is only the most recent episode in a string of debt and financial sector crises to hit since the early 1980s.

Yet given the magnitude of this most recent crisis and depth of the Great Recession that has ensued, the global return to Keynesian-style stimulus, a practice long since rendered disreputable by neoliberal orthodoxy, did mark a break from previous crisis responses. As a result, many heralded the return of Keynesianism and the fall of neoliberalism. However, as time went on it became clear that not only were the stimulus packages shallow and selective, but reforms of this nature were also temporary. While in 2010 most stimulus packages were set to expire by early 2011, the lack of global economic recovery prompted the OECD to advise its members that "Monetary policy stimulus should largely remain in place during 2011." Economic imbalances in Europe, deflation in Japan, and slow recovery in the U.S. were cited as being among the main concerns (Deen 2010). The effects of the prolonged crisis are especially visible in the U.S. economy as there continued to be lower than expected rates of growth, job creation, personal income earnings, and consumer spending (RBC 2010). The fragility of overall economic recovery, and prolongation of economic woes in the U.S. specifically, foreshadows significant problems for the Canadian economy given that its relatively small, export-dependent economy has become deeply integrated with the rest of

North America since the signing of the Canada-U.S. Free Trade Agreement and NAFTA. Furthermore, and of concern more broadly, the G-20 and other international organizations have thus far failed to initiate any significant reforms of the international financial architecture and the style of global governance remains the same as it was in the neoliberal era. Neoliberal rule has not been challenged, and the same conditions that led to the meltdown remain with us today. Somewhat paradoxically, the failures of neoliberalism could very well prove to be a recipe for future neoliberal rejuvenation as imminent public debt repayment will come through future fiscal austerity imposed on citizens rather than tax increases imposed on capital (see chapter 5).

Canadian policy reaction to the crisis illustrates this business-as-usual pattern nicely: first the crisis was denied and then minimized. Canada's potential for leadership internationally due to its banking sector stability has also been used by the Conservatives as a tool to manipulate the types of reforms implemented internationally. Thus at the July 2010 G-20 meeting Canada used its position as host nation to promote measures such as increasing capital requirements and strengthening liquidity that have found fertile ground, whereas proposals for significant change (such as a bank tax which would ensure that the taxpayer was not on the hook for future financial sector imprudence) were opposed and lack the broad-based support needed within the competitive context of neoliberal globalization.

Chapter 2

THEORIES OF CAPITALIST CRISES

Our focus in this book is on the connections between politics, institutions, policies, ideological currents, and economic crisis. As we showed in chapter 1, the global crisis that began in 2007 emerged first as a financial crisis and later morphed into a generalized economic crisis with widespread effects like job losses, recession, bankruptcy, and housing foreclosures. While our analysis is largely at the political level, it is predicated on the recognition that this crisis is not an isolated incident; rather, it is one of a series that have afflicted the political economy over the last few decades. It will be helpful to our project, therefore, to review some of the voluminous literature that has emerged on this subject.

There have been a series of financial crises occurring on a fairly regular basis throughout the neoliberal period. Examples include Mexico (1994), East Asia (1997), Russia (1998), and Argentina (2001). The central difference between these earlier crises and the current one is that the neoliberal heartland, Wall Street and the city of London, for example, had until now not been subjected to the extreme volatility and instability that accompanies the neoliberal financial regime. Instead crises in the past had remained confined largely to particular states or regions in the global south. Or, as with the recessions in the developed north in the early 1980s and 1990s, they were concentrated in the real economy and lacked the spectre of a complete financial collapse associated with the 2007 crisis.

The series of financial meltdowns experienced during the neoliberal era indicates that instability is intrinsic to the operation of the neoliberal global political economy. On top of this, and taking a long-term view, the capitalist system has shown itself inherently crisis-prone, with system-wide or generalized crises occurring on a fairly regular basis over time (for example, the economic depressions in the 1870s to 1890s, the Great Depression in the 1930s, followed by global stagflation in the 1970s). Adequate explanation calls for the phenomenon and regularity of economic/financial crises to be understood from a systemic perspective, even if each crisis may have historically specific forms that require detailed investigation (see Panitch and Gindin 2011: 5–6).

The reigning ideological orthodoxy in economic neoclassical theory fares particularly poorly in this respect. Instead neoclassical economic theory emphasizes the rational, self-regulating, and self-equilibrating nature of the capitalist system.

At the heart of neoclassical theory rests the general equilibrium model, which assumes that prices clear all markets and once equilibrium is reached (as always, *ceteris paribus*) the market is essentially "failure-free" (Pitelis 1992: 14). Consequently, theoretical insights into crises are fairly shallow in the mainstream tradition. This is not to say that it holds no perspective on crises as exogenous factors such as sudden, random technological transformation are often blamed for instigating a crisis. Alternatively, monetarist economists (for example, Milton Friedman) reject the notion of market failure altogether (i.e., the argument advanced by Keynes) and instead suggest that serious crisis episodes, like the Great Depression of the 1930s, are due to government failure — namely excessive state intervention. Similarly, the stagnation that occurred in the 1970s has been explained by this school of thought as a problem of government regulation (for example, see Feldstein 1974 on the expansion of social security in the U.S. as a cause of declining rates of capital accumulation). More recently, neoclassical contributions include seeing market failure as being induced at the micro-level by certain transaction costs involved with market activities — such as search and information costs, bargaining costs, and policing and enforcement costs (Pitelis 1992). In sum, orthodox economic theory holds that markets may not clear, or other distortions may occur, should there be inadequate information, irrationality on the part of consumers or workers, or blockages created by monopolies, labour unions, and state regulation (Jessop and Sum 2006: 5). Thus policies such as neoliberal deregulation or re-regulation of financial markets and the privatization of authority over financial market governance are key components of the neoclassical solution to crises and are not considered to be the cause of them (despite ample evidence to the contrary).

Beyond the orthodoxy exists a rich critical political economy tradition which has long recognized that crises are endemic to capitalism. While multiple theories abound, those which are particularly insightful with respect to how and why periodic capitalist crises occur are long wave theory, including the social structure of accumulation approach and regulation theory; Brenner's study of "the long downturn"; and the Marxist overaccumulation perspective of capitalist crises, exemplified here by Harvey and McNally.[1] Despite the diversity that exists between these various heterodox approaches, a common element remains: they see capitalism as an inherently crisis-prone mode of production that is riddled with contradictions and conflicts. This challenges not only the neoclassical understanding of the self-equilibrating nature of capitalism, but also calls into question those who mainly blame the recent crisis on financial market regulatory changes introduced early on in the neoliberal period. By implication, these critical theories show that the recent exercise in light Keynesian stimulus and token alterations to financial market governance and regulation will not, and cannot, be an entirely sufficient solution to crises in the long run. Thus the purpose of this chapter is to review these general theories of crisis in order to situate our discussion in the following chapters within a wider understanding of capitalism and its ongoing propensity for crisis.

We have little to say with regard to the relative merits of these theoretical perspectives. Nor do we deal in any detail with analyses of specific crises.[2] Rather, for our purposes, this tradition of critical political economy represents a rich tapestry of complementary and sometimes competing interpretations, which points to the systemic nature of the current crisis and the inadequacies of the "solutions" to contain it. Thus the perspectives presented here help to make sense of the current crisis by contextualizing it within the larger pattern of crisis and recovery that is an intrinsic feature of the capitalist system.

Long Waves

Long wave theories hold that capitalism routinely moves through phases of long-term development that involve periods of relative growth and predictability followed by instability and stagnation. These dynamics present themselves in various timeframes, with some cycles being hundreds of years long, while others last for forty to sixty years (Kondratieff cycles). Until the 1940s, theorists writing from within this tradition focused their debate on the mechanism that initiated this tendency — be it Kondratieff's durable capital, Schumpeter's innovation, or Lenoir's price (O'Hara 2006: 13). This debate largely died out as a consequence of the surge in popularity of Keynesian employment theory and policy beginning in the 1940s. Keynes, of course, suggested that cycles could be smoothed out by state manipulation of levels of aggregate demand.

With the onset of significant economic turmoil in the 1970s (rising inflation concurrent with economic stagnation, dubbed stagflation) and the subsequent lack of recovery in profitability and growth when compared to the postwar era, there has since been a revival of interest in the long-term evolutionary dynamics of the capitalist system. Today two principal long wave theories are the social structure of accumulation approach and regulation theory. These long wave perspectives are interested in the variety of economic and extra-economic arrangements that facilitate successful growth and development, yet which ultimately break down and lead to crisis.

Social Structure of Accumulation

Insights into the long wave dynamics of the capitalist system form the basis of the social structure of accumulation (ssa) perspective. For this approach, during the first half (upswing) of the forty- to sixty-year long wave (or Kondratieff cycle), strong growth is guided by institutional innovations that provide for a few decades of relative stability and prosperity. However, these institutional arrangements will eventually mature, and once they have run their course they will begin to generate their own unique contradictions. Problems could include a loss of confidence as a result of growing social or financial instability, lack of effective demand, excess competition, heightened global tensions, or the loss of other forms of stability, predictability, and coordination support for private accumulation (O'Hara 2006: 12). A downswing will then inevitably set in and recessions and financial instabilities will grow more frequent and severe.

The institutions that form the ssa are crucial as they "condition the process of capital accumulation, relationships between industrial and financial capitals, capital and labor, capital and the state, and nation-state set within the global economy" (O'Hara 2008: 89). Ultimately, it is the extra-economic institutions that produce the stability, predictability, coordination, and compromise that are needed in order to facilitate long-term investment, demand, and growth within a capitalist economy. Since an institution is held to be a "durable structure outside the direct control of individual firms," they are the product of negotiation and often of class compromise (O'Hara 2008: 89). Institutions are of an economic, social, and political nature.

The capitalist system requires these extra-economic institutions in order to help facilitate accumulation as there are certain inherent conflicts generated by this mode of production. A central conflict for ssa theorists is class conflict (between both capital and labour and among various fractions of capital) that arises over the distribution of surplus value, control over the production process, influence over the state, and other related tensions. Thus, the institutions of the ssa smooth out conflicts of this sort and provide for stability and predictability, accomplished through class compromise or outright repression.

Conversely, crises are said to occur as a result of the breakdown of institutional arrangements that support accumulation. Simply put, "the dynamic behind the successive periods of growth and stagnation are located squarely in the construction and breakdown of the ssa" (McDonough 1999: 9). Crisis is therefore "a period of economic instability that requires institutional reconstruction for renewed stability and growth" (Gordon et al. 1994: 19). Just as the capitalist system is aided through the upswing by a supportive ssa, the resolution of a crisis "requires collective action and the creation of a political consensus" (Gordon et al. 1994: 19) as it cannot be accomplished by capitalists alone. For the ssa approach it is also possible for the accumulation process itself to generate crises (for example, through underconsumption or overaccumulation), but these processes are again related to the ssa. Crises of accumulation, for example, will undermine the resources required to sustain the ssa, and thus it is problems with the ssa that are of fundamental concern (Kotz 1994: 57).

The key institutions that supported growth during the postwar upswing (in the U.S. and other western states) were: Pax Americana (U.S. international hegemony); a capital-labour accord (described below); a moderation of competition; the Keynesian welfare state (which enhanced stability, provided for conflict resolution, enhanced effective demand, and so on); a system of regulated finance (the Bretton Woods agreement); and family-community stability and trust (O'Hara 2006: 48).[3] Given that the moderation of class conflict is of central importance for ssa theorists, a key concern for this approach is how capital-labour relations are institutionalized. Stability must be present within this institution in particular in order for growth to occur despite the inherent class conflict built into capitalism.

During the postwar upswing, the capital-labour accord provided for mutual tradeoffs and benefits, which generated decades of prosperity. A stable and cooperative collective bargaining system was implemented in the advanced capitalist countries, which allowed employers to reap benefits associated with innovations in technology and the organization of work, and in exchange workers received regular wage increases and social welfare benefits from the state (Gordon et al. 1994: 22). Stability was crucially beneficial for both capital and labour. Over the years this began to strengthen and embolden the working class, as expectations had formed around the ideal of continually rising benefits and real wages. However, these demands produced a "profit squeeze" and added a measure of rigidity within labour markets, ultimately hindering adjustment to changing conditions. Thus the capital-labour accord that helped to generate significant prosperity during the postwar era would later create a barrier to rapid capital accumulation in the 1970s.[4]

Despite widespread agreement within the ssa approach that a downswing was initiated in the mid-1970s, there is much debate surrounding whether or not the next upswing has begun. Many theorists argue that we are still in the downswing (Moseley 1999; Brenner 2006; Aglietta 1998; O'Hara 2004). The lack of stability and growth is said to be the result of inadequacies within the key institutions of the neoliberal governance system. These key institutions are: in the place of the Keynesian welfare state is a consensus around small government and privatization; controls on international financial flows have since given way to deregulated domestic financial systems; labour markets are deregulated and worker power has been rolled back; free trade agreements allow capital to invest around the globe; and the hegemony of the U.S. has effectively collapsed. Upon evaluation of these institutions (the neoliberal state, free trade and international institutions, deregulated financial systems, and a flexible system of production), O'Hara (2000: 284) concludes that:

> Neoliberalism is riddled with contradictions such that there is a large degree of instability, not enough profit for industrial capitals,

and insufficient resolution of conflict. Neoliberalism has too many contradictions to solve the major problems of modern capitalism. Hence, either the contradictions are too great for neoliberalism to constitute a new SSA, or any minimal degree of SSA reconstruction that has emerged is not sufficient for the system to evade deep recession and instability for any substantial period of time (for instance, for a decade).

The narrow consumption base of the neoliberal SSA alone is extremely problematic as it promotes high levels of indebtedness, equity bubbles, and overall instability. Consumption by the working class and the poor has not been supported by real wage growth since at least the 1990s.

The inadequacy of the institutions that form the neoliberal SSA is illustrated through the lack of significant recovery since the onset of the downswing. For instance, while the 1980s–2000s saw the growth of newly industrialized East Asian countries, within the world economy as a whole "there has been little or no success in promoting growth since the early 1970s" (O'Hara 2006: 54). This is not to say that there has been no growth at all over the past three decades. It is important to make the distinction, as Schumpeter did, between short cycles and long waves. If short cycles (three to five years; seven to eleven years) are mistaken for the upswing phase of a long wave then short-run growth will erroneously appear to indicate significant recovery and the beginning of a new phase of sustainable growth (O'Hara 2006: 12).

In this sense, short-term growth is not enough; there must be a fundamental change in the institutions that support accumulation in order to initiate a long wave upswing. If the SSA is not suitable, developing, or in place, then "periodic deep recessions and major financial instability are likely in the foreseeable future and long wave upswing is not currently operating" (O'Hara 2006: 138). This prediction is particularly ominous given the locking in of neoliberal reforms through disciplinary neoliberalism and new constitutionalism (Gill 1995).

Regulation Theory
In many ways regulation theory is similar to the SSA approach. Both are long wave theories that share an interest in the ways in which capitalist crises are stabilized through extra-economic arrangements and in how growth and development are facilitated through the restructuring of these arrangements. Thus, the social structure does not stand apart from the capitalist system, it is endogenous and interrelated for both perspectives. However, there are also some significant differences between the two. Regulation theory contains a central concept absent from the SSA approach: the regime of accumulation (explained below). This makes it more structuralist/materialist, as it tends to

emphasize processes of accumulation and technological forces as opposed to the ssa focus on class struggle, relationships, and conflicts (O'Hara 2006: 17).

Regulation theory contains four levels of analysis: the mode of production; the regime of accumulation; the mode of regulation; and its accompanying institutional forms. The mode of production is nearly everywhere dominated by the capitalist system today. The regime of accumulation describes the regular patterns that ensure the progress of capitalist accumulation (key concepts being production, circulation, consumption, and distribution), and how inevitable crises are postponed. The mode of regulation supports and steers the regime of accumulation and refers to a "set of mediations which ensure that the distortions created by the accumulation of capital are kept within limits which are compatible with social cohesion within each nation" (Aglietta 1998: 44) and therefore ensures compatibility between the regime of accumulation and the range of institutions that support accumulation. The institutional forms are codifications of social relations, the key institutions being the monetary regime, the wage-labour nexus, the forms of competition, the methods of insertion into the international regime, the forms of state, and the fiscal/financial regime (Boyer and Saillard 1995: 6).

Markets are therefore embedded in a series of institutional arrangements that temper the propensity for crisis inherent in the capitalist mode of production. Like the ssa approach, regulation theory also suggests that there are "alternating periods of stable capitalist accumulation and crisis-induced restructuring, rescaling and reregulation" (Jessop and Sum 2006: 1). Capitalism does not have auto-generated periods of stability, nor can the economic system heal itself in response to crises. It is the historically particular combinations of economic and extra-economic institutions and practices that create stability, predictability, and resolution following crises, however temporary these successes may be.

Regulation theory holds that "every society displays the economic evolution and crises that correspond to its structure" (Boyer and Saillard 1995: 15). Crises can take many forms for regulation theory, including those that are exogenously triggered (similar to the neoclassical focus), endogenous (taking place within the mode of regulation within a given country), occurring within the accumulation regime (limits are reached within the essential institutional forms), and occurring within the mode of production itself (Boyer and Saillard 1995: 41).

The concept of an accumulation regime is central to this perspective. The accumulation regime is formed by the relationship that exists between technical progress and income distribution (Juillard 1995: 153). The postwar accumulation regime is defined as Fordist (referring to its mass production and mass consumption macroeconomic regime). Ideal typical features of this regime of accumulation are self-reinforcing: mass production is defined by national boundaries, rising productivity is based on economies of scale, rising incomes are based on these productivity gains, increases in mass demand are achieved through rising wages, and profits are based on full capacity utilization encouraging greater investments in mass production (Jessop and Sum 2006: 60).

The term Fordism is also used to describe the postwar mode of regulation in the sense that it contained an "ensemble of norms, institutions, organizational forms, social networks and patterns of conduct" that guided the Fordist regime of accumulation (Jessop and Sum 2006: 60). Relevant examples include corporatist labour relations and collective bargaining (linking gains of labour to productivity and other corporate gains), Keynesian welfare state management of aggregate demand (ensuring mass consumption, aiming for full employment), and hierarchically organized credit relations and controls on finance capital (privileging reinvestment within production). Thus for regulation theorists the success of the postwar era was in large part the result of the mode of regulation at the time: it "reconciled rapid increases in productivity with the growth of real income and with stability in its distribution" (Aglietta 1998: 57). This provided for self-sustained long-term growth.

Unlike the ssa approach, regulation theory grounds the crisis of the 1970s within the regime of accumulation. The crisis of the mid-1970s was a crisis of the Fordist regime of accumulation: given the interrelated nature of the high-productivity, high-growth, and wage gains of the Fordist regime of mass production and consumption, the slowdown in productivity and growth in the late 1960s was deeply problematic for the institutional forms described above. For example, for the Keynesian welfare state the slowdown in growth spelled financial disaster, producing significant budgetary problems. Financing the policy of countercyclical spending, still held as a key way for government to support the regime of mass consumption, became problematic (Andre 1995: 99). For the monetary regime, Guttmann suggests that "the acceleration of inflationary pressures during the 1970s was an expression of structural crisis" as it indicated "the deterioration of underlying accumulation conditions in production" (Guttmann 1995: 60). Ultimately, the institutional arrangements of the postwar monetary regime were undermined through stagflation. Whether we are able to identify a new post-Fordist regime of accumulation and mode of regulation is open to debate (for example, see O'Hara 2006; Jessop and Sum 2006).

Brenner and the Long Downturn
Brenner has coined the phrase the "long downturn" to describe the relative condition of the global economy since the 1970s. This phrase refers to the long-term and system-wide economic downturn evidenced by a deterioration in many macroeconomic indicators: in addition to the series of world-wide

recessions and regional financial crises experienced over the past four decades, "average rates of growth of output, capital stock (investment), labour productivity, and real wages for the years 1973 to the present have been one-third to one-half of those for the years 1950–73, and the average unemployment rate has been more than double" (Brenner 2006: 2–3). This description of a long downturn may at first blush resemble the forms of long wave analysis mentioned above but it is Brenner's account of how this stagnation occurs which sets him apart.

As we saw earlier, for ssa theorists, crises are initiated by a breakdown of key national institutions that form the ssa, such as the capital-labour accord described above. Brenner takes exception to this analysis and devotes a portion of his *The Economics of Global Turbulence* to a critique of what he calls the "supply-side" or "contradictions of Keynesianism" approach to explaining the crisis. While he agrees that "the power of labour... can skew the operation of the labour market in favour of workers" and that workers' gains can undercut capital accumulation in the short run, he maintains that these actions "cannot, generally speaking, make for an extended downturn because it cannot, as a rule, bring about a spatially generalized (system-wide) and temporally extended decline in profitability" (Brenner 2006: 22–24). Simply put, a profit squeeze could have taken place in specific areas for a short amount of time, but this cannot account for why the downturn has been so long lasting and why it is systemic rather than local (given that capital accumulation and profitability operate at the level of the capitalist system as a whole).

The approach that he forwards is instead based on an analysis of the drive to accumulate and the paradoxical problems for profitability that are produced by cost-cutting innovations which undermine older masses of fixed capital investments. While prosperity during the boom period of the postwar era was widespread, international development during this time also proceeded in an uneven fashion, which created regional blocs in the 1960s: an American bloc, and the later-developing European (centred on Germany) and East Asian (centred on Japan) blocs that benefited from the hegemony and technological leadership of the U.S. (Brenner 2006: 37). Although innovations introduced by the newer bloc competitors created lower-cost, lower-priced exports, American firms were initially able to maintain their incumbent position because the scale of their prior (albeit less efficient) fixed capital investments had been so great. As competition for international market share grew in the 1970s, market-clearing adjustments (in the form of less efficient U.S. firms exiting the market) did not take place. Instead, producers from all blocs restructured and reinvested. This dynamic led to systemic overproduction, overcapacity, and a dramatic decline in profitability. Uneven development continued through the 1980s and 1990s as new East

Asian manufacturers expanded into world export markets by combining advanced production techniques with low wages, which once again forestalled an end to the downturn and the recovery of profitability as overcapacity and overproduction in manufacturing continued (Brenner 2006: 39).

During the 1970s, expansion was initially maintained in the face of overaccumulation (excess capital) through the ratcheting up of public and private debt loads, which made it possible to sustain demand (Brenner 2006: 270). However, with the introduction of monetarist and neoliberal policies in the U.S. in the early1980s, significant changes were initiated — namely a rationalization and restructuring of American manufacturing, the beginning of financialization (the relocation of capital toward financial activity), and the initiation of a low-wage economy (Brenner 2006: 271). Despite these changes and their emulation elsewhere, the advanced capitalist world as a whole remained mired in stagnation until the mid-1990s, the main exceptions being the emerging market economies of East Asia (Brenner 2006: 280). Thus economic recovery witnessed after this time was based largely on the creation of successive bubble economies and not underpinned by real growth. The trend was exacerbated by "stock market Keynesianism," which subsidized demand not through government expenditures but through private debt, enabling corporations and households to spend more than they earned, with the same main exemptions as previously mentioned of emerging market economies in East Asia (Brenner 2006: 293). Ultimately, the bubble produced by massive and unsustainable levels of household and corporate debt, concurrent with significant disparity between actual profits and the wealth generated by paper assets, was bound to end in disaster. After a series of regional financial crises (for example, the Asian financial crisis in 1997) and sectoral bubble crashes (for example, Dot.com in 2000–2002), the financial crisis of 2007–08 would prove systemic.

Insights Offered by Long Wave Theories
The principal insight offered by Brenner, and why his analysis may be seen for our purposes to be complementary rather than contradictory to the other long wave theories discussed here, is that real recovery never did take place after the end of the highly successful postwar era. Instead, the world economy remained mired in a long downturn that began in the early 1970s and continues to this day. Regulatory changes that permitted financialization did allow a narrow segment of the population to experience tremendous prosperity and affluence, but this was accomplished without a sustained recovery of real growth. Bubble economies resulted, and thus financial instability became a hallmark feature of the neoliberal era.

Similarly, from the SSA approach and regulation theory we can take the importance of extra-economic support needed to facilitate capital accumulation (growth). This stands out as their central contribution and influences our discussion in the chapters that follow. Although there are differences between these two long wave theories, they also share features and may be used together in a heuristic fashion to highlight the correspondence between an emerging institutional structure and the needs of capital accumulation. In this vein, they indicate that while the forms of institutions may change, their importance in underpinning a successful accumulation process is a constant. These approaches suggest that if a particular social structure of accumulation (or mode of regulation) can no longer deliver, then crisis results and can only be resolved on terms consistent with continued capitalism by constructing new institutions that can perform this function.

Harvey: Overaccumulation and Spatio-Temporal Fixes

The underlying cause of crises in David Harvey's account is not the institutional contradictions of the SSA approach, nor is it regulation theory's exhaustion of regime of accumulation–mode of regulation compatibility; it is instead a product of capitalism itself. For Harvey, crises are the result of overaccumulation. Periods of crisis within global capitalism are not unique but rather are expressions of the internal contradictions within the capitalist system itself. Harvey describes three central contradictions within the capitalist mode of production which produce these periodic crises: those that arise within the capitalist class as individual capitalists act in a competitive profit-seeking manner; antagonisms that exist between labour and capital create class struggle over the wage-profit split; and contradictions that arise due to the potential for strife between the capitalist production system and non- or pre-capitalist sectors (Harvey 2001: 79–80).

Ultimately, these contradictions lead to crises of overaccumulation, which are "particular manifestations of excess capital 'held up' in all of the states it assumes in the course of circulation" (Harvey 2006: 195). Surplus capital is thus the root cause of crisis. Overaccumulation can take many forms of appearance, including a glut of commodities on the market, idle productive capacity, and surpluses of money capital lacking outlets for productive and profitable investment (ibid.).

Crises are not only inevitable, they are also in a certain sense beneficial from the perspective of the system as a whole. In this account, crises can have a constructive role to play by "forcing new technologies, and forging new organizational structures that are more in accordance with the law of value in that they provide a basis for renewed capital accumulation through the production of surplus value" (see Harvey 2006: 301–304 on the accumulation cycle). The accumulation cycle has five parts to it: stagnation; recovery; credit-based expansion; speculative fever; and crash. The crash is needed to devalue excess capital and labour (for example, as witnessed through the collapse of inflated paper assets), and stagnation produces adjustments, which bring production processes into accord with what is needed for more successful accumulation. Extraneous elements must be eliminated, production rationalized, and weak links severed. In contrast, SSA theorists reject the notion that recessions have a restorative effect. They hold that there is no automatic mechanism that leads stagnation into expansion (Kotz 1994: 57). Resolving crises requires a new SSA.

However beneficial crises may be for the system as a whole, the high level of misery associated with crashes and stagnation can mean serious hardships for many in society, raising the spectre of significant social unrest, and thus strategies are devised to manage this painful readjustment. These strategies take the form of what Harvey calls fixes. An important area of his work has been to theorize the ways in which the inherently crisis-prone nature of capitalism is assuaged, however temporarily, through the establishment of a fix. In furtherance of this goal he has proposed that overaccumulation can potentially be resolved by resorting to one of three strategies of crisis prevention: spatial displacement; temporal displacement; or a combination of the two (spatio-temporal fixes) to help overcome difficulties. Jessop (2002) counters by arguing that institutions are needed to facilitate capital accumulation as the capital relation alone cannot provide for this — there is a need to add a "social fix" to Harvey's concept of a spatio-temporal fix.[5] The role of neoliberalism as a set of ideas and of the policies of the neoliberal state would seem to be important in articulating, implementing, and managing these strategies.

For Harvey the periodic crises experienced by capitalism do not signify a collapse of the system but instead represent moments in which social reaction operates to resolve the problematic features of one mode by replacing them with a shift to what Harvey calls a new plane of accumulation which structures new, more successful domestic arrangements (Harvey 2001: 241–42). This new plane will typically involve the following elements: the penetration of capital into new spheres of activity by reorganizing pre-existing forms of activity along capitalist lines; the creation of new social wants and needs; and a geographic expansion into new regions. In addition to geographic expansion and spatial reorganization, Harvey adds the concept of temporal displacement to account for long-term investments in physical and social infrastructure, which he then terms spatio-temporal fixes (Harvey 2001: 312–44; Harvey 2003a: 64–68). He describes how this process absorbs surplus in the following way: "temporal displacement [encourages] investment in long-term capital projects or social expenditures that defer the re-entry of current excess capital values into circulation well into the future; and spatial displacement... open[s] up new markets, new production capacities and new resources, [and new] social and labour possibilities elsewhere" (Harvey 2003a: 64). Finance (credit) is therefore a key pivot around which fixes are formed as it allows for both spatial and temporal displacement of surplus capital. However, this is a risky endeavour as it can only disguise the appearance of crises in the short run, and eventually value has to be generated through production in order for the credit to be repaid.

Another way of attempting to restore profitability is through the use of accumulation by dispossession. Whereas Marx's *Capital* focused on valorization through expanded reproduction, Harvey insists that the processes of "original accumulation" identified by Marx are ongoing features of the system and not relics of a pre-capitalist or proto-capitalist period (Harvey 2003b: 144). For Harvey, dispossession remains continually important as it devalues assets and/or strips away rights so as to create an "outside," which can then be incorporated into the circuits of capital accumulation at low, or no cost (Harvey 2003b: 149). In this fashion, new spaces for capital accumulation are opened up, and overaccumulated capital can be valorized — an effective way to resolve accumulation problems. Although dispossession is by no means unique to the current era, it is especially prevalent with neoliberalism. This includes the creation of new mechanisms to enclose the commons (e.g., privatization), the creation of new markets (e.g., trading in carbon credits), and devaluation through currency speculation (Harvey 2003b: 145–48). In these processes the institutions and policies of the neoliberal state play important roles (Harvey 2005; 2003b).

While the spatio-temporal fix can temporarily avoid devaluation, and accumulation by dispossession can open new areas for investment of surplus capital, crises cannot be eliminated forever. The promise of the fix is that by creating new markets, spatially realigning capitalist activities, and creating the possibility that overaccumulated capital can lead to greater profitability in the future, crises are deferred or pushed elsewhere. Similar to the insights provided by the SSA approach and regulation theory, it is recognized that future crises are then generated by today's solutions. In fact, spatio-temporal fixes can lead to an intensification of crisis tendencies as well. If the fix is unable to generate real recovery in the future and/or when it inevitably begins to break down under the weight of its own contradictions (for example, if/when fixed capital becomes a drag on future accumulation), the underlying problems will again be made manifest.

David McNally also views overaccumulation as a root cause of crises and uses insights forwarded by Harvey to analyze the mechanisms underlying the recent global financial/economic crisis. Unlike what Brenner, O'Hara, and others suggest, McNally argues that real recovery did take place under the neoliberal accumulation order during the 1990s. He says that a "dramatic social, technical and spatial restructuring of capitalist production… occurred across the neoliberal period, all of which significantly raised rates of surplus-value and profitability" (McNally 2009: 43). Thus recovery did take place under neoliberalism even though turbulence, uneven development, and chronic recessions were the norm. World-wide forms of accumulation by dispossession and increased exploitation of the working class were endemic to the neoliberal era (McNally 2009: 55). However, the resumption of growth that began in the early-1980s, largely in East Asia, began to drop off by 1997 and overaccumulation began to set in (for example, warehouses with excessive inventories or factories running far under capacity). After 1997, McNally argues that economic expansion did occur but it was largely credit-fueled and thus unsustainable. The credit-fueled expansion was able to stave off crisis for roughly a decade, but confidence in the bubble economy burst in 2007, exposing both the precariousness of financialization and the underlying problems of overaccumulation (as witnessed by the problems experienced within sectors as diverse as manufacturing, construction, auto, and electronics).

Insights Offered by the Overaccumulation Perspective
McNally's description reveals how processes of overaccumulation can manifest as financial crises. Thus crises in the financial sector can be linked to production problems, and maintaining a rigid dichotomy between finance and the real economy can lead to mistaken analyses of crisis episodes. For his part, Harvey reminds us that fixes, however successful at avoiding crises, are temporary in nature. Crises cannot be eliminated as a facet of the capitalist system due to deep, intrinsic contradictions and conflicts. Crises can be deferred or pushed elsewhere, but they cannot be avoided forever. In fact, crises can also result from the spatio-temporal fixes established in an earlier era as they eventually create problems for future accumulation.

In this sense, these arguments are similar to those of the ssA approach and regulation theory. The principal difference, and the main insight of the overaccumulation perspective for our purposes here, is that these crises are ultimately crises of capital and therefore rooted in production, not in the extra-economic structures that support accumulation, although all approaches recognize that institutional supports can certainly help or hinder economic recovery.

Policy Paradigms
The insights provided by these theories of capitalist crises help to situate the recent economic crisis within its wider historical context as well as point to the different facets of the crisis-prone nature of capitalism. Yet the political-economic paradigms that guide policy development, under-examined by all of theories discussed above, are also of central concern. Thus, with these deeper theoretical critiques of capitalist accumulation in mind, in subsequent

chapters we turn to the macro-level policy paradigms which have guided the Canadian state (federal and provincial) since the postwar era and the ways in which they create their own set of contradictions which must ultimately be resolved. In using the term paradigm we follow Hall's (1993: 279) depiction of the concept, using the example of the dominance of the Keynesian paradigm in Britain. From this perspective a paradigm consists of ideas that "specified what the economic world was like, how it was to be observed, which goals were attainable through policy, and what instruments should be used to attain them. They became the prism through which policymakers saw the economy as well as their own role within it." Much policy change consists of incremental adjustments to existing policies or major policy alterations without changing the goals of policy. But from time to time, paradigmatic change involving different goals as well as instruments occurs (Hall 1993).

In the last century two major paradigm shifts took place in the western, capitalist liberal democracies, which changed state policies in dramatic fashion. The first was the rise of Keynesianism in the 1930s and 1940s; the second was the shift to neoliberalism in the 1970s and 1980s, first domestically and later in the global arena. Such sea changes in public and elite opinion are rare, and many factors are involved in changes of this magnitude. The most important is the development of a crisis that challenges old practices and demands the development of new ones. One effect of crises is that they can undermine confidence in the existing dominant approach or paradigm. However, in itself this will not produce change. Another necessary condition is the existence of an alternative paradigm within which the crisis can be framed differently and alternative responses developed. A third would be a period of political struggle followed by the emergence of a bloc of social and political actors committed to the alternative paradigm.

Thus we use the term paradigm to represent the ideational and policy content that comes to characterize a particular era in the development of capitalism, national policy regimes, and their socio-economic and political systems. Paradigms are located in a broader set of relationships — institutional, social, economic, and political — and are therefore part of the wider social structure of accumulation and promote a particular accumulation strategy.

It is important to note that often summarizing policies in terms of paradigms overstates the degree of policy conformity that existed in particular periods. Keynesianism in Canada was often more diluted or less interventionist in practice than elsewhere, and neoliberalism often exists in hybrid forms, and can vary in emphasis between jurisdictions. The purpose of identifying the various paradigms that have guided Canadian policy is therefore not to imply homogeneity but instead to illustrate dominant tendencies and the boundaries of the practicable (delineated by international pressures and the need to promote and restore capital accumulation, as illustrated by both the long wave and overaccumulation theories discussed in this chapter).

Ultimately paradigms inform processes of implementing new forms of social rule, which involves continual contestation, compromise, and the production of contradictions that urge new policy and eventually new paradigms. The paradigm approach offered here is interested in identifying guiding forces, with policy often adopted in an uneven or incomplete fashion when compared with the ideological prescription. Further, a paradigm is not an ahistorical given as the potential for contention is continual, and a common sense must be renewed by the dominant actors involved. In what follows we turn our attention to the nature of Keynesian and neoliberal reform in Canada, as paradigms that inform policy, shape state-society relations, and guide state support for accumulation. Accumulation crises, along with the contradictions generated by the social fix, have played an integral role in acting as catalysts that lead to changes in the paradigm of the capitalist state.

Conclusion

Within the tradition of political economy there are many perspectives on capitalist crises. Mainstream approaches, such as neoclassical economics, emphasize the self-regulating nature of the capitalist system and place the blame for disturbances on market-distorting mechanisms such as insufficient information, state interference and over-regulation, and irrationality on the part of labour. This leaves the mainstream analysis in a particularly impoverished state — unable to see the patterns which link the most recent systemic crisis to previous crises — and therefore it is unable to make sense of recent events except by pointing to regulatory failures, corruption, and other one-off explanations. Policy makers are equally myopic, as is reflected in the desire of politicians to get back to the status quo as soon as possible, at the expense of initiating any significant structural (or even regulatory) change. Denial is thus the order of the day, and this creates a serious barrier to change and ultimately to recovery from the Great Recession in the long run (i.e., an escape from the long downturn).

Beyond the mainstream exists a multitude of perspectives that reject this narrow and ahistorical focus, and instead point to the crisis-prone nature of the capitalist system and the ways in which the state and other extra-economic institutions and arrangements are integral to ensuring that growth and stability occur. Long wave theories such as the ssa approach and regulation theory are particularly well positioned to provide a rich analysis of moments of stability, and overaccumulation perspectives are adept at uncovering the ways in which production problems and surplus capital can undo the temporary solutions to crisis that are forged.

Thus the theories discussed here provide insight into the underlying causes of the economic crises that have triggered paradigm shifts in the past. The ssa emphasis on institutions of the state and Harvey's description of overaccumulation lend themselves quite well to analyses of changes in the postwar era from a Keynesian to a neoliberal form of capitalism, and the institutional implications that follow (a task we take up in chapters 3 and 4). This also alerts us to the possibility of future institutional and paradigmatic change as a result of the recent financial and economic crisis.

Chapter 3

THE KEYNESIAN WELFARE STATE

Drawing from the theories of crisis literature reviewed in the previous chapter, we begin, in this chapter and the next,[1] to trace the precursors of the economic crisis of 2008. Focusing on Canada, though with reference to other examples from time to time, we will present an historical account of the country's responses to previous crises, making use initially of two related concepts. The first, policy paradigm, enables us to focus on the ideas that underpinned the responses; the second, social structure of accumulation, illuminates the institutional architecture associated with the ideas and policies.

Here we examine the incremental adoption of Keynesianism in Canada as the dominant policy response to the Great Depression of the 1930s — arguably the worst crisis episode in the history of capitalism. The Keynesian interpretation of how to resolve the problems that plagued the Depression era — stagnant economic growth and persistently high levels of unemployment — involved a common element which changed the face of public policy in the west. This was the need for greater state intervention in order to help smooth out the ups and downs of a capitalist economy. This marked a sharp break from the previous paradigm of classical laissez-faire liberalism. In Canada, as is the case elsewhere, it facilitated the creation of a welfare state focused on propping up employment levels, providing a social safety net, and ensuring some degree of compromise with respect to the demands of organized labour. As with other social structures of accumulation, however, the institutions of the Keynesian era were supportive of the needs of the capitalist system as a whole. Encouraging employment and providing a safety net to make up for the deficiencies of the market were intended to support consumption and therefore aggregate demand. Compromises afforded to labour were circumscribed and operated to create a relatively stable, predictable system of labour relations (largely curtailing the more radical expressions of the labour movement). Thus the stability and prosperity engendered by these institutional arrangements make the Keynesian era the prime example of a successful and well-functioning social structure of accumulation. While this is not the only explanation for the successes of the postwar economic order, it is certainly an integral component. We now turn to an elaboration of the Canadian version of the Keynesian policy paradigm as well as its core institutional features.

Keynes's Theory of Crisis

Keynesian ideas began to take hold in the Great Depression of the 1930s, a profound crisis that shook capitalism to its roots. Some capitalist nations, attempting to adjust to the new circumstances and end the crisis, engaged in wide-ranging political experiments, varying from fascism to social democracy. Others remained rooted in the orthodoxy of the existing paradigm (Gourevitch 1986). Either way, the period's legacy would be the emergence of the modern welfare state in the advanced capitalist nations. After the Great Depression and World War II, the classical laissez-faire doctrine of minimal state intervention was temporarily laid to rest in most western countries including Canada. There was a marked change in the approach to social policy, and the state's role in managing and regulating the economy was enhanced. Even supporters of the capitalist system had come to believe that "without state intervention and regulation in the economy, the market simply would not survive" (Savage and Robins 1990: 3).

In *The General Theory of Employment, Interest and Money* (1936) John Maynard Keynes provided the theoretical justification for state intervention within modern capitalism, and over the course of the next decade his views became widely accepted. Classical economics had rested on the belief that there existed "natural built-in equilibrating forces which ensured that a capitalistic economy would generate continuing prosperity and a high level of employment" (Buchanan and Wagner 1977). Economic downturns might occur, but they would trigger adjustments that would set the equilibrium right. The Depression of the 1930s, however, undermined the belief in the existence of such equilibrating forces, and Keynes set forth a major challenge to the classical paradigm by denying "the very existence of the self-equilibrating forces of the capitalist economy" (ibid.: 25).

Writing in a period of mass unemployment which the neoclassical economic orthodoxy of his day was unable to explain, Keynes's ideas challenged several postulates of that orthodoxy, particularly the neoclassical claim that there was an automatic tendency, via adjustments in prices, wages, and interest rates, towards full employment. In this view such unemployment as occurred was either frictional, as with persons temporarily out of work while looking for a job, or voluntary, as in the case of workers who priced themselves out of jobs by insisting on excessive wages. Keynes accepted that these types of unemployment did exist but considered that most 1930s unemployment was neither frictional nor voluntary. Instead, he argued, most of it was involuntary and caused by insufficient aggregate demand in the economy — an eventuality regarded as impossible by the neoclassical paradigm because of its acceptance of Say's Law, which held that supply creates its own demand.

Aggregate demand is made up of consumption, investment, net exports, and government spending. In the event that these did not equal potential output a deflationary gap could be said to exist and unemployment would result. In Keynes's opinion there was no reason to suppose that supply and demand would tend towards equilibrium at a full employment level and demand deficiency was, therefore, quite a likely occurrence under capitalism. If governments wanted full employment it was up to them to manipulate aggregate demand to the necessary level. This might be achieved either by adjusting the government's own spending, or by stimulating private sector consumption or investment through tax cuts, or by changes in interest rates. These examples indicate that either fiscal or monetary policy instruments could be used to achieve the desired result, although it was anticipated that fiscal policy would play the greater role.

Though extensive state intervention had previously been anathema from the point of view of capitalist economics, it is quite clear that Keynes's ideas, both in general and in detail, were designed to save rather than subvert the capitalist system. Keynes's context was the delegitimizing effects of mass unemployment in the 1930s and the threat to capitalism from communism and to liberal democracy from fascism. In this context his ideas, as his perceptive contemporary Harold Macmillan was quick to observe, offered a "middle way" between communism and fascism that involved reform of the system but preservation of its essentials.

Under the influence of Keynesianism, the capitalist state not only made full employment an economic priority but came to embrace a welfare state function based on the provision of material benefits to subordinate classes. However, the Keynesian welfare state was also economically functional in that it sustained aggregate demand and thus the potential for profitable investment in other sectors of the economy. In any case, under conditions of full employment its costs were sustainable.

The pursuit of full employment would necessitate the "socialization of investment." But this was not to be understood as involving extensive state ownership (Keynes 1936: 378). The attraction of these ideas, once an adequate theoretical account was constructed of how they might be realized, was obvious. A commitment to full employment was a massive advance for labour. Similarly the Keynesian paradigm adopted a relatively benign view of trade unions, saw positive benefits in the encouragement of collective bargaining, and supported welfare state measures including unemployment benefits for those temporarily out of work. All of this was very positive from a labour perspective.

Equally importantly, permanently high levels of aggregate demand offered seemingly endless opportunities for expansion by capital. Policies derived from the Keynesian paradigm seemed capable of maintaining the necessary conditions for capital accumulation while legitimating the system at the same time.

However, there were drawbacks from capital's point of view identified at the time that were to loom large in the debates of the 1970s (cf. Kalecki 1943; Gonick 1987: 81–84). First, full employment posed an authority problem for capital. Second, full employment could trigger a profit squeeze for capital and an inflation problem for society. For Kalecki, at least, there was little doubt that the authority problem was the more serious source of capital's ambivalence about and ultimate opposition to full employment. The problem should really be understood as one with two dimensions. Capital's authority over its workforce was threatened by full employment. But so also was capital's authority vis-à-vis the state. As Sawyer's (1985: 137) discussion of Kalecki's ideas puts it:

> Under laissez-faire capitalism the level of employment strongly depends on the "state of confidence." If the confidence falters, then so does investment, and thereby output and employment. Confidence is a fragile flower which needs great care, i.e., policies which industrial leaders approve of. Thus the use of public expenditure to maintain the level of demand is seen to remove considerable power from capitalists, whose threats not to invest if confidence is harmed become less potent…. the social function of the doctrine of "sound finance" is to make the level of employment dependent on the state of confidence.

In the context of the recent historical memory of the Depression and the need for postwar reconstruction for most observers such concerns lay in the future. The genius of Keynes was his ability to devise a technical solution to the crisis of capitalism, one that sanctioned a measured degree of government intervention while maintaining market dominance. Keynesian economics thus held the promise of making capitalism function better without at the same time upsetting the "underlying social relationships" of the system.

In Canada, as in other western countries, Keynesianism was adopted as a policy paradigm, albeit more cautiously than in some other states. The focus was on the demand side of the economy, leaving the supply side to look after itself or, more accurately, leaving it to the private sector to take care of. This minimized the scope for state intervention that was possible within a Keynesian framework.

In terms of the components of aggregate demand, which the state was henceforth committed to managing, the 1945 *White Paper on Employment and Income* laid particular emphasis on the contribution of exports. In this respect Wolfe (1984: 55) noted, the white paper represented "a rather unique synthesis of the traditional staples-led approach to economic development with the Keynesian theory of demand management and fiscal stabilization." Throughout the postwar period there were supply-side interventions on the part of the state in such policy areas as immigration, commerce, taxation, transport, and energy. Most of these can be best understood as applications of Canada's traditional state-based economic development policies rather than being derived from a more interventionist version of Keynesianism. As such they were very much directed towards capital accumulation (Gonick 1987: 91).

Nevertheless, a second national policy[2] (Neill 1991: 173) was articulated following World War II. A Keynesian demand-management economic strategy complemented by the construction of a social welfare state was the main feature (Brodie and Jenson 1988: 293; Smiley 1975: 47–48). The approach went along with an active pursuit of a liberalized international trading system (see Eden and Molot 1993: 235–40). According to Robin Neill (1991: 183), where Keynes had assumed a closed, mature economic system, "By introducing considerations relating to development and trade into Keynesian general equilibrium analysis Canadians… made major contributions to the development of economics." Canadian Keynesians, such as W.A. Mackintosh, were responding to factors that today would be associated with globalization. Intimately aware of the realities of staples dependency, the early Keynesians knew that the application of their approach would be difficult in Canada because "the Canadian economy was open, regionally diversified, relatively dependent on primary product exports, and governed by a federated state" (Neill 1991: 173).

The Keynesian Welfare State — Social Base

In Canada, as elsewhere, many scholars have interpreted the postwar Keynesian era[3] as a tacit class compromise between capital and labour. Certainly both these social actors received benefits from the social contract constructed in Canada after World War II. Capital had to tolerate a more active and interventionist state, but the intervention was largely confined to fiscal and monetary policies designed to maintain aggregate demand at a level sufficient to sustain high and stable levels of employment and income. As a result, economic growth and profit-making opportunities were good. Keynesianism did not imply higher levels of public ownership or state control of investment or other investment decisions. Labour won collective bargaining rights, even though legally circumscribed, and commitments that the state would construct a welfare system and aim for high employment levels in its economic policies. The adoption of Keynesianism by most western countries in the postwar world was a response to the deep interwar economic crisis, the challenge of an ideological competitor in the shape of the Soviet Union, and the pressure from below for full employment, labour rights, and economic security. Another factor was the experience of World War II: it seemed that an active state was quite capable of organizing not only a military victory but the economic activity that made it possible — a practical refutation of classical economic doctrines.

The Keynesian Welfare State — Programs in Canada

By the 1960s, the responsibilities of government throughout the western world were decidedly Keynesian: "full employment; a high rate of economic growth; reasonable stability of prices; a viable balance of payments; and an equitable distribution of rising incomes." In short, the state had come to be responsible for ensuring a measure of "equity, efficiency, stability, and growth" (Stewart 1991: 92). Keynesianism helped to complete the logic of what is sometimes termed the Fordist regime of accumulation (see chapter 2 on regulation theory), the major elements of which have been characterized "as the era of the dominance of mass production (economies of scale, assembly-line production, detailed division of labour, separation of execution, and control at the level of the workplace), balanced by high levels of mass consumption maintained by institutional supports which include Keynesian demand policies, and an accord between business and labour" (Macdonald 1991: 182).

During the twentieth century, state involvement in the areas of education, health, social security, and the economy in general mushroomed in all the advanced capitalist nations. In Canada government spending as a portion of Gross Domestic Product (GDP) increased from 15.7 percent to 26.4 percent between 1920 and 1950, and by 1984 it had reached 46.5 percent (Banting 1986: 2; Bakker 1990: 429, Table 2.1). This pattern of state expansion was not exclusive to Canada, but represented part of a trend common to all western democracies. In comparative terms, in fact, Canada fell into the lower third of developed nations with regard to levels of social spending (Canada 1985: Vol. 2, 554). Comparatively speaking then, Canada remained a welfare state laggard, although in the context of North America its social welfare status was "advanced."

The social contract constructed in Canada after World War II respected the key interests of capital: investment decision-making power was left in the hands of private enterprise. In exchange the state made four major concessions to labour that, together, constitute the postwar welfare state. It made commitments to pursue policies ensuring high, stable levels of employment and incomes. For individuals unable to participate fully in the labour market, the state would provide assistance, thus sanctioning the various aspects of the social welfare state. Third, a limited number of universal social programs, notably health care, were instituted. Last, the state extended recognition to a number of labour rights, including free collective bargaining.

Full Employment

As we have seen, the Canadian version of full employment Keynesianism (cf. Campbell 1987: ch. 2) was launched by the 1945 *White Paper on Employment and Income*. It stopped short of promising full employment, preferring instead the phrase "high and stable levels of employment" (Canada 1945). Given this ambivalent beginning, doubts have been expressed about the strength of the commitment to full employment in Canada. For much of the postwar period unemployment, though low, exceeded levels in other western countries (see McBride 1992: ch. 2). Some commentators have drawn attention to the passivity of fiscal policy in this period (Campbell 1987). The view that the Keynesian era in Canada was not as Keynesian as it might have been certainly has some validity. Such criticisms help explain why neoliberalism was able to sweep away the commitment to full employment with such apparent ease after 1975. The point, of course, is that doubts about Keynesianism had deep roots and its adoption and practice were hardly institutionalized.

Nonetheless, the critics do miss something. The notion that the adoption of Keynesianism may have been more rhetorical than real was not apparent to observers at the time. The terms of economic policy discourse had changed dramatically since the 1930s. Accepting the concept that achieving high and stable levels of employment was an essential function of government changed the terms of political debate and the practice of politics itself. This is entirely consistent with the claim that Keynesianism was the dominant policy paradigm of its day; this need not be reflected in each and every policy, but instead informs how policy makers view the economy overall, which types of goals ought to be set, and the instruments that are to be used to help achieve those aims. Moreover the Canadian state was operating, during this period, in an international economic environment shaped by Keynesianism and in which many nations' policies did implement the paradigm. This had real implications in Canada as well and the depiction of a Canadian Keynesian era is not entirely a misnomer.

A Social Safety Net

The Canadian version of the welfare state was constructed piecemeal and gradually. World War II provided a stimulus and saw the creation of some programs, but the process as a whole continued for years, culminating with the reform and expansion of the unemployment insurance system in 1971. The process had various origins: the demands of ordinary citizens for a better future; demands that under wartime full employment conditions became more vocal and insistent; the realization of the elite that suitable plans for postwar society were an important motivating force in prosecuting the war; and the intellectual influences of Keynes's economic theories and the Beveridge report on postwar reconstruction and social policy in Britain (Guest 1987).

Canada's own version of the Beveridge report, Leonard Marsh's *Report on Social Security in Canada*, appeared in March 1943. It recommended full employment policies, supplementary programs for occupational training, comprehensive systems for social and medical insurance (covering unemployment, sickness, maternity, disability, old age, and health), family or children's allowances, and general welfare assistance for those who, should the full employment policies fail, had exhausted unemployment insurance benefits or were not covered by them (Guest 1987: 212–13).

The immediate policy impact of the Marsh report was modest: Canada's implementation of the report's recommendations proved tepid and unenthusiastic and this applied to the principle of full employment itself (McBride 1992; Campbell 1987, 1991).

Despite these important caveats, a version of Keynesianism was officially adopted in Ottawa; henceforth policy discourse took place in Keynesian terms and full employment was a legitimate goal of economic policy. In these respects Canada differed from its neighbour to the south, where the official reception of Keynesian ideas and policy goals was considerably cooler and occurred later. The same point can be made about the creation of a welfare state in the two countries. Canada was not in the vanguard internationally, but the gradual piecemeal extension of programs did result in a more comprehensive social network than found in the United States, and the role of the state in promoting economic stabilization and social welfare arguably became an important element of political and national integration in Canada.

The federal government set up an unemployment insurance system in 1940 after a constitutional amendment had established federal jurisdiction in the area. Some suggest that the move would have come earlier but for a genuine constitutional problem that made jurisdiction unclear (Pal 1988: 151–52); for others the constitution served as a useful excuse for inaction (Struthers 1983: 209–10). In any event, the initial scheme was a cautious, actuarially sound system of insurance, which covered only 42 percent of the workforce (see Pal 1988: 38–41 for a summary). From 1941 to 1971 the scheme's coverage was steadily expanded and the qualifying criteria were eased. The *Unemployment Insurance Act* of 1971 significantly expanded coverage (to around 96 percent of the workforce), introduced more generous income-maintenance provisions, relaxed entrance requirements and increased their sensitivity to regional disparities in unemployment, and offered coverage for maternity leave. By the early 1970s the UI system had undergone significant development and was considerably different from the truncated system available in the United States.

In 1945 the federal government introduced a universal family allowance system. Its stated purposes were to contribute to the well-being of all Canadian children (indicative of determination to leave the Depression era behind) and to the maintenance of postwar purchasing power should the anticipated slump occur (Guest 1985: 128–33). The legislation was passed unanimously on its second reading in the House of Commons, a sure indication that a version of Keynesianism, however qualified, had attained hegemonic status in postwar Canada.

Other elements of social security included the Canada Assistance Plan (a cost-shared federal-provincial program providing welfare and social assistance services); old age pensions; a variety of job creation and training programs that expanded considerably in the late 1960s and early 1970s; and a number of regional development programs to encourage economic diversification in disadvantaged regions. Most of these programs were implemented or extended gradually over the course of the postwar decades. The 1960s stand out as a particularly active period in the construction of the Canadian welfare state.

Health care in Canada is primarily a provincial responsibility, but through its spending power Ottawa gradually acquired a significant role in shaping the health care system. The end result was that health care in Canada was publicly organized and universally available. The federal *Medical Care Act* (1966) established five criteria that provincial health programs had to meet to qualify for funding: universality; comprehensiveness; portability; accessibility; and public administration. The *Established Programs Financing Act* (1977) seemed to establish a long-term federal funding commitment for the health area, and the *Canada Health Act* (1984), as well as reiterating the principles of the 1966 legislation, permitted the federal government to withhold funding from provinces that implemented direct user costs, a device that had emerged as a significant challenge to the universality principle. The contrast between Canada's cheaper, universally accessible health care system and the costly U.S. system, under which coverage varied dramatically with individual income and wealth, is a frequent object of commentary in Canada, and the Canadian health care system has become a source of national pride.

Thus, in the years following World War II, the Canadian state established for itself an active profile in social policy. Its adoption of a version of Keynesian economic theory was followed by the development of stabilization policies that contributed to full employment. Together these activities involved a significant modification of market forces and the individualist values associated with them. Collective provision of social benefits and collective (in the sense of state) management of the economy became features of Canadian political life and society to an extent that clearly differentiated this country from the United States. In comparing Canadian and U.S. social policy at the beginning of the 1980s, Robert Kudrle and Theodore Marmor argued that Canadian social programs were "usually... more advanced in terms of program development, coverage and benefits.... In every policy area it appears that the general public as well as elite opinion… [is] more supportive of state action in Canada than in the United States. This support appears to underlie not just the typically earlier enactment of policy in Canada but also subsequent changes… (and expansion)" (1981: 110–18).

Canadian social policy in the postwar period also had a decidedly regional dimension as befitted a federal society. The new social welfare measures approved by the central government "would not only benefit individuals, but also would help protect the regional communities" from the ravages of poverty and unemployment. The Keynesian policies of providing minimal levels of social and economic security were viewed as "economically advantageous and fair" in the peripheral provinces (Simeon and Robinson 1990: 134). Initially the Keynesian social and economic management policies designed for national development were viewed as containing within them an inherent regional development component. However, by the 1950s, as part of the Canadian state's commitment to greater fairness and equity, more explicit policies were designed to address the persistent problems of regional economic disparities (Norrie, Simeon, and Krasnick 1986: 281). These included equalization payments to have-not provinces and targeted regional development programs. The goal was to ensure "a more equitable distribution of the national benefits of the economic union" (Simeon and Robinson 1990: 134) and thus alleviate some of the tensions that arose from the geographic disparities and discrimination stemming from uneven national development. The Canadian social contract was expanded in this period to include a territorial equity provision. In this respect Canadian social and economic policy was "intended to foster east-west interregional links in order to offset or lessen north-south pressures" (Doern and Purchase 1991: 9). The Keynesian welfare state in Canada was thus designed to meet the challenge of regulating not only class struggles but also territorial ones.

Labour Rights

Early in the Keynesian era labour rights were expanded by P.C. 1003, an order-in-council establishing a new legislative environment for industrial relations. P.C. 1003 is often, but inaccurately, regarded simply as a Canadian imitation of the Roosevelt era U.S. *Wagner Act*. Like the *Wagner Act*, it included acceptance of trade unionism and collective bargaining as a right, provided there was evidence of a certain level of worker support, and the establishment of an enforcement machinery (Woods 1973: 64–70, 86–92). However, Canada's postwar legislation also contained provisions for compulsory conciliation and mediation before strikes could occur, banned strikes during the duration of collective agreements, and placed a number of other restrictions on the way unions could operate. These provisions built upon earlier Canadian labour legislation such as the *Industrial Disputes Investigation Act*, and entrenched a corporatist dimension into the postwar industrial relations system (McBride 1996).

The growing acceptance of Keynesian theories did something to reconcile Canada's political and economic establishments to an enhanced role for trade unions. In the Keynesian paradigm unions could play a positive role in sustaining levels of aggregate demand. More importantly, unprecedented working class pressure, both industrial and political, produced the concessions which are represented in the 1944 order-in-council and in postwar legislation (cf. Panitch and Swartz 2003: 16–20). Cold war coercion against radical unions and unionists also played a role in ushering in the new system. The legal framework was not an unqualified victory for labour. It was characterized by elaborate certification procedures, legally enforceable contracts, no-strike provisions for the duration of contracts, and liability of trade unions and their members if illegal strikes occurred. On the other hand, the legislation did guarantee the right to organize and to bargain collectively, it forced employers to recognize unions once certain conditions were met, defined unfair labour practices, and provided remedies under the law for violations.

Although the balance of class power had shifted in labour's favour during World War II the unions had still lacked sufficient power to force the employers into recognition and bargaining unassisted by the state. The price of state assistance was regulation and the continuation of the compulsory conciliation and "work stoppage delay" features of earlier legislation (McBride 1983: 508–09). The cumulative effect of the restrictions was to severely curtail labour's right to strike (Woods 1973: 93). Most labour relations fell under provincial jurisdiction. However, a Canada-wide system of collective bargaining existed because most provinces adopted legislation patterned after P.C. 1003. A significant change to this situation only came with the development of special provisions for public sector collective bargaining in the 1960s and early 1970s. Growing differences in policy towards public service labour relations tended to undermine the existence of the national industrial relations system that developed in the immediate postwar years.

The economic crisis of the 1970s and the displacement of Keynesianism first by late Keynesian tinkering such as wage control programs, and later by monetarism, was reflected in attacks upon the collective bargaining rights of unions generally, and of public sector unions in particular. The "postwar consensus" proved particularly fragile concerning the rights of unions, which, however moderately they might conduct themselves, represent a challenge to the rights of property owners.

Institutional Base

Canada's adoption of Keynesianism was complicated by the federal system and the way it had evolved between 1867 and the 1930s. By the 1930s, Canada's federation had become considerably decentralized. The causes of these developments lie in the complex interaction of social forces, institutional developments (including judicial reinterpretation of the *British North America Act*), and a dominant ideology at that time that leaned increasingly to laissez-faire economics once the nation-building stage of Canada's economic and political history was judged complete by the 1920s. The constitutional preference of that ideology was for a weak state accomplished through decentralization.

As the desperation of the Depression increased and the example of Roosevelt's New Deal resonated in Canada, along with the threatening spectre of communism and fascism in Europe, the constitutional impasse did create a genuine obstacle to social reform, additional to that created by the ideological blinkers of the governing class. The ultimate resolution of this impasse by 1945 depended only partly on formal constitutional amendment, such as the transfer of unemployment insurance to the federal level in 1940. More important was the use of Ottawa's spending power in the postwar period to engineer shared-cost programs, meeting national conditions or standards, in areas of provincial jurisdiction.

This system became known as "cooperative federalism," and it was under this label that the Canadian version of the postwar Keynesian welfare state was created. Many of the programs involved federal and provincial cooperation. Indeed, the heyday of the Keynesian welfare state in Canada was also the heyday of cooperative federalism. Shared-cost arrangements emanated from the fact that much of the social policy area was under provincial jurisdiction while the predominant power of taxation was in the hands of the federal authorities. Since the federal level was inclined to pursue an agenda of building national standards in social policy over the postwar years, the scene was set for bargaining between the two orders of government about the generosity and shape of that policy. Some of the programs, such as family allowances, were universal and funded from general revenues. Others, such as the Canada Pension Plan and unemployment insurance, were based partly on insurance principles. In addition to providing income-support programs, the federal government made dollars available to the health, education, and social assistance systems. Frequently, as with the *Medical Care Act* or Canada Assistance Plan, Ottawa would attach conditions to its funding. Provincial health systems, for example, had to meet the criteria of universality, comprehensiveness, portability, accessibility, and public administration to qualify for federal financial contributions.

The impact of the provision of these benefits had profound effects in Canada, including providing an ingredient of national identity. Gradually Canadian citizenship came to mean more than simply having a formal set of "negative" constitutional rights such as "life, liberty, and security of the person." Over time, the idea of a Canadian citizenship evolved and broadened. As late as the 1990s, official documents could claim that a national system of health care, an array of income support programs, free public and secondary education, and affordable post-secondary education symbolized "Canadians' sense of themselves as members of a community where solidarity and mutual responsibility are fundamental social norms" (Ontario Ministry of Intergovernmental Affairs 1991: 2). Thus the Keynesian consensus, in its attempt to produce a stable and efficient capitalism, pursued universal social programs and other policies embodying principles of mild redistributive justice, and this helped to promote "a sense of common social citizenship" (Doern and Purchase 1991: 9).

Crisis of the Keynesian Welfare State

In the Keynesian era there was an emphasis on building a social consensus that would outline the acceptable boundaries within which political contests were to be waged. Broadly speaking, there were two versions of the consensus, one that "talked about the 'mixed' (i.e., still overwhelmingly private-enterprise) economy," and another that stressed the social democratic elements, emphasizing to a much greater degree the state sector, welfare, and planning (Leys 1980: 49). The mixed-economy version predominated in Canada, although it still resembled the social democratic version enough to differentiate the country from its southern neighbour.

In political terms, the consensus meant that the major political parties and forces accepted the Keynesian welfare state and Keynesianism was adopted as the new "common sense." On questions of policy and style of government there was a substantial degree of cross-party agreement. Political opposition and conflict over the extent of welfare provision did occur, but within mainstream politics it was unquestioned that the state should play a central role in welfare provision and be active in economic regulation (Savage and Robins 1990).

The long economic boom that had begun in the expansionary climate of post-World War II reconstruction was brought to an abrupt end in the early 1970s, signaled by, but not solely due to, the 1973 Arab oil embargo and the subsequent dramatic increase in oil prices by the Organization of Petroleum Exporting Countries (OPEC). This event was the first shock wave of an economic earthquake that rocked the international economy. One indicator of the changing times, some have argued, was the decline of profits and the onset of overaccumulation (see chapter 2). Another was capital flight, as multinational corporations rapidly shifted their manufacturing investments to the newly industrializing centres of the Third World, where cheap pools of labour could be readily found. A process of deindustrialization, "a widespread, systematic disinvestment in the nation's basic productive capacity" (Bluestone and Harrison 1982: 6), was set in motion in the industrial core.

The traditional smokestack industries—steel-making and other heavy manu-facturing — rapidly declined, causing unemployment in the industrial belts and a transformation of the structure of employment. In Canada, employment in goods-producing industries fell from 34.8 percent of the labour force in 1951 to 26.7 percent in 1981, a pattern replicated in most other OECD nations (Economic Council of Canada 1984b: 157, Table 11-5).

The global jockeying of investment and production was paralleled by a technological revolution as corporations attempted to modernize their enterprises, thus lowering labour costs and boosting profits. The impact of technological change on employment opportunities alone was vividly illus-trated by the Economic Council of Canada. Throughout the 1971–79 period, advances in technology made it possible to produce the 1979 level of output with 8 percent fewer jobs in the commercial sector of the economy than would have been required under 1971 conditions. This represented a labour saving of approximately 630,000 jobs. As expected, the impact of technology varies from one industry to another. Only in seven of the thirty-nine industries did the introduction of new technology call for additional labour skills. In all others, labour saving ranged from 37 percent of total employment in knitting mills to 1 percent in the construction industry (1984a: 75).

During the 1950s and 1960s unemployment in OECD countries stood at about 3 percent, a level generally regarded as full employment. This scenario changed dramatically during the 1970s. In Canada, the ever expanding army of unemployed caused the federal government to officially abandon this full employment definition in 1972 along with its policy commitments to maintain full employment (Gonick 1987: 24–25; also see McBride 1992). The official unemployment figures steadily advanced from 3.6 percent in 1950 to 5.9 percent in 1970, finally peaking in 1983 at 11.9 percent (Marr and Paterson 1980: 427, Table 13:3; Ruggeri 1987: 322, Table 3). For the OECD area as a whole the problem worsened but remained less serious than in Canada as the unemployment rate climbed from an average of 3.5 percent in 1973 to 5.5 percent in 1975 to 8.4 percent in 1983 (Gonick 1987: 341).

Increased unemployment was initially accompanied by upwardly spi-raling prices. Economic assumptions concerning a tradeoff between unem-ployment and inflation were turned on their head as a new phenomenon, stagflation, the co-existence of economic recession and high inflation, made its appearance. Inflation rates rose steadily during the 1970s, reaching double-digit figures and easing only after 1982 (see, for example, Ruggeri 1987: 297, Table 3).

The twin evils of recession and inflation stimulated the revival of the neoliberal policy paradigm. Proponents pointed to the apparent inabil-ity of Keynesianism to explain or counter inflationary pressures. Similarly Keynesianism's lack of concern about government deficits and the public debt became a major plank in the neoliberal platform. According to the Royal Commission on the Economic Union and Development Prospects for Canada (the Macdonald Commission): "In the past, economists who subscribed to Keynesian views on demand management usually argued that the size of the deficit was not a matter for concern. The important point was 'to balance the economy' rather than 'to balance the budget'" (Canada 1985: Vol. 2, 294). But for most economists the perceived failure of Keynesian policy to correct economic difficulties served to undermine its logic concerning deficits. Management of the public purse soon became a heated topic of policy debate; public deficits were cited as a major factor in the economic decline.

During the 1950s and 1960s, periods of deficits had been followed by surpluses, which limited the growth of government debt. After 1974 government revenue shortfalls rapidly increased. Public debt consequently "increased not only in absolute value but as a proportion of the country's gross national expenditure" (Economic Council of Canada 1984b: 35). The fiscal crisis generated by the public debt problem led many to question the legitimacy of the Keynesian welfare state (Resnick 1989: 105), even though the debt burdens currently experienced by the state were in no small measure a consequence of neoliberal economic policy itself.

To some extent, of course, the welfare state does operate as a restraining agent on private profit and accumulation, which together serve as the basis for the expansion of the capitalist system. The reason for this is not because welfare policies attempt to redistribute wealth to any significant extent. Leo Panitch has referred to welfare's redistributive effects as "socialism in one class" (cited in Leys 1980: 52), because the transfers are largely "from younger, employed workers, to retired, unemployed workers, workers' widows and one-parent families." However, the welfare state can act to constrain profit levels by introducing barriers to the free market mechanism. Prior to the welfare state, the reserve army of labour under free-market conditions served to undermine labour's demands, whereas the welfare state's existence placed labour in a stronger position than otherwise (Gough 1981: 14).

Such perceptions partly explain the withdrawal of support for the Keynesian welfare state by the capitalist class. Russell has observed that the welfare state, once "portrayed as an important adjunct to Keynesian economic policy," increasingly was "depicted as a destabilizing influence that has indeed given rise to a new set of economic problems" (1991: 489). The driving force behind this redefinition in Canada was the corporate sector speaking through its peak organization — the Business Council on National Issues — and through business-funded think tanks like the Fraser Institute and C.D. Howe Institute.

With the advent of economic crisis and global capital restructuring, the Keynesian consensus unraveled and its institutions were questioned. Even the quintessential Keynesian economist, Paul Samuelson, concluded that "our last consensus was wrong" and would have to be replaced by a "new one" (1983: 19). The economic crisis generated political strains. The Macdonald Commission reported, "Clearly, in recent years, political consensus on social policy has given way to more active ideological debate and uncertainty" (Canada 1985: Vol. 2, 578). By the mid-1980s, a decade after Keynesianism was declared to be in crisis, the active ideological debate had concluded. The neoliberal paradigm had emerged as the new conventional wisdom.

Conclusion

In this chapter we have outlined the paradigmatic ideas, policies, and institutions that comprised the Keynesian era in Canada. The ensemble can be viewed as a social structure of accumulation, in terms of the theoretical material we presented in chapter 2. It was able to accommodate the needs and demands of both capital and labour. In doing so, it met the accumulation requirements of capital while simultaneously legitimating the system by concrete measures that benefited labour and other subordinate groups. By these means Keynesianism became hegemonic for a prolonged period, roughly thirty years, and presided over a stable yet economically expanding political economy.

There is a temptation to attribute the success of that period to the hegemonic ideas and the policies and institutions in place. Certainly, the paradigm gave way to an alternative once it failed to address new policy challenges that arose. But, of course, underneath the surface of the Keynesian SSA other factors were at work. For example, part of the success of Keynesianism rested on the destruction of capital and infrastructure that resulted from the war. Replacing those stocks provided many seemingly limitless opportunities for profitable investment. But when the backlog was addressed and the economically devastated countries of East Asia and Europe recovered, business began to encounter problems that fitted the crisis of overaccumulation described by David Harvey. In that context the battle of ideas between Keynesianism and neoliberalism picked up steam.

At that level, there were certainly alternatives on offer and the outcome was far from pre-determined. Greater state intervention in the economy, and the market system specifically, could possibly have extended the achievement of the Keynesian goal of full employment. But this would have meant a stronger and bigger state using greater coercion, either against labour through wage control programs, or against capital by insisting on more planning and interference with market prices. And, of course, the attraction of Keynesianism had been that it represented a class compromise. Policies such as those mentioned would end the compromise, a step social democratic parties and their labour allies were unwilling to take.

Once capital came to the view that its interests could no longer be met under the Keynesian formula, its organizations and associated think tanks and political parties undertook the task of developing an alternative that would. This tended to leave labour and its associated social democratic parties as defenders of a paradigm and SSA that had lost its social base. The compromise had been breached from the political right.

Chapter 4

THE NEOLIBERAL STATE

As the Keynesian social structure of accumulation began to give way to rising contradictions, conflicts, and economic stagnation, the nascent neoliberal paradigm was able to emerge from obscurity. In Canada this process was gradual, marked by incrementalism and stealth. After a period in which various alternatives and options seemed available, and adherents of each contended for advantage, we can see that the achievement of an electoral majority by Brian Mulroney's Progressive Conservatives in 1984 marked the triumph of neoliberalism. The paradigm was sustained and significantly deepened during the 1990s under the Chrétien Liberals and continued under Stephen Harper's government. As such, neoliberalism has always been a political project, not a necessary outcome of Keynesian contradictions. The onset of stagflation and other difficulties with the SSA in the 1970s provided the opportunity and justification for the paradigm shift, but did not require it. The ascension of key tenets of neoliberal policy — balanced budgets, inflation control, retrenchment of public programs, and reduction of government intrusion into economic and social affairs — have not only produced a crisis in the institutions which are largely a holdover from the Keynesian era (for example, public health care) but are also intentionally designed to widen the sphere of private accumulation, enhance private authority and control, and make the state more "market-like." This domestic emphasis of neoliberalism also means that globalization, often used as a justification for neoliberal policy, is in fact largely a consequence of the paradigm shift. In this chapter we examine many of the key features of the Canadian neoliberal policy paradigm, and begin to delve into the implications of this shift (although this topic is also taken up in chapters 5 and 6). In what follows we discuss the neoliberal account of the Keynesian crisis, the connection between globalization and neoliberalism, free trade and the social base of neoliberalism, neoliberalism at home, and the institutions of the neoliberal era.

The Neoliberal Account of the Crisis of Keynesianism

The Keynesian postwar consensus was in its heyday from 1945 until around 1975. Thereafter its decline began, but some attachment to the Keynesian approach lingered in Canada until the defeat of the Liberal government in 1984 (Lewis 2003). Since then neoliberalism has been the dominant policy paradigm, and while dismantling the Keynesian institutions and programs proceeded only gradually, neoliberalism has altered the entire context within which public policy is conceived. Parallel to domestic developments, neoliberalism has proved to be the ideology of globalization.

As well as "rolling back" the programs and commitments of the Keynesian welfare state (Peck and Tickell 2002) neoliberals have tried to "roll-out" their own alternative prescriptions and to alter the institutional arrangements to reflect their priorities. A significant component of the package was connected to enthusiastic participation in what can be termed neoliberal globalization. A new generation of trade and investment agreements was a key vehicle, not least because by embedding the neoliberal principles in binding international agreements they locked them in place. It was conceivable for states to change course and repudiate neoliberalism, but this was made much more difficult by international commitments.

While Keynesian ideas held sway, most people concerned about national-level public policy saw the active involvement of government in achieving goals such as full employment as a legitimate function. Although the practice of Keynesianism was less enthusiastic in Canada than in some other countries and certainly proved to be imperfect (Campbell 1987), the framework was encouraged until the early 1970s by an international economic regime that was tolerant of national economic management. Everywhere there were strong domestic pressures for more interventionist states to provide economic stability and social security, political goods that differentiated the postwar state from its predecessor before World War II.

By the mid-1970s, the long postwar economic boom that, in reality, had its shares of ups and downs was widely recognized as being over. The demise of the Bretton Woods system and the rise of a new generation of intrusive trade and investment agreements were characteristic of the 1970s and succeeding decades. The space for domestic policy autonomy shrank. In the 1970s, America's financing of the Vietnam War and two international oil crises drove inflation higher, though in political debates rising prices were often attributed to domestic causes. Two broad explanations focusing on domestic factors were available: one emphasized labour costs, the other the role of government budget deficits. Both contributed to the termination of the Keynesian order.

Discussion of inflation initially focused on increased wages stemming from the power of labour under a full employment regime. Labour's ability to extract higher money wages from employers seemed to fit the popular definition of inflationary pressures as "too much money chasing too few goods." This explanation entirely overlooked the possibility that wages were chasing externally induced inflation. From this point of view, wage controls became the remedy for inflation. Later, high interest rates and resultant unemployment were to achieve the same end.

It was commonly argued that a second source of inflation was government itself. Here profligate government spending, and financing this through government budget deficits, was held to increase the money supply with no commensurate increase in production. Once more too much money pursued too few goods. Based on this interpretation the solution lay in balanced budgets to be achieved, primarily, through reducing expenditures and reducing the size of government in the economy.

Some commentators argued the real problem was that a decline in profits had occurred (Gonick 1987: 341–42; Heap 1980–81). Timothy Lewis (2003: 104–05) linked the profitability crisis to corporations' search for new political strategies that would escape the confines of the nation state. Others noted the phenomenon of capital flight — multinational corporations shifting their manufacturing investments to the newly industrializing centres of the Third World, where cheap pools of labour could be readily found. The deregulation of the international monetary system with the termination of Bretton Woods also led to instability (O'Brien and Williams 2004: ch. 8). The move to a fuller integrated global economy represented a spatial fix for capital in searching for profitable investment outlets.

Domestically, a new phenomenon called stagflation, the co-existence of economic recession and high inflation, made its appearance in public discourse. Analyzing these developments through the lens of policy paradigms, the sense of crisis in the 1970s provided the opportunity for long-standing critics of the Keynesian revolution in economic thought to emerge from obscurity. The economics profession, undergoing what amounted to a paradigm shift, returned to a version of neoclassical orthodoxy of the kind that Keynes and like-minded economists had overturned, in the context of the Great Depression, two generations earlier. The revived ideas found powerful backers, mostly in a business sector concerned about increasing state intervention in the economy.

This coalition of neoclassical economists and corporate interests pushed right and centre political parties to a decisive break with Keynesianism. Moreover, the electorate proved susceptible to the appeals of the incoming paradigm, particularly its claim that balanced budgets and sound finance would eventually restore a degree of economic security that inflation and declining real incomes had eroded. The left, as represented by social-democratic parties in office, later followed the new orthodoxy as well.[1] The shift of paradigms between 1975 and 1984 was contentious, and other options such as interventionist nationalism certainly seemed achievable at the time. Generally, however, these years saw an incremental retrenchment of public programs, efforts to minimize the public's expectations of government, and advocacy of a reduced role for the state in the economy and social affairs.

The fiscal crisis generated by budget deficits contributed to the questioning of the legitimacy of the Keynesian welfare state. A more balanced assessment might have led to the conclusion that major problems of public debt occurred *after* the abandonment of Keynesianism and the adoption of neoliberalism. Implementation of that alternative paradigm, with its arsenal of high interest rates that cured inflation by driving the economy into recession, led to government revenue shortfalls on the one hand and, despite less generous social provisions, growing social expenditures on the other.

Nonetheless, the neoliberal argument that it was the social welfare state that created economic distortions won the day. The welfare state to some degree did decommodify a portion of the potential labour force and enhance the bargaining power of labour. Under conditions in which a fundamental reorientation of economic strategy was on the agenda, social welfare policy became a target. Increasingly critics depicted the welfare state as "a destabilizing influence" (Russell 1991: 489).

Globalization and Neoliberalism

Part of the rationale for the abandonment of national-level Keynesianism was the putative impact of globalization. It was suggested that because of competitive pressures emanating from the global economy national politicians had little choice but to downsize and restructure the state and clear the path for market forces to operate more freely. Economic forces, and actors such as multinational corporations, were said to have outgrown national boundaries, with the economic basis of national autonomy eroding. Thus, "Keynesian fiscal and monetary policy is rendered largely ineffective in open global financial markets" (Simeon 1991: 47–48, 49). Or, as Thomas Courchene argued, "This situation poses major concerns for national welfare states since they were... geared to national production machines" (quoted in Simeon and Janigan 1991: 39). These trends are linked to the state's emergence as a "competition state," in which governments react to perceived threats from international economic activity and seek to compete in this arena by creating a competitive advantage for their territorial economies (Cerny 1997).

What is distinctive about the performance of this role in the globalization period is the degree to which states have transformed themselves by becoming more market-like through initiatives like new public management, while at the same time privatizing authority and capacity by forging closer and more collaborative relationships with private actors in certain areas and handing over jurisdiction to them in others. Business organizations pressed the view that much state regulation was both ineffective in advancing its goals and a barrier to the economic success of the private sector. To the extent that regulation was required an enhanced role for the private sector in its own regulation was advocated.

International agreements like the WTO and NAFTA embedded neoliberal rules that preclude certain types of national (and supranational) political control of the operation of markets and hence also constrain the reach and operation of national democracy. Thus market relations and outcomes are less constrained by the kind of democratic pressures and procedures that historically, at the nation-state level, grafted democracy onto a pre-existing liberal society (Macpherson 1972).

International economic agreements can directly affect the outcomes of the balance of domestic political forces by significantly diminishing the legal potential for states to take (sovereign) decisions on matters of concern to their citizens. The agreements specifically preclude certain outcomes that used to be within the purview of states. International economic agreements are systems of power whose effect is to enhance liberalism and the liberal market society and to diminish democracy insofar as that concept includes the potential to go against or even modify significantly the results of market processes. Notwithstanding the key role that the state has played in promoting neoliberal globalization, limiting certain of its capacities is a central goal of international economic agreements. This is because of the "tremendous potentialities of the state as a centre for alternative forms of economic organization" (Petras and Veltmeyer 2001: 55). These restrictions on state actions may be particularly significant on the semi-periphery, where state-centred policies aimed at achieving more autonomy, diversified development, and redistribution of incomes were common as a response to the influences of powerful core countries.

Strong states were catalysts and facilitators of globalization (Weiss 1997). In North America, the U.S. consolidated a regional bloc in which common trade and investment rules apply. The Canadian state, responding to business preferences, facilitated this process. Thus the diminution of state capacity was acceptable to Canada's economic and political elite, as shown by the fact that Canada initiated the original free trade agreement with the United States and remains deeply wedded to market liberalization at home and abroad.

Thus, the neoliberal fix was one response to the perception of economic crisis in the 1970s and 1980s. Although some of the causes of the crisis originated in the international economy, much of neoliberalism's early emphasis was domestic. Its actions in reducing the state's role and prioritizing market forces served to clear the domestic obstacles to international liberalization. In this sense globalization is as much or more of a consequence of neoliberalism at the national level than the reverse. Neoliberalism involved political action aimed at reducing or removing impediments to the operation of market forces, including global market forces. Various justifications, economic and moral, were advanced for placing markets in this privileged position. An economic argument, for instance, was that markets enhanced competitiveness in a global economy and that international competition had beneficial effects on efficiency in the domestic economy. A moral argument, applied to both domestic welfare and foreign aid recipients, was that people removed from the discipline of the market lost their independence and became undesirably dependent on government programs.

Free Trade and the Social Base of Neoliberalism

A key component of the transition from Keynesianism to neoliberalism was the drive to closer global and regional economic integration represented by a new generation of trade and investment agreements. The agreements played complementary roles in the neoliberal order. First, they signaled and facilitated an export-oriented growth strategy. Henceforth, international competitiveness would replace management of domestic demand in governments' priorities. Second, because the agreements reached deep into domestic decision-making capacity, they had the potential to lock neoliberal reforms in place through entangling them in international commitments that might otherwise be reversible at the national level. International economic agreements accomplish this result through their impact on the sovereignty of states and through a *de facto* rewriting of national constitutions. In the process, economic liberalism is privileged at the expense of potential and future democratic choice. Considered at the level of states, international economic agreements have increased the external constraint on policy making for most states. However, this is less true of the major powers and least of all true of the hegemonic power, the United States. Considered at the level of class interests within countries, this situation empowers some interests (capital), while disempowering others (labour). Ricardo Grinspun and Robert Kreklewich (1994: 33) argue that free trade agreements, for instance, "serve as a restructuring tool or, put differently, as a conditioning institutional framework that promotes and consolidates neoliberal restructuring. These international treaties serve as a mechanism whereby domestic ruling groups, with the encouragement of the United States government, can advance economic and social reforms that are inherently anti-democratic." International conditioning frameworks are, then, rooted in the societies to which they apply.

The international agreements are "anti-democratic" in the sense that their provisions foreclose certain options that the populations of nation-states may want to preserve or adopt in the future, and the governments that have agreed to these provisions reflect the interests of domestic and international economic elite.

In Canada, the push to free trade would serve both the material interests of the Canadian capitalist class and its political ambitions to refashion Canada along explicitly pro-market lines. Linda McQuaig provided a compelling account of how leaders in the Canadian business community saw free trade in part as a vehicle by which they might achieve a massive overhaul of Canadian society (McQuaig 1992: 194). Certainly, business was the driving force behind the negotiation and provision of political support for the free trade agreement with the United States, NAFTA, and the WTO. The great change in state policy was preceded by a consensus among Canadian business organizations around the desirability of free trade with the United States. Within the state, sectors of the bureaucracy, notably those concerned with foreign trade and external affairs, worked hard to engineer a shift to free trade. These efforts received a major boost from the election of the Conservative government and the subsequent pro-free trade report of the Macdonald Commission. Both Jack Richardson (1992) and William Carroll (1986, 2004) suggest that these transitions represented a strengthening of the capitalist class relative to other social forces and that mature Canadian capital began to see its own interests as being furthered by continentalist arrangements. These trends found a voice with the formation of the Business Council on National Issues (BCNI), composed of the CEOs of 150 leading corporations based in Canada, which not only wielded enormous structural power, but which also which had the capacity to lead and convince the business sector as a whole. It is here that we must locate the social base of the neoliberal turn in Canadian politics. From the outset the BCNI had a clear set of "reforms" in mind for Canada. It favoured "the free flow of goods, capital, services and people" and proposed free trade with the United States as a strategy for restraining both the federal and provincial states. Further North American integration would confine the federal government to market-reinforcing reforms (Bradford 1998: 106).

The Neoliberal State at Home

The state under neoliberalism has been seen as the chief impediment to the free operation of markets. Measures were thus advanced to reduce or at least redefine its role in areas such as fiscal policy, government employment, privatization, social policy, labour-market policy, and health policy.[2] However, the process of neoliberalization has been underway now for several decades and a number of processes, both sequential and co-terminous, have been identified. One is the distinction between roll-back and roll-out policies (Peck and Tickell 2002). The roll-back concept refers to the partial demolition or reduction of the key institutions and programs of the Keynesian era. Roll-out, on the other hand, identifies a phase of constructing new institutions and programs that embed the neoliberal approach to governance. Similarly, reviewing roll-out mechanisms as part of the ongoing practice of neoliberal governance, Peter Graefe (2006) has drawn attention to the distinction between measures that deepen and extend the basis of neoliberalism and those that operate as "flanking mechanisms." The latter are measures that ameliorate or address the contradictions between the various forms of privatization inherent in neoliberalism and the need for social inputs if it, or any other system, is to be sustainable. Strategies of social investment (Jenson and Saint-Martin 2003) and versions of "inclusive liberalism" (Mahon 2008) might serve as examples.

Expenditure Restraint

The main neoliberal themes — that government is too large, deficits unacceptable, the tax system in need of reform, and spending priorities in need of revision — entered public discourse in Canada before the election of the Mulroney government in 1984. But with that event they moved from the status of ideas that might reluctantly be endorsed, out of crisis-driven necessity, to the centre of policy discussions (Wilson 1984), where they have remained since. In practice, the Liberal governments of Jean Chrétien and Paul Martin pressed the neoliberal fiscal agenda much more vigorously than did their Conservative predecessors (see Lewis 2003: ch. 6 and 7). The minority Conservative government under Stephen Harper essentially continued the Liberal policy (Jackson and Weir 2008). Even the temporary stimulus spending necessitated by the 2007 financial crisis has not shaken its faith in diminished public spending. The government has repeatedly called for a swift return to neoliberal normality as soon as possible.

The government justified expenditure restraint by declaring the need to balance the budget. However, neoliberal governments were ideologically committed to the means of expenditure restraint (cutting state expenditures) as well as the end of a balanced budget (which could also have been achieved by tax increases). This approach was taken because reduced expenditures typically mean a smaller role for the state, especially in the crucial economic and social areas.[3] In the recession of the early 1980s, spending on programs climbed to 19.4 percent of GDP. In the 1990s recession this item accounted for a peak of 17.5 percent of GDP before falling dramatically to 12.4 percent by 2000, the lowest level for decades.

By 2001–02, program spending had fallen further to 11.3 percent of GDP, its lowest level since 1948–49. More recently, in the face of 2008–09 recession, program spending has increased slightly to 13 percent of GDP (DOF 2009: 16). But compared to the recessionary peak in the 1980s (19.4 percent) or the 1990s (17.5 percent) this figure highlights an inexorable downward trend. Government "effort" to respond to recessions, as measured by its spending, therefore fell steadily through the neoliberal period. Early signs of this imbalance in successive governments' treatment of expenditures and revenues led some observers to depict the deficit as a "Trojan horse" for a somewhat different agenda: reduction of the state's role (Doern, Maslove, and Prince 1988: 28). There is evidence that Canada was much more aggressive in its expenditure reduction campaign than the OECD average (Stanford 2004: 35).

Expenditures, including those on personnel, bore the brunt of neoliberal policies despite considerable evidence suggesting that expenditures by government were not the cause of deficits and rising public debt. Rather, these phenomena were the product of foregone tax revenues, high interest rates, and recessions that were partly due to the implementation of neoliberal economic policies. Rather than originating in the Keynesian era, these problems flourished after the monetarist economic theories favoured by neoliberal politicians took root.[4]

A number of writers have drawn attention to the scope and impact of the loopholes, tax breaks, and tax expenditures that led to the shortfall in revenues after 1975 (Maslove 1981; McQuaig 1987; Ternowetsky 1987; Wolfe 1985). Apart from this revenue shortfall, the main cause of increased deficits was high real interest rates resulting from monetary policy (Chorney 1988; McQuaig 1995). A Statistics Canada project attributed 50 percent of the increased deficit incurred between 1975–76 and 1988–89 to revenue shortfalls relative to GDP, 44 percent to an increase in debt charges relative to GDP, and only 6 percent to higher program spending relative to GDP (McIlveen and Mimoto 1990; Klein 1996).

Thus many of the problems associated with fiscal policy, such as the deficit, which provided the pretext for implementing neoliberal, expenditure-cutting and state-reducing policies, had their origins in neoliberal political choices made in the monetary policy area.

Government Employment

Another indicator of the shrinking state is the number of people employed by it. Government employment between 1990 and 1999 fell by 9 percent. In the early years of the twenty-first century there was some reversal of the trend at the federal and provincial levels in that numbers of public sector employees began to edge back up. It is important to note, however, that as a percentage of the total labour force the decline was long-lasting: from 21.25 percent of the labour force in 1990, to 17.5 in 1999, to 17.0 in March 2003, and rising slightly to 18 percent in 2009 (compiled using Statistics Canada CANSIM data, table 183-0002 "Public Sector Employment"). As a result, despite economic growth, the imprint of the public sector in employment terms has never recovered from its 1990s levels. Future cuts to the public sector also appear imminent as the 2010–11 federal budget seeks to save $17.6 billion over five years through "streamlining and reducing the operating and administrative costs of government departments" (Evans 2010).

Privatization

A central thrust of neoliberalism has been the privatization of state-run activities. This may take a variety of forms, some of which we describe below. Typically rationalized in terms of the efficiency of goods and services provision, we suggest that privatization has had a more fundamental role in the neoliberal project. We have seen that accumulation by dispossession can be considered a hallmark feature of neoliberalism. Reminiscent of "original accumulation" as described by Marx, it involves the expansion of market relations in a number of ways, namely through new mechanisms to enclose the commons, such as privatization, and the creation of new markets, such as trading in carbon credits (Harvey 2003b: 145–48). Both facilitate an expansion of the breadth and depth of capitalism. Although dispossession is by no means unique to the current era, it is especially prevalent with neoliberalism. Considered together, neoliberalism and its propensity for dispossession are meaningful ways to explain not only the waves of public asset divestiture in the 1980s, but also the less obvious forms of privatization that continue today through contracting out and the use of public-private partnerships (P3s).

With full-scale privatization, dispossession occurs in the most overt of ways. The sale of public assets, such as in Crown corporations, directly converts public property into private property through ownership rights. In Canada this process has included some of the most potentially profitable assets in the country. For example, federal sales have included the Canadian National Railway in 1995, Air Canada in 1988, and portions of Petro Canada in 1991. Provincially, this has included Alberta Government Telephones in 1990, Nova Scotia Power Corporation in 1992, and the Potash Corporation of Saskatchewan in 1989 (McBride 2005: 103–04). Once transferred, these assets then become sources of private accumulation. It is also common for these assets to be devalued and sold off well below their anticipated exchange value. For instance, in 1994 the cable network portion of Manitoba Telephone Service (MTS), a then sixty-one-year-old Crown corporation, was sold for $11.5 million, which translated to only 18 percent of its $63 million valuation according to an internal MTS assessment (Black and Mallea 1997: 11).

However, dispossession is not an unambiguous or unidirectional process of ever-increasing plunder. In the Keynesian era publicly owned enterprises were commonly encouraged by the private sector as a way of providing cheaper infrastructure, utilities, and services, and to ensure that natural monopolies did not fall into the hands of rival firms (Gordon 1981: 19). This meant that in some cases the establishment of public corporations and utilities involved the conversion of private property into state property. Take the example of MTS provided above. Manitoba's telephone network was first established by the private sector (the Northwest Telegraph Company in 1878, and taken over by Bell Telephone Company of Canada in 1880), and it would be three decades before the province purchased these private assets, which later became the property of MTS, incorporated in 1933 (Muir 1964–65). This means that some of the now privatized assets under the neoliberal fix ought to be more accurately described as having been recommodified: first transformed from private capital to state capital, and then back into private capital (Ashman and Callinicos 2006: 123). Thus solutions to overaccumulation involve complex and potentially contradictory processes of dispossession and repossession, and decommodification and recommodification occurring over time, with a different rationale appropriate during different fixes.

Similar to full-scale privatization, P3s are best understood as examples of accumulation by dispossession (Whiteside 2009). Whereas traditional public works projects (physical and social infrastructure) are wholly owned and controlled by the public sector, with contracts awarded to a private company for a limited and specified role (such as the construction portion), P3s establish binding long-term contracts that incorporate the logic of the private sector into the provision of public goods (Hodge and Greve 2005: 64). This is reflected in Daniel Cohn's definition of P3s as "instruments for meeting the obligations of the state that are transformed so as to involve private property ownership as a key element in the operation of that instrument" (Cohn 2004: 2). Therefore, although public assets are not directly divested, P3 contracts nonetheless carve out avenues for profitable private sector investment by contractually guaranteeing future revenue streams in areas that would otherwise prove potentially unprofitable, or too politically sensitive to privatize.

P3s in Canada typically occur in the area of public infrastructure provision, such as hospital buildings, water and sewage facilities and roads. These projects will involve the private sector in a variety of ways. The most common forms of P3s are Build-Own-Operate-Transfer (boot), Design-Build-Finance-Operate (dbfo), and Design-Build-Operate (dbo).[5] This means that while partnerships between government and the private sector have, to one extent or another, been present for centuries, the novel feature of contemporary P3s is the amount of control that the private sector has over all stages of the formulation and implementation of public policy.

The standard assumption behind the adoption of a P3 is that it is able to harness the efficiencies, innovative capacities, and financial resources of the private sector in order to more effectively deliver services or infrastructure (Akintoye et al. 2003: 4). This assumption is derived from new public management prescriptions that aim to transform the government and its agencies into the procurer of services rather than the provider (Edwards and Shaoul 2003: 397). This transformation is achieved by using a variety of alternative service delivery forms, such as contracting out and partnering with the for-profit private sector. However, the promotion of alternative service delivery involves not only a series of policy reforms but also the introduction of a new style of governance and administration, making its transformative agenda both ideational and practical. With P3s in particular, there is an assumption (derived from its roots in the public choice school and neoclassical economics) that partnering with the private sector will avoid the problems associated with an inherently inefficient public administration. This translates into P3s being presented as a net gain for the taxpayer: they are able to deliver value for money through lower costs over the lifetime of the project by transferring risk to the private partner who, it is believed, will operate in a more innovative, efficient, and financially prudent fashion (Edwards and Shaoul 2003: 397–98).

In contrast, contracting out public services, which occurs with public service delivery of all sorts, including hospital maintenance and dietary services, involves far less decision making on the part of the private contractor. As opposed to asset divestiture or partnering with the private sector, with this form of privatization "the government entity retains ownership and overall control but employs the private vendor to actually render the service" (Seidenstat 1999: 7).

Nonetheless, in terms of our theoretical discussion in chapter 2, all of these forms of privatization are equally part of a neoliberal spatio-temporal fix using dispossession. First, they all provide for spatial displacement by enhancing the breadth and depth of profitable private accumulation. Second, temporal displacement is achieved by opening up investment in long-term capital projects and social services to surplus private capital rather than the previous pattern of "crowding out" private investment in these areas. Thus the various forms of privatization have played a crucial role in the neoliberal accumulation strategy and in explaining business enthusiasm for it.

Diminishing Social Protection
The establishment of the Canadian version of a Keynesian welfare state was largely complete by 1971. Almost immediately the edifice came under attack. Some programs, such as unemployment insurance, were reduced in generosity during the 1970s (McBride 1992: ch. 6), but, for the most part, the main features of the welfare state remained in place when the neoliberal Mulroney Conservatives took office in 1984.

The precise impact of the Mulroney government on existing programs was a matter of debate in the 1980s and early 1990s. The prevailing view was that change was incremental and consisted of erosion rather than outright dismantling (Banting 1987: 213). In retrospect it appears that incrementalism and "stealth" over a protracted period produced fundamental change, especially when the same direction was sustained by the Liberal governments of the 1990s. However, the means of implementing changes in social programs indicated a cautious approach on the part of Canadian neoliberals. Common techniques included transforming universal into selective programs, tightening eligibility requirements, and imposing ceilings on program costs — or, alternatively, attempting to make programs self-financing or subject to "clawbacks" over a certain benefit level (Houle 1990). Stephen Phillips (2000:

5–6) noted that in 1979 universal programs paid out 43 percent of income security benefits and, by 1993, zero percent.

The 1995 federal budget marked a fundamental shift in the role of the federal state in Canada. Erosion of social programs had ended, and demolition began. The budget was depicted as an "epiphany in fiscal federalism and national social policy" (Prince 1999: 176) and as the end of an era: "It is now clear that the Minister of Reconstruction's White Paper on Employment and Income of 1945 can be regarded as one bookend on a particular period in Canadian history, and Paul Martin's February [1995] budget as the other" (Kroeger 1996: 21).

The case for viewing 1995 as the termination point of the Keynesian welfare state rests on the primacy of deficit reduction over maintenance of the social safety net. The determination to reduce the deficit through spending reductions in the social policy area quickly resulted in declining federal transfers to provinces and a fundamental redesign of the unemployment benefit system. The reduced federal commitment to social programs was accomplished not only by eroding transfer payments but also by diminished federal conditions attached to the funds transferred. The major change occurred in 1996 with the introduction of the Canada Health and Social Transfer (CHST).

In 1996 a number of federal transfers to the provinces were rolled into the Canada Health and Social Transfer, a single block funding scheme. The CHST removed most remaining federal conditions attached to the transfers. No matching expenditures were required of provinces, as had been the case, for example, under the Canada Assistance Plan (CAP). The CAP had established several other conditions. Provinces should provide assistance to every person in need; take into account people's needs in setting assistance rates; provide an appeal mechanism to enable challenges to eligibility decisions; not discriminate on the basis of province of origin; and not require work as a condition for receiving assistance (Anderson 2004). The new scheme eliminated the other conditions attached to CAP, with the exception of a prohibition on residency requirements. The CHST contained no conditions as far as post-secondary education was concerned, and federal enforcement mechanisms were either diminished or less direct than formerly. Moreover, welfare, traditionally not as well regarded in public opinion as education or health, came into the same funding pool, which placed it at a competitive disadvantage (MacDonald 1999: 77).

The changes made possible considerable experimentation by provinces in the design of assistance programs. As provinces were motivated as much by deficit reduction priorities as the federal government, the effect in terms of eligibility and benefit levels was dramatic. Welfare recipients declined from just over 3 million people in 1995 to 1.68 million in 2005 (NCW 2006).

Of course, not all the reduction can be attributed to policy changes. Some must be accounted for by the slow economic recovery that began in the late 1990s. However, the reductions are dramatic and clearly policy accounts for a good deal of it. The annual Welfare Incomes publication produced by the National Council of Welfare (NCW) shows the severity of the impact. For instance, welfare incomes continue to decline, "making life more difficult for the nearly 1.7 million children, women and men who relied on welfare" (NCW 2008: 66). This was largely due to the fact that welfare rates remained flat in the face of rising inflation. For some family scenarios this meant that in 2006 and 2007 welfare incomes were at their lowest point since 1986 (ibid.: 68). On top of the reduction in purchasing power, those in need of social assistance must now contend with more punitive, workfare-oriented social programs, which make qualifying for and maintaining assistance very difficult, especially for the homeless (Wallace, Klein, and Reitsma-Street 2006; Bezanson 2006).

Federal funding under the Canada Health and Social Transfer has few conditions attached to it. Other federal funding has been provided since 1998 with the introduction of the National Child Benefit. However, part of this is regarded by some provinces as part of welfare for families with children; hence their own welfare payments to these families are reduced accordingly. The end result is a patchwork of fourteen programs, one in each province and territory. In general, payments are way below the low income cut-off levels (LICO), often regarded as the "poverty line," and in real terms have declined over time.

Growing Inequality

The government's approach to social policy, combined with tax policy, had predictable results, including the growth of various types of inequality (Yalnizyan 1998: 127). Always unequal, ownership of wealth has become even more skewed, with the richest 10 percent of the population increasing its share of total wealth in Canada from 51.8 percent in 1984 to 58 percent in 2005 (Kerstetter 2002: 12; Morissette, Zhang, and Drolet 2002; Morissette and Zhang 2006).

Income statistics show a similar trend. Between 2000 and 2007 average after-tax income increased by roughly 13 percent, from $50,700 to $57,400 in 2007 dollars (compiled using Statistics Canada CANSIM data, table 202-0603, "Average After-tax Family Income"). If taken at face value, this increase would appear to indicate that Canadian families were better off during the 2000s than they were during the 1990s. However, the benefits of economic expansion during this period went disproportionately to the most wealthy. Incomes of the richest 20 percent of Canadian families rose by 10 percent from 1990 to 2000, while those of the poorest 20 percent stagnated over that same period (Statistics Canada 2005). Furthermore, from 2000 to 2005 earnings fell by 3.1 percent for the lowest income group yet rose by 6.2 percent for the top group. When seen from a longer historical perspective, increases in income inequality become even more apparent. Using the latest census data, from 2006, we see that from 1980 to 2005 earnings increased by 16.4 percent for those in the top income group, they stagnated for those in the middle income group, and they fell by 20.6 percent for those in the bottom group (Conference Board of Canada n.d.).

Statistics Canada data on family income found that after-tax income in 1998 had risen only slowly over the previous decade and exceeded, by only 1.7 percent, average after-tax income in the pre-recession peak year of 1989. In itself this speaks volumes about the impact of neoliberal policies on incomes. Especially pertinent is the observation that income inequality increased during the second half of the 1990s. The study noted that in the early part of the decade, "Taxes and transfers held the ratio of highest-to-lowest after-tax incomes at just under five to one. During the second half of the 1990s, as transfers declined, the ratio widened from about 4.8 to one in 1994 to 5.4 to one in 1998" (Statistics Canada 2000: 4). By 2001 the ratio had increased slightly to 5.5:1 (Statistics Canada 2003). A study by Roger Sauvé for the Vanier Institute (2001) attributed the slight increase in family incomes in the late 1990s almost entirely to an increase in the number of hours worked rather than to increased hourly wages. Average incomes for unattached individuals, who made up one-third of all households in Canada, were down by 2.6 percent over the decade from 1989, with much of decline being concentrated among young adults. For families, 60 percent experienced an after-tax real income decline in the 1990s. The poorest 20 percent of families, with an average income in 1998 of $17,662, had the biggest decline at 5.2 percent; the richest 20 percent, with an average income in 1998 of $96,175, experienced a 6.6 percent increase (Sauvé 2001: 7–8) While economic and income growth picked up in the late 1990s, the overall picture remained inferior to the postwar Keynesian years. Growth in real disposable income per capita was 1.3 percent in the 1980s and 0.1 percent in the 1990s, though it was 2.3 percent in the period from 1997 to June 2000. This finding compares to figures of 2.2 percent for the 1950s, 3 percent for the 1960s, and 4.2 percent for the 1970s (Maxwell 2001: 6).

Health Care: Domestic and Global Influences
Although the Canadian health care system is better protected than most social programs, it has felt the effects of the shift to neoliberalism. Such effects include creeping privatization, primarily through the contracting out of services (CCPA 1995a: 5), and Bill C-22, which anticipated NAFTA provisions on intellectual property rights (Fuller 1996: 18). Under Bill C-22

patent protection for name brand drugs was originally extended from four to ten years. In 1993 the protection was extended to twenty years. The result has been rapidly escalating pharmaceutical costs. Some provincial health plans reduced coverage in order to contain costs (CCPA 1995b: 9). There is also what Mike Burke (2000: 180–81) terms the discourse of efficiency, which is linked in business rhetoric to globalization. When applied to the health care sector this discourse promotes markets, decentralization, and individualism. And in areas like home care, where Canadians might want a publicly funded system, NAFTA and the WTO's General Agreement on Trade in Services (GATS) may constrain decision makers' options (Hankivsky and Morrow 2004: 60). In 1984 the federal government reaffirmed the conditions stipulated in the 1967 *Medical Care Act*. These provisions consist of five core principles (McBride 2005: 112–13):

1. Public administration: the administration of the health care insurance plan of a province or territory must be carried out on a non-profit basis by a public authority;
2. Comprehensiveness: all medically necessary services provided by hospitals and doctors must be insured;
3. Universality: all insured persons in the province or territory must be entitled to public health insurance coverage on uniform terms and conditions;
4. Portability: coverage for insured services must be maintained when an insured person moves or travels within Canada or travels outside the country; and
5. Accessibility: reasonable access by insured persons to medically necessary hospital and physician services must be unimpeded by financial or other barriers.

The *Canada Health Act* also contains provisions that ban extra-billing and user charges:

1. No extra billing by medical practitioners or dentists for insured health services under the terms of the health care insurance plan of the province or territory;
2. No user charges for insured health services by hospitals or other providers under the terms of the health care insurance plan of the province or territory.

The 1984 legislation also provided that federal funds would be withheld, on a dollar for dollar basis, for every dollar of extra billing or hospital user fees that provinces permitted.

Two debates dominate discussion of the financing of the health care system. One relates to the respective shares of the federal and provincial governments. The other relates to the split between private and public provision. Since neoliberal governments favour a greater role for the private sector in delivery of health care and health insurance the two debates intersect at various points.

The decline in the public portion of the total health bill (from a normal level of 75 or 76 percent to 69.8 percent in 1997) seemed to indicate "passive privatization," characterized as "a generalized retreat of the state from the provision of health care services and an enlargement of the health space occupied by the private sector" (Burke 2000: 182). However, the proportions as far as funding is concerned appear to have stabilized for the moment. In 2003 the public to private ratio remained 70:30 (Canadian Institute for Health Information 2004). In 2008 the public to private ratio was 71:29 (Canadian Institute for Health Information 2008). If public "tax expenditure" subsidies are included the publicly funded share rises somewhat, perhaps to around 75 percent (Evans 2002: v).

As Burke (2000: 183–85) noted, the shift toward increased private funding that did occur was but one part of an ongoing and intense commodification of the health system. In a careful analysis of the determinants of the increased private share of health care costs in Canada, Livio Di Matteo (2000) concluded that the decline in real per capita health transfers from the federal government had eroded the public share in health expenditures, a factor combined with the effects of changes in the distribution of income since those in higher income brackets have a greater preference for privatization of health care expenditures (Di Matteo 2000: 108). The reasons for this are not hard to detect: "Tax finance distributes health costs according to tax liability — roughly proportionate to income. User charges distribute them by use of care, very closely related with illness. Any shift from public to private financing will transfer costs from those with higher incomes to those with lower incomes, and from the healthy to the ill" (Evans 2002: v, 15–23).

Most analysts link declining CHST transfers and subsequent provincial budget cuts to the increased public perception of a crisis in the Canadian health care system. Hospital closures, reductions in the numbers of beds, waiting lists for elective surgery and emergency room services, and reductions in the number of nurses and other medical personnel made newspaper headlines and created concern over the sustainability of the system (Maioni and Smith 2003: 305–06; Boychuk 2002: 13–16). Growing public concern, and some business leaders taking issue with the erosion of the "competitive advantage" of Canada, urged a rise in health care spending once again.[6] By 2001 spending had increased to almost $60 billion, well above its 1992 level of $52 billion (Rachlis, Evans, and Lewis 2001: 6). However, despite this increase, expenditures on hospitals remained well below their 1992 levels, and jobs eliminated (primarily nursing staff) were not restored (ibid.). Analysts were beginning to recognize that health care funding was not the only issue, as poor management and organization were also to blame (Rachlis 2004: 22). This theme was emphasized in the Romanow and Kirby reports of 2002, both suggesting that innovation in service delivery would be needed to resolve the problems of medicare. The exact nature of this innovation has been largely left up to the provinces. In many cases "alternative service delivery" has meant turning to the private sector (via P3s and contracting out), rather than innovations made within the public sphere. Provincial autonomy was further enhanced in 2004 when the federal government committed to transfer an additional $41 billion over ten years to the provinces without any conditions attached (Armstrong and Armstrong 2008: 24).

Yet, as Boychuk (2002) and Evans (2002) pointed out, the perceptions of unsustainability, notwithstanding public perceptions, were overdrawn, or incorrectly drawn. Evans, for example, showed that claims that public spending on health care was absorbing a rising share of national income or of public tax revenue were "simply false" (Evans 2002: 27). Provincial expenditures on health were absorbing a higher proportion of public expenditures but this was due to prioritizing reductions to other expenditures in order to achieve balanced budgets (Evans 2002: 27–28) under conditions where many provincial governments also wished to implement tax cuts. Thus the health spending "crisis" was rather artificial and an artifact of political choice. This point is reinforced by Boychuk (2002: 12), who showed that federal budget cuts provided the provinces with "perverse incentives" to magnify issues of fiscal constraint, declining quality of health services, and rigidities imposed by the *Canada Health Act*.

Labour Market Policy

In comparative terms Canada spends little on active labour market policy (Haddow 2003: 243) and is compliant[7] with the neoliberal recommendations of the OECD Jobs Study (McBride and Williams 2001). Responding to high unemployment levels that emerged in the 1980s, the OECD directed its secretariat to conduct a study and make substantive proposals for policy reform. Recommendations produced by the Jobs Study subsequently formed the basis of the 1994 OECD Jobs Strategy, a detailed set of policy prescriptions for each member state. The theoretical basis of the Jobs Study rested on the non-accelerating inflation rate of unemployment, or NAIRU; this led to an identification of the bulk of contemporary unemployment as structural rather than cyclical. The policy implication of this, for the OECD, was that the vast majority of unemployment, being structural, was impervious to macroeconomic management (OECD 1994: 66–69). The core hypothesis and central policy implication then was that labour market rigidities such as employment protection legislation, or financial inducements which cushioned workers from changing market conditions (unemployment benefits, early retirement schemes, and social programs generally), served ultimately to reduce employment and harm the workers they were intended to help (Kuhn 1997). Thus grounded in neoclassical or neoliberal economic theory, the Jobs Study represented a sustained plea for policies to promote greater labour market flexibility by removing politically constructed obstacles to the unfettered operation of market forces.

While cognizant of the need to avoid social disruption, the OECD identified social policies as a key area for change if adequate flexibility was to be achieved. Members should examine "the full range of policies that have been put in place over the last 30 years to see where, and to what extent, each may have contributed to ossifying the capacity of economies and the will of societies to adapt; and then to consider how to remove those disincentives without harming the degree of social protection that it is each society's wish to provide" (OECD 1994: 30).

Unfortunately it turned out that there was no statistically significant relationship between Jobs Strategy compliance and improved labour market performance. So the logic stating that they had to reform their policies in the directions demanded by globalization (towards greater flexibility etc.) or face worsening economic conditions could not be supported by the data (McBride and Williams 2001). As with some other areas of domestic policy, this leaves the explanation for the shift in policies firmly in the domestic sphere, in particular the rise of the neoliberal ideology and the social forces backing it to hegemonic status.

In the earlier periods in this policy area, before the shift to neoliberalism, active labour market policy was underpinned by a relatively generous system of unemployment insurance, one that was often criticized for its generosity and passivity.[8] In 1996 the federal government announced its withdrawal from the training sphere and began a radical restructuring of the renamed employment insurance system along with the transfer of responsibility for active employment measures to the provinces.

Despite the asymmetrical arrangements that emerged as a result of devolution to the provinces, some common neoliberal principles ran through the new labour market development agreements. The federal authorities planned to retain only a limited range of labour market policy responsibilities: employment insurance benefits; provision of a national system of labour market information and exchange; support for interprovincial sectoral development and developing responses to national economic crises; and jurisdiction over a one-time transitional jobs fund (HRDC 1996: 1). It was claimed that these reforms would complete a long-term trend to ending federal consolidated revenue funding for employment measures. Any future federal money for these purposes was to come from the employment insurance account.

The federal government also restructured the unemployment insurance system (HRDC 1995). The program had already ceased to be generous by international standards. The 1996 changes to the system (HRDC 1996) included calculating qualification periods in terms of hours worked rather than weeks worked. The department claimed that this would be more equitable for part-time workers and women workers in particular, and that it reflected the labour market reality of increasing part-time work. Other changes reduced the benefit replacement rate for repeat claimants; introduced a supplement for low-income family claimants; increased the clawback of benefits from high-income earners; and reduced premiums and maximum insurable earnings.

Coverage declined sharply. A Canadian Labour Congress (1999) study based on Statistics Canada data showed that in 1997 the percentage of unemployed workers covered by EI was less than half of what it had been in 1989 — 36 percent as compared to 74 percent. Women, whose coverage had declined from 70 percent in 1987 to 31 percent in 1997,[9] and young people — 55 percent to 15 percent — were hit particularly hard. An updated version of the study (CLC 2003) revealed slight increases in coverage, as measured by the ratio of EI beneficiaries to the unemployed, but the situation was essentially the same and the gender gap persisted. A government study (HRDC 1998) estimated the decline in the beneficiaries to unemployed ratio at almost 50 percent in the 1989–97 period (83 percent to 42 percent). The report attributes just under half of the decline to policy and program changes. The rest is due to labour market changes such as increased long-term unemployment. The effects were to increase the number of "exhaustees," produce more unemployed people who lacked previous work experience, and increase the number of people who were "self-employed." Be this as it may the CLC study drew a rather close relationship between the introduction of regulatory changes to the EI system and subsequent reduced coverage (see Table 1).

Table 1 Impact of Higher Eligibility Requirements on Insurance Coverage Rates

	1990	1993	1994	1996	2001
Legislative change	Bill C-21	Bill C-113	Bill C-17	Bill C-12	
% of Unemployed receiving EI	74	57	51	42	39

Source: CLC 2003: 3

In addition to the coverage issue, the duration of benefits was shortened and the benefit rate fell steadily from 66.6 percent to 55 percent. The bottom line was that the employment insurance system assisted far fewer of the unemployed in the 2008–09 recession than in earlier recessions: 46 percent compared to 71 percent in 1981–82 and 76 percent on 1990–91 (Mendelsohn and Medow 2010).

Institutions in the Neoliberal Era

Early globalization theorists suggested that an entirely new institutional structure was emerging in which the nation-state was superceded by global and local actors, and the state by markets and by civil society. Subsequent research has demonstrated that this was an extreme view. The state as nation-state and as system of government is central to the neoliberal order. However, its role has changed in a number of significant respects that include a tendency to global and private governance.

In the Canadian case, the provisions of international agreements should be integrated into discussions of the political system. Similarly, federal-provincial agreements, such as the Agreement on Internal Trade (AIT), and interprovincial ones like the Trade, Investment, and Labour Mobility Agreement (TILMA), which parallel the international agreements, should also be taken into account. A key, and related, issue is the extent to which the implementation of neoliberalism, domestically as well as internationally, has altered the operation of Canadian institutions.

The entanglement of the federal government in the international system, and of federal and provincial jurisdictions in various cooperative arrangements, both enhanced tendencies to executive dominance. Once intricate agreements were worked out at intergovernmental meetings, they were very difficult to alter after the negotiators returned to home base. The lines of accountability became quite blurred under this system, which further diminished the possibility for effective legislative scrutiny of the executive.

Indeed, some analysts have noted an even further concentration of power within the executive. In this view the Cabinet is almost as redundant as Parliament in terms of real decision-making power, which now resides overwhelmingly with the prime minister.[10] According to Donald J. Savoie (1999: 362), the full picture is:

> Cabinet has now joined Parliament as an institution being bypassed. Real political debate and decision making are increasingly elsewhere — in federal-provincial meetings of first ministers, on Team Canada flights, where first ministers can hold informal meetings, in the Prime Minister's Office, in the Privy Council Office, in the Department of Finance, and in international organizations and international sum-

mits. There is no sign that the one person who holds all the cards, the prime minister, and the central agencies which enable him to bring effective political authority to the centre, are about to change things.

Neoliberal Globalization and the Courts

The role of the courts has been diminished by the new generation of international economic agreements as important issues have been transferred to the jurisdiction of international trade panels. Under NAFTA, for example, a binational review panel has displaced judicial review of most issues concerned with dumping and anti-dumping, at least for disputes between NAFTA members. The investment chapter of the agreement gives foreign investors the option of pursuing disputes through domestic courts or arbitration panels. Whereas under the anti-dumping and countervailing subsidies provisions the panels are applying domestic law, under the investment chapter they apply international law and are able to award damages (Lemieux and Stuhec 1999: 146).

The courts would seem, then, to be losing authority in an important area of property rights. Investors increasingly have access to special disputes procedures, and questions of whether a government is acting in accordance with its treaty obligations, and whether it is applying Canadian law and regulations appropriately, are matters on which the courts can be bypassed.

Similarly, once attempts at consultation and mediation fail to produce a mutually acceptable resolution, the WTO refers disputes arising under its jurisdiction to panels. The scope of regulations under the WTO expanded dramatically as a result of the Uruguay Round. The organization also strengthened its dispute resolution mechanisms to eliminate delays and the right of the "guilty" party to eventually veto decisions. Enforcement mechanisms include elimination of the regulation or legislation found to be in breach of WTO provisions; payment of compensation; or, should the offending party fail to implement panel findings, sanctioned retaliation by the injured party. The WTO has already deemed both Canadian magazine legislation, promoted as defence of Canadian culture, and the Auto Pact to be contrary to WTO provisions. These examples alone indicate the scope of the WTO and its extraterritorial adjudication mechanisms.

Neoliberal Globalization and the Parliamentary System

Neoliberal globalization, in the shape of involvement in the new generation of multilateral and bilateral trade and investment agreements, has significantly modified the doctrine of parliamentary supremacy.

It is true that Parliament could pass legislation withdrawing from these agreements. In Stephen Krasner's (1999: 9) terms the state does retain international legal sovereignty. Short of that, however, its reach is circumscribed and constrained in ways that would hardly have been imagined even two decades ago. In a book on NAFTA, international trade lawyer Barry Appleton (1994: 207) concluded:

> The NAFTA represents the supremacy of a classical liberal conception of the state with its imposition of significant restraints upon the role of government. All international trade agreements entail some self-imposed limitation on government authority, for example governments regularly agree not to increase their tariff rates. However, the NAFTA appears to approach an extreme. It does this by the extensiveness of its obligations which attempt to lock-in one perspective of governmental role for all successive North American governments.

Accountability of decision making to Parliament and the public has been reduced. But other forms of scrutiny and accountability have emerged. The international organizations to which the country belongs continuously monitor domestic policy. Conducted in the name of "transparency," this monitoring function exercises a strong "moral suasion" effect for compliance not only with the letter, but also with the neoliberal spirit, of the agreements to which Canada is a signatory.

Under the WTO the Trade Policy Review Mechanism (TPRM) regularly reviews trade policies of member nations. The TPRM would "contribute to adherence by all members to rules, disciplines and commitments made… by achieving greater transparency" (Laird 1999: 742). Opinion among scholars is divided on whether this is an enforcement mechanism or simply a tool aimed at improving public policy through providing transparency and information about each state's practices. In general the latter seems more plausible as a legal interpretation, though the impact of moral suasion should not be underestimated.

We have noted above the proselytizing activities of the OECD. The OECD operates as an important site for the construction and dissemination of transnational research and policy ideas. More broadly, the OECD is a "purveyor of ideas" and ideas play an important role in contemporary transnational governance. Institutions and interests (of nation-states, international organizations, and social forces) are important, but ideas also play a critical role. In the broadest sense, transnational norms identify what a modern state "is" (Porter and Webb 2008: 43–44) and thus sanction appropriate modes of internal and external conduct. In policy terms, the ideas sanctioned by international organizations help to identify problems and to map out the range of "best practice" solutions (Mahon and McBride 2008a).

Beyond the moral suasion activities of some international organizations, international agreements impose significant restrictions on state capacity. Often these restrictions play on the state's capacity to engage in industrial policy. Under the provisions of the treaties, many of the key instruments that might be used — such as performance requirements on foreign investment, discrimination in favour of domestic producers, and using energy resources to support domestic industry — are prohibited. Unexpectedly, as a result of the magazines case, Canada is also prevented from applying some of the measures it has used to promote Canadian culture.

Steps that might be contemplated to protect public health or the environment must now meet the test of being the "least trade-restrictive" possible, and the test will be applied by dispute resolution mechanisms established under the international agreements. Even though social policy retrenchment has been driven by domestic factors, there is a constant danger that control over social services will slip out of national jurisdiction because of the investment provisions under NAFTA and the danger that GATS exemptions, even if the political will exists to sustain them, will be bypassed because of the content of other WTO agreements or NAFTA articles. In a wide range of policy areas, Canadian law makers must now factor in the terms of complex international agreements or face the possibility that their work will be challenged from outside the Canadian political system. These constraints apply just as much to provincial decision makers, who have had no control over the negotiation of the international economic agreements, as to Ottawa decision makers, who have had some control.

Public Administration

The institutions of the state have been shrunk, reshaped, and redirected. Reducing the role of government generally, and in particular reducing the role of the welfare state, has been a central feature of neoliberalism (Marchak 1991: ch. 5; Shields 1990). Economic and social interventionism has been curtailed. But in certain spheres of activity, such as defence and law and order, a "strong state" has been retained. Strong government is necessary to uphold authority in society, which clearly implies a role for the state in defence of the institution of private property and, perhaps, of institutions such as the family (see Gamble 1988: 35–36).

Peter Aucoin (1995; 1996) notes the centralization of budgetary control and the simultaneous decentralization of operations to maximize efficiency. The professional public service has been circumvented as a source of policy advice in favour of private, often corporate-funded, sources such as think tanks and polling firms. Indeed, the partial privatization of state functions has been a feature of neoliberal administrative reform. Often described in technocratic terms as the "new public management," these techniques have served as a conduit for neoliberal ideology and transmitted its values and practices into the public sector (Shields and Evans 1998). As Daniel Cohn (1997) argues, the doctrine of new public management not only represents an elite consensus on a changed role for the state, but also carries with it the potential to be a technique for the avoidance of blame for the costs incurred in the transition to a new policy paradigm. Other examples of the paradigm in operation are the tendency to go outside the public service for appointments to key public service positions (Savoie 1995); the contracting out of government services to private suppliers; and the general intrusion of commercial principles into government operations (Pierre 1995; Russell 2000: 43–46). Broader than contracting out, alternative service delivery systems include "single-window service centres, the outsourcing of functions to not-for-profit organizations and public-private partnerships" (Clark 2002: 783).

These practices have been linked to globalization (Doern, Pal and Tomlin 1996: 1–2) as well as to domestic neoliberalism. Summing up these trends, John Shields and B. Mitchell Evans (1998: 81) propose:

> The new state being constructed is not simply a leaner state but a state with an entirely different purpose. The redistributive market-controlling dimensions of the Keynesian welfare state are being replaced by a focus on market flexibility and wealth accumulation. The apparatus of the state is being redesigned to facilitate this transition from a regime of national economic management to one of global competitiveness.

The public administration of the new "lean state" (Sears 1999) has thus been calibrated with the purposes of neoliberalism. As part of this transition, Evans (2004: 9–10) argues that within the public service the value of neutrality and commitment to a rational, evidence-based policy process are waning, and those values associated with neoliberalism, including a commitment to policy making informed by political considerations emanating from the Cabinet or premier's office, are on the rise.

Neoliberal Globalization and the Federal System
The operation of the federal system has also been altered by the terms of international agreements. Indeed, the conjunction of domestic neoliberalism, which has tended to decentralize Confederation, and international economic agreements (themselves infused with neoliberal content), which tend to enhance the role of the federal government, has been somewhat contradictory.

Some activities, such as placing export restrictions on energy resources, are now denied to either the federal or provincial governments. That these limitations on government were negotiated by the federal authorities, which consulted the provinces (though without treating them as full partners), could be taken as tilting the constitutional balance towards the federal level. The agreements essentially legislate, at least negatively, in areas of provincial jurisdiction. On the other hand, provincial demands for consultation are "not going to diminish. This has implications for the federal government's policy flexibility, both domestic and international" (Kukucha 2008: 57). Indeed consultations have advanced to a new level in the Canada-E.U. trade talks, partly as a result of E.U. insistence that provinces be involved in key areas like government procurement, which would have major implications for them (Kukucha 2010).

The situation is certainly complex as the terms of some of the agreements cast the federal government in a supervisory role vis-à-vis the provinces through the injunction to take "all necessary measures" (NAFTA) or all "reasonable" measures (WTO) to obtain the compliance of subnational governments. An analysis of the implications of NAFTA chapter 11, which deals with investment and to some degree intrudes on provincial regulatory capacity, concluded that the provinces were bound by chapter 11 under the federal trade and commerce power. Moreover, it concluded that it would be constitutional for the federal authorities to enact legislation compelling a province to pay any compensation due as a result of a provincial law in violation of chapter 11 provisions (Luz 2001). The international agreements thus put the federal government in the position of acting as "the domestic enforcer of an international system that reduces the scope and effectiveness of provincial policy instruments" (Robinson 1995: 251).

The Agreement on Internal Trade (AIT) and the Trade, Investment, and Labour Mobility Agreement (TILMA)

Proposals to strengthen the economic union by reducing the capacity of governments to regulate markets have a long history, and they seemed to gather momentum in the 1970s and 1980s (Safarian 1974; Canada 1979; Courchene 1986) when they featured in early rounds of constitutional negotiations. In 1991, the federal government took advantage of renewed constitutional discussions that eventually became the Charlottetown talks to pursue the issue. In its original 1991 constitutional proposals, the federal government adopted a stance similar to the Business Council on National Issues' view that one of the key ingredients of future competitiveness rested in strengthening the free market basis of the economic union (Canada 1991: 9). After the failure of the Charlottetown talks, the government, urged on by business (*Globe and Mail* 1992: B3) but largely ignored by the general public, began trying to achieve a stronger economic union through a new approach to intergovernmental negotiations (Doern and MacDonald 1998: 4).

The influence of pre-existing international trade agreements was felt from the outset. A formal set of negotiation rules for the AIT rested on GATT, FTA, and NAFTA precedents, such as the most-favoured nation and national treatment provisions of GATT and dispute-settlement procedures from the FTA (Doern and MacDonald 1998: 4).

Despite this impressive ancestry, for some the Agreement on Internal Trade, signed on July 1, 1995, turned out to be a damp squib — a non-binding political accord that provided little enforcement to back up the stated goals of removing internal trade barriers in Canada (Howse 1996). This was certainly the position of business groups such as the Canadian Chamber of Commerce (Doern and MacDonald 1998: 152). Big business pressure had, of course, been a major impetus behind the negotiations (ibid.: 55), and business and neoliberals expressed some disappointment at the limited results. The weakness of the enforcement mechanisms — the result of provincial resistance to any supervisory powers for Ottawa — stands at odds with the provisions of international trade agreements to which Canada is signatory. According to trade consultant Peter Clark, "The more and more we get into international trade agreements, the onus falls on the federal government to ensure that the provinces play by the rules" (*Globe and Mail* Nov. 13, 1995).

Yet the Agreement on Internal Trade is not without institutional or even constitutional import. Proponents of the AIT tend to depict it as part of the government's "trade agenda" and as having no constitutional implications. The preamble to the agreement itself proclaimed its lack of constitutional effect. Yet opponents, including several provinces, tended to view it in governance terms (see Doern and MacDonald 1998: ch. 1). G. Bruce Doern and Mark MacDonald (1998: 152) observe that the existence of the agreement shapes the decisions of policy makers. It may enhance the federal government's trade and commerce powers, they say, because its anti-discriminatory provisions have the greatest impact on provincial governments (ibid.: 162–63).

Nor have its results been negligible. Reviewing the agreement after five years, Daniel Schwanen (2000) concludes that while its record in dismantling many internal barriers to trade had been disappointing, the agreement had brought some progress. Negotiations towards mutual recognition agreements regarding qualifications in many professions had made headway, and advances had been made by including the MASH sector (municipalities, academe, schools, and hospitals) in the government procurement provisions.

The AIT permitted parties to conclude additional agreements to further liberalize trade, investment, and labour mobility and the provinces of British Columbia and Alberta concluded such an agreement, the Trade, Investment, and Labour Mobility Agreement (TILMA), in 2006. Among its other liberalizing and privatizing measures the agreement introduced a direct investor-state dispute resolution mechanism, very similar to NAFTA chapter 11 and provisions in some international bilateral investment treaties.

Conclusion

In describing the ideas, policies, and institutions of the neoliberal package we have been depicting a new social structure of accumulation (SSA). As well, following Peck and Tickell (2002) and Graefe (2006), we have been sensitive to the distinction between measures that rolled back the previous SSA, others that rolled out the neoliberal successor, and others, such as the development of inclusive liberalism in some policy areas, that might moderate the full impact of the hegemonic paradigm. Institutionally, the most remarkable feature of neoliberalism has been the construction of global and regional institutions, agreements, and rules that are intended to bind states to the neoliberal principles embedded in these arrangements.

A number of points stand out. First, the gradualism of the roll-back stage of the project testifies to the strong public support that Keynesianism had enjoyed. Second, though, even if the roll-back was never total, as the persistence of a public health care system shows, it was effective. A new paradigm did triumph and significant policy and institutional changes did ensue. Third, however, not only have gains made during this era been disproportionately enjoyed by the most wealthy, but as we will examine next in chapter 5, the neoliberal SSA is unstable and crisis-prone. Despite this, neoliberalism has thus far proven resilient. Alternative ideas certainly exist but no social force capable of pushing them to the forefront is on the scene. Labour is disaffected. But, never having been part of the coalition that launched neoliberalism, its opposition is nothing new. In any event, labour's influence has been reduced by the impact of globalization and by the neoliberal repudiation of full employment and diminution of the social wage. Furthermore, changes made to key political institutions during the neoliberal roll-out phase, have held serious implications for the depth and functioning of democratic control in Canada. International agreements have produced greater executive dominance and concentration of political power, reduced the role of the courts, and provided new mechanisms for investors alone to initiate dispute procedures. Accountability of decision making to Parliament has also been dramatically reduced, and thus, so too has public control over decision making in the neoliberal era. Later we argue that this has produced an unprecedented degree of "democratic malaise" in Canada (see chapter 6).

Chapter 5

A TALE OF THREE CRISES

In choosing the lens of "crisis" through which to view Canadian political developments in the early twenty-first century, we have not been influenced solely by the global financial and economic crisis that developed in 2007. Rather, it seems that taking into account the record of neoliberalism in practice over the last three decades, the political economy and polity of Canada has been characterized by recurrent crises. In contrast to the deep, structural (generalized or system-wide) crises of the Great Depression in the 1930s and the dismal decade of global stagflation in the 1970s, here we are referring to the pattern of regularly occurring episodes of instability and economic downturn that have plagued the neoliberal era. In Canada (as is certainly the case elsewhere) this has taken the form of three major recessions occurring each decade since the emergence of neoliberalism. Thus neoliberal-era crisis episodes have been of different degrees of severity, but the phenomenon of frequent crises, as opposed to the minor fluctuations of the normal business cycle, is reminiscent of the period before World War II and contrasts with the three decades that followed that war. In that respect, postwar Keynesianism is the exception in the history of capitalism, rather than the norm, as its own sense of hubris in the postwar period suggested.

Of course, neoliberalism, as is the case with all policy paradigms that achieve hegemony, originated in a crisis. So the Keynesian era did ultimately produce a crisis situation that led to its replacement. But interestingly, neoliberalism has itself proven crisis-prone throughout the period in which it has dominated political discourse and practice, but without this instability having so far undermined its hegemony.

The neoliberal era was born out of stagflation — simultaneously high levels of unemployment and inflation — in the mid-1970s. Keynesianism seemed to have few answers to the problems posed by stagflation. It was predicated on the goal of full employment, an objective that, where realized, conferred advantages on labour in its battles with capital over wages and working conditions. The 1970s crisis was frequently framed in terms of "wage-push" inflation. One solution to the stagflation issue was to regulate the outcomes of wage negotiations, thus using the state to moderate labour's presumed bargaining power under full employment conditions (McBride 1983). More radical solutions would have seen more planning and a diminished role for markets including the price system (see, for example, Holland 1975).

For the emerging neoliberal paradigm, rolling back the gains labour had made in the postwar period, whether directly through confrontations at the bargaining table or indirectly through diminishing the state's provision of a "social wage" in the form of widely available social programs, became a prime objective. As well, tight monetary policy and ensuing recession would restore the role of unemployment as an instrument of labour discipline. Apart from its social programs and its role as guarantor of full employment, the Keynesian state came under further scrutiny from capital as a perceived obstacle to new profitable investment opportunities for capital. In this capacity, it blocked business solutions to any crisis of overaccumulation that might exist (see chapter 2). We can see two ways in which this might have occurred.

First, although the Keynesian era was one in which progressive liberalization of trade in goods took place, the fact that Keynesianism was a system of national economic management meant that controls of various kinds continued to be important. For many forms of trade and, more importantly, for mobility of capital it meant that potential areas of foreign investment were highly regulated and difficult to enter. The drive for freer trade and an end to restrictions on foreign investment, essential components of what came to be known as globalization, were key features of the neoliberal assault on Keynesianism and analogous policy paradigms, such as import substitution industrialization, in developing countries. Second, significant sectors of the economy and social provision in most western capitalist countries were occupied by state monopolies or had a significant state presence. Depending on the country in question, such economic sectors might include transport, utilities, mining, key manufacturing like steel and automobile and aircraft production, airlines, and even banks. Social policy areas like education and health, pensions, and other social programs tended to be state preserves. As a result of state domination of these sectors, a host of potentially profitable locations for private investment were ruled out. The drive to alter this situation, by advocating progressive privatization, was the second key feature of the neoliberal revolution. In short, neoliberalism can be understood as a political project aimed at maximizing opportunities for private profit through globalization and privatization.

During the Keynesian era, various accounts of state policy described a balance in state priorities between accumulation and legitimation activities (for example, O'Connor 1973). Indeed, one of Keynesianism's claims to fame was that by providing full employment and also sustaining aggregate demand by various social wage expenditures, it could satisfy both priorities. As noted above, however, business interests came to view such interventions into the private enterprise system as blocking the path of opportunities for private capital accumulation.

In terms of the policy paradigm seeking to replace the Keynesian one, its discourse focused initially on the trade-off between inflation and unemployment and the apparent inability of Keynesian policies to produce low rates of both. Gradually an alternative neoliberal account of the inflation-unemployment relationship gained currency, a theoretical perspective that offered a clear explanation and prescription for poor labour market conditions. Central to the emerging neoliberal version of the issue were the concepts of a natural rate of unemployment — the rate of unemployment where the demand for and supply of labour are in equilibrium, notwithstanding any remaining amount of unemployment — and the concept of a non-accelerating inflation rate of unemployment (NAIRU). The NAIRU is that rate of unemployment, determined by the supply side of the economy, at which the inflation rate will be constant (see Sawyer 2004: 33–36).

These concepts had several policy implications, all of which helped flesh out the neoliberal fix for the problems faced by capital in the 1980s. Fiscal policy had little role to play. It lost its privileged position, with monetary policy being increasingly favoured as the means of accomplishing macroeconomic goals. This was partially due to the end of the Bretton Woods monetary regime, a development that liberated monetary tools once the exchange rate was no longer fixed. The demise of fiscal policy was also due to globalization, a process that impeded the effectiveness of fiscal tools because of spending leakages associated with trade liberalization. These rendered demand management policies counterproductive.

Second, even in the context of a closed economy it was argued that there was an inflation barrier to full employment. It was held that beyond a certain level, decreases in the unemployment rate could only be purchased by spending levels that triggered increased inflation. Any level of unemployment above the natural rate was caused within the labour market itself by market imperfections that reduced demand for labour or prevented the labour market from clearing. Examples include strong trade unions, and labour market rigidities (employment protection legislation, social supports, and unemployment insurance), which, by this interpretation, far from actually achieving their goals, increased unemployment above its natural level (Kuhn 1997). Thus policy action against these obstacles or rigidities could be justified in the name of employment creation.

Later, as inflation declined and the fight against it lost its power to justify continuing restrictive policy measures, the size of government budget deficits and measures designed to stimulate private investment — such as privatization, deregulation, tax cuts, and expenditure cuts to balance budgets — assumed greater prominence. There was no advance blueprint for this sequencing of justifications. Rather, neoliberalism has proved flexible and opportunistic in supplying arguments, though quite principled and unwavering in its objectives.

In the process of shifting priorities, Keynes and his legacy became subject to demonization by proponents of the neoliberal model. However, it is important to recall that his theories and policies were constructed to save capitalism from possible collapse occasioned by its delegitimization as a result of prolonged mass unemployment. In the 1930s, liberal democratic capitalism was only one of a number of alternatives available and being practised somewhere in the world (Gourevitch 1986). From the perspective of capital in the 1970s, however, yesterday's solution or fix had become today's problem. And the solution to that problem lay in the restoration of the process of capital accumulation, at the expense of legitimation activities, to be accomplished through an expansion of the market and the authority of market forces. The failure of the neoliberal social structure of accumulation to win the hearts and minds of the population behind its accumulation project can be counted as a failure of legitimation, one that contributes to the democratic malaise characteristic of this era, which we explore in the Canadian context in the next chapter.

As we shall see, this fix to the problems of the 1970s has itself been crisis-prone at the global level and in the experience of many of its constituent states. Here we provide an analytic sketch of neoliberalism's role in Canada in imposing public austerity amid private affluence and its long survival despite successive crises. The juxtaposition of affluence and austerity has been a feature of recent decades as labour market inequality has increased and the capacity of the state to modify market outcomes has been diminished.

Recession in the 1980s: The First
Crisis of Neoliberalism in Canada

The change of paradigm took place over an extended period in Canada, the trend beginning in 1975 and largely complete by 1984. From 1975 the government prioritized inflation control over full employment, and this found expression in a variety of policy areas. The emphasis on inflation control is hardly socially neutral. Protecting the value of money against inflationary erosion privileges lenders over borrowers, with the result that not only do the affluent generally benefit from such priorities, but also financial interests are better served than industrial ones. The origins of "financialization" — a process whereby financial markets, institutions, and actors gain influence over economic policy and economic outcomes at the expense of participants in the real economy of production and distribution of real products — which figures in many accounts of the 2007 crisis — may thus lie thirty years earlier in the move to inflation-control as the chief economic priority of government.

Fiscal restraint saw federal program expenditures remain below the 1975 level of 20.8 percent of GDP until 1982, when still-existing Keynesian automatic stabilizers were triggered by the deep recession of the early 1980s. Notwithstanding expenditure restraint, however, government deficits rose sharply. In time, these deficits would come to serve as the rationale for further rounds of expenditure reductions. However, the increasing size of the annual deficit had little to do with the expenditure side of the ledger. The deficit was largely due to revenue shortfalls, themselves the product of neoliberal fiscal policy choices, and to increased debt-carrying charges, the result of monetary policy measures aimed at controlling inflation (McIlveen and Mimoto 1990). On the fiscal side, governments created tax loopholes, offered tax breaks to business, and made widespread use of tax expenditures (McQuaig 1987; Ternowetsky 1987). Overwhelmingly, the benefits of these measures flowed to higher income taxpayers (Maslove 1981).

Monetary policy became restrictive from 1975 onwards. In that year the Bank of Canada announced a policy of "monetary gradualism." Under this approach the bank set targets for the growth of money supply that were steadily reduced over time. Control of inflation was the stated goal and high interest rates a key instrument that followed logically from the restraint in the money supply. Apart from directly contributing to government deficits through higher carrying charges on accumulated debt, high interest rates affected revenues indirectly through depressing economic activity and thereby increasing unemployment and slowing economic growth. Fiscal and monetary measures were supplemented by general wage and price controls at the federal level (1975–78), the effect of which was similarly to redistribute income from individuals to businesses (Gonick 1987: 184–85).

The impact of these policies in terms of rising levels of unemployment was clear, and was felt with a vengeance in the early 1980s recession. Unemployment had averaged 5.7 percent in the early 1970s, rising to an average of 7.3 percent in the last half of the decade, and 9.8 percent in the 1980–84 period. Indeed, for the five-year period 1982–86, the rate averaged 10.8 percent, before gradually declining later in the decade. Unsurprisingly, the inflation rate also dropped, as demand was squeezed out of the economy. But rather than this providing leeway for restoration of the state's social role, the size of the government deficit began to serve as a rationale for continuation of the neoliberal policy mix, and especially measures that circumscribed the state's ability to modify market outcomes. Payments on the public debt had risen to more than a third of state revenues by the end of the 1980s. In this context, efforts to restrain spending and to raise revenues by privatizing state assets found willing supporters. Greater priority was to be given to the accumulation needs of capital and the state's role was transformed. However, in many respects, it remained important, in contradiction to some theorizations of state obsolescence. For example, the state was active in the redistribution of wealth in an upward direction, engineering a new global governance architecture, significant financial market re-regulation, and in coercing labour through measures like wage and price controls, reform of industrial relations legislation, back to work legislation, and so on. Beyond such activities, however, there is a sense in which accumulation was largely handed over to private actors. Another way of putting this is that the process of capital accumulation was less subject to public influence or control and increasingly privatized, though with a supportive state in the background.

In the run-up to the 1980s recession the state's domestic economic and social policy stance proved responsive to the articulated preferences of capital as represented in Canada by the Business Council on National Issues, an organization founded in 1976 by the chief executive officers of the 150 leading corporations. The same picture held true in foreign economic policy. The repudiation of Keynesianism meant that the notion of a national economic space, lightly managed by state intervention to massage the level of aggregate demand, was also repudiated. In spite of opening up new scope for profit making activities through policies such as privatization, business required a wider scope, ultimately a global one, to optimize accumulation. Thus, the sequence of domestic policies that culminated in the crisis of the 1980s also served as a launching pad for moving to free trade and export-led growth strategies to replace the notion of national economic management.

Internationally-oriented capital and powerful states began to construct a new architecture of international trade and investment agreements. Traditionally cast as a middle power or semi-peripheral actor in the global economy, the Canadian state cast in its lot with its hegemonic neighbour to the south and enthusiastically advocated what would become known as globalization. From differing points of view this could either be represented as the result of the growing maturity of Canadian capital, which increasingly defined its future prosperity in continental if not global terms (Carroll 1986; 1989), or, in the words of Donald Macdonald, head of the influential royal commission which launched Canada's free trade initiative with the U.S., referring to Canadian business spokespersons: "If these people say they can compete in a free market, who am I to say they cannot?" (quoted in Doern and Tomlin 1992: 55).

When compared to earlier trade agreements like the GATT the resulting trade and investment agreements — some bilateral, some regional, and others global in scope — were far more intrusive and disciplinary as far as national regulations were concerned. The agreements covered more topics. As well as the trade in goods provisions of earlier agreements, trade in services, intellectual property rights, and investment were often included. Applying trade rules like non-discrimination, most favoured nation, and national treatment to these spheres involved much greater penetration of national borders than had the tariff-focused trade regime typical of the Bretton Woods-GATT era. As a result, states would become more circumscribed than formerly. However, this does imply they became less powerful. Indeed their role in creating, implementing, and enforcing the new system of rules and regulations remained essential. But in other areas, by institutional design in which they played a key architectural role, their capacity was limited.

In the Canadian case, these developments would see a reversal of a long-standing preference for engaging with the United States in multilateral contexts in favour of increased bilateralism. This found expression in the Canada-U.S. free trade agreement, subsequently expanded to include Mexico in NAFTA, and later in the 2010 Canada-U.S. Government Procurement Agreement.

The effect of the first crisis of neoliberalism was thus to reinforce the constraints on state activity that neoliberalism demanded. The apparent compulsion of dealing with the deficit and accumulated debt rendered innovation or responsiveness to social issues problematic. And if economic prosperity was to be achieved in the global order, it seemed to demand greater emphasis on competitiveness and conformity with the rules of the global economy as these became articulated in international agreements. Although states were the architects of the agreements, once in place such rules tended to further reduce states' room for manoeuvre and to privilege market solutions and the interests of private actors.

Recession in the 1990s: The Second Crisis of Neoliberalism in Canada

Canada entered a recession in 1990 and experienced only a slow, sluggish recovery over the course of the 1990s. Unemployment exceeded 10 percent from 1991–94 and, over the decade as a whole, averaged 9.5 percent, the highest decade-long figure since the Great Depression. Thereafter the rate fell and remained lower for the first decade of the new century. Various factors were involved in the move into recession and the slow recovery. They include the anti-inflationary monetary policy pursued by the Bank of Canada and the inflexibility of fiscal policy, which was partly the result of the high debt charges triggered by the high interest rate policy of the bank. This second crisis of neoliberalism was to coincide with the move to globalization, which could be represented as a potential solution to economic stagnation and was used as an opportunity to intensify the battle against Keynesianism's institutional legacy, notably the relatively generous, by North American standards, welfare state.

In its first decade from 1975, the neoliberal project was largely focused on modifying the policies that defined Keynesianism. Success was not guaranteed: hence the gradualism of the process and its incomplete success. For example, polls through the mid-1990s continued to show public preference for an active state motivated by a desire to see job creation promoted and social programs protected. Such views found little support at the elite level (see McBride and Shields 1997: 78–79). But public and social movement opposition was not ineffective. In the late 1980s there were signs that the institutions of the Keynesian welfare state were proving resilient (Banting 1987; Mishra 1990). Similarly, the escape from the national to the global really only took hold in the 1990s, some twenty years after the dominance of neoliberalism began to be asserted. The 1989 Canada–United States free trade agreement was an early indicator of this, but the main developments took place later, with the implementation of NAFTA and the WTO in the mid-1990s. The new agreements had institutional effects, as noted in chapter 4. The impact of these conditioning frameworks was generally to enhance and embed economic liberalism and to render it more difficult for states to alter market relations (McBride 2003).

A little noticed aspect of Canada's ongoing constitutional debates in the 1980s and early 1990s was the attempt to insinuate neoliberal constitutional measures into a process largely dominated by efforts to reconcile national, linguistic, and regional cleavages within the country. Such efforts can be seen as part of an attempt to construct a social structure of accumulation, or mode of regulation, suitable for the neoliberal project. The principle mover seems to have been the Business Council on National Issues though it, in many respects, drew inspiration from the institutional analysis of the Macdonald Report (McBride 1993). Neoliberal preferences included a modicum of decentralization of federalism, especially in the classic Keynesian areas of health and welfare, with binding rules in areas like the economic union, from which both levels of government would be barred from tinkering. In the so-called Canada Round of constitutional negotiations, federal proposals gave a great deal of space to the constitutional requisites of the prosperity agenda. Concretely, this found expression in proposals to strengthen the Canadian economic union, to better harmonize federal-provincial policies, to reform the mandate of the Bank of Canada by making its sole goal the preservation of price stability rather than its rather broader mandate that included attention to employment levels and recognition of property rights, a constitutional provision that could serve as a hindrance to social legislation and the welfare state. In the event, many of these proposals had fallen by the wayside by the time that the Canada Round itself, as embodied in the Charlottetown agreement, was defeated in a constitutional referendum. Nonetheless, the agenda put forward represents an interesting case of an attempt to construct, by formal constitutional means, a social structure of accumulation appropriate to neoliberalism. The formal constitutional route having been blocked, less direct means were found to achieve some of these ends.

These included legislative attempts to impose balanced budget legislation. A key Keynesian policy prescription is the use of counter cyclical demand management. The idea is that during times of recession, government spending can be used to stimulate the economy by propping up effective demand. The flip side is that spending austerity can play a role during boom periods as a way of discouraging inflation. This technique would therefore help smooth out the upswings and downswings inherent to capitalism (although critics argued that in practice spending seldom dropped during upswings). Balanced budget legislation, or similar laws which limit fiscal policy making powers, effectively eliminate the ability of government to spend during downturns (given that tax increases are also discouraged or capped through legislation). In this way the Keynesian policy option was legislatively removed from the tool-kit of governments. Constitutional doctrines in Westminster-type political systems, such as parliamentary supremacy and the related notion that no Parliament can bind its successors, limit the legal consequences of these measures. Like other legislation, these laws can be repealed by a subsequent Parliament and, as noted below, under pressure from the recession some were. Thus they can best be understood as politically symbolic measures designed to make it more difficult, but unable to make it constitutionally impossible, for governments to engage in deficit spending.

The introduction of balanced budget legislation occurred in most provinces and territories across Canada in the 1990s. Spending control and/or balanced budget legislation was first introduced by the federal and Alberta governments in 1992, followed by Nova Scotia in 1993, the Northwest Territories, Manitoba, New Brunswick, and Saskatchewan in 1995, Quebec in 1996, Ontario in 1999, and B.C. in 2001. The idea behind this trend was that deficits cause debt and, regardless of the state of the economy, "the best level of government debt is no debt at all" (Stanford 1999: 60). Spending cuts are thus encouraged by locking in neoliberal reasoning, attempting to tie the hands of future governments should they seek to promote greater social equity and full employment.

However, it must be noted that the recent economic crisis has prompted a temporary reprieve from inflexible balanced budget legislation in some jurisdictions. For instance, B.C. amended its balanced budget law in 2009 to allow for two years of deficits (CBC 2009d), and in March 2010, Manitoba made revisions in order to allow for four years of deficit spending (Kusch 2010). This raises the question of the future of balanced budget policy in Canada. As the Canadian Taxpayers Federation said in reaction to the B.C. amendments, "they [governments] need to stick with these things in the tough times. That's supposedly why they have them to keep them on track in the tough times" (CBC 2009d). Despite these neoliberal fears, allegiance to austerity remains strong. The B.C. government "seems determined to run as small a deficit as possible" through current and future spending cuts (Ivanova 2009).

In addition to this balanced budget legislation, as we saw in chapter 4, various domestic institutional changes also typify the 1990s. These changes relate largely to the process of becoming embedded in the international economic agreements that typify the era of globalization, and some were minor while others were quite significant. They affected the way that federalism operates, the role of the courts and of Parliament, and the organization and ethos of the bureaucracy. Most of the changes that can be partially attributed to the influence of global factors were also reinforced by the preferences of governments at the domestic level, strongly influenced as most of them were by the ideology of neoliberalism. The ongoing policy initiatives of neoliberalism are also recounted in chapter 4; the shrinking of government as measured by the percentage of GDP it spent, the reduced impact of government as an employer, ever-advancing privatization of government functions and operations, reductions in social spending, and federal withdrawal from most areas of labour market programming characterized the period after the second crisis of neoliberalism. Many of these measures had institutional as well as policy implications.

Thus, the neoliberal policy paradigm has drawn on some combination of the following over the past few decades: budgetary austerity, implementation of regressive taxation, deregulation and re-regulation, privatization, liberalization, and the adoption of free trade agreements. However, the exact nature of neoliberal reform has also evolved, as crises produced have necessitated policy learning and adjustment. Peck and Tickell (2002) describe three phases, though these should be considered heuristically rather than as chronologically distinct phases. First, during the 1970s, neoliberalism was mainly an intellectual project, a critique of the Keynesian orthodoxy at the time. Second, global stagflation and a massive expansion of public debt were used to promote a change in policy orientation in the 1980s under ideologically motivated governments such as the Reagan, Thatcher, and Mulroney administrations. This 1980s phase is dubbed roll-back neoliberalization to refer to the process of tearing down the old Keynesian policy system through the introduction of monetarism, massive budget and social spending cuts, regressive taxation, privatization, and deregulation, which all became reigning policies of the day. Unlike Peck and Tickell, however, we argue that in Canada neoliberal reforms actually precipitated the crisis of the Keynesian welfare state (see chapter 4; McBride 2005: 97). This was then used to intensify the neoliberal policy package.

By the mid-1990s it was becoming clear that further reforms, internal to the state and more pragmatic and technocratic (less political) in nature, would be necessary to cement the paradigm shift. This would serve to help normalize the new common sense. For Peck and Tickell (2002) this is the third phase, the roll-out, prescriptive phase of the neoliberal project.[1] Common policies now include social program reform (rather than program cuts), tax expenditures as new forms of the welfare state (rather than removing all support), establishing partnerships with the private sector (rather than full-scale privatization), and re-regulation (rather than deregulation).

The roll-back and roll-out distinction is an important one to make because it demonstrates the ways in which the neoliberal project has evolved over the years, often out of a need to deal with the contradictions and dislocations that result from its hallmark austerity. However, it would be misleading to suggest that the roll-out phase does not promote austerity. Four examples of continuing austerity in Canada are: reduced spending on social programs; less generous social programs; erosion of government employment; and a locking in of these changes through balanced budget legislation. Thus areas once crucial to Keynesian policy have been steadily undermined, eroded, and altered by waves of roll-back and roll-out neoliberal policy in Canada.

Global Financial Meltdown and the Attempt to Restore "Business as Usual"

In chapter 1 we provided an account of the course of the global financial crisis which developed in 2007 and which, for a time, shook neoliberal certainties to their foundations. Emergency, not to say panic-stricken, reactions included bailouts and de facto nationalization of banks and financial institutions. As well, significant spending plans to sustain consumption were also undertaken around the world in order to combat the crisis. A global recession followed the financial crisis and credit crunch, though a worse depression was averted due to the stimulus packages put in place. However, with the benefit of hindsight it is clear that the emergency responses such as stimulus packages denoted no change of mind on economic fundamentals on the part of the neoliberal elites, nor was any alternative political force able to wrest the initiative from those who had presided over the crisis-prone neoliberal era. Indeed, almost before they had fully taken effect, policy discussions turned to the issue of how quickly they could be terminated and the ironically named doctrines of sound finance restored. In this process, it must be said that Canada has been in the forefront of neoliberal orthodoxy. Moreover, the G-20 and other international organizations have thus far failed to significantly reform the conduct of private international financial transactions, and the substance of global governance remains much the same as formerly. Meanwhile the vast sums expended in bailing out financial institutions deemed too big to fail are now slated for repayment. A new age of austerity looms in which state budgets and particularly social programs will be ravaged to pay for the excesses of financiers.

In short, neoliberal rule seems to be on the point of repeating its recent history by attempting to use the crises its policies have regularly created to push its agenda to the next stage. This means, of course, that the policies and institutions that led to the meltdown remain in place and some are being extended. For example, Canada is seeking to negotiate a NAFTA-style agreement with the European Union, one that could expose its government procurement sector to foreign competition to a far greater extent than is the case with either NAFTA or the WTO (Sinclair 2010; for a contrary view see Kukucha 2010). Similarly, as multilateral trade negotiations have stalled there has been a proliferation of bilateral trade agreements in the 2000s. That said, all is not as it was. Some of the institutions and policies of neoliberal globalism have encountered an impasse in terms of their further development. The best example is the Doha Round of WTO negotiations, launched in November 2001, which still seem deadlocked despite repeated setting of new deadlines for completion. And the cozy club of the G-7 and G-8 has been opened up to a broader range of participants (the G-20), reflecting in part the rise of strong developing states such as Brazil and China, with somewhat different agendas, than the countries of North America, Europe, and Japan, which had held undisputed sway over the global political economy.

Conclusions

Neoliberalism is a political project, distinct not for its stability or widespread social prosperity but instead for its promotion of expanded private markets and market relations, leading to great insecurity and systemic instability. This market expansion is achieved in a number of ways, with features relating to both the accumulation process and state policy. Though not mutually exclusive, these two features of the neoliberal project have the propensity to generate their own unique contradictions. Changes within the accumulation process associated with neoliberalism are the emergence of financialization and reliance on debt to stimulate prosperity, and an enhancement of accumulation by dispossession and exploitation. Changes to state policy include budgetary austerity (in the form of deficit fixation, an end to demand management, and a dramatic decline in the generosity of social programs), deregulation and re-regulation both at home and in the international economy, and privatization in multiple dimensions. Neoliberal policies greatly affect state-society relations and hold particular implications for social reproduction. These two broad categories of the neoliberal project are interrelated and reinforce one another, leading to significant social inequalities. These contradictions render neoliberalism inherently crisis-prone, as the evidence of the past thirty years shows. Interestingly, the many crises engendered by neoliberalism so far have not led to an undermining of the project. It has even been argued that a great strength of neoliberalism is its ability to be reconstituted, and thus rejuvenated, through the crises that it produces (Peck and Tickell 2002: 392). Whether this capacity to survive, adapt and intensify can continue indefinitely is less certain.

Chapter 6

CANADA'S COMPOUNDED POLITICAL CRISIS

Neoliberalism and Democratic Malaise

The 2008 financial crisis has provoked widespread comment on the threat economic instability poses to democracy. For example, the Economist Intelligence Unit's Index of Democracy (2008) concluded that a financial crisis and global recession could be threatening to democracy and not just in areas typically regarded in the western media as unstable, such as Russia, China, the Middle East, and Latin America (Petrou 2009: 22–27). The Economist Intelligence Unit considered that "In the developed West, a precipitous decline in political participation, weaknesses in the functioning of government, and security-related curbs on civil liberties are having a corrosive effect on some long-established democracies" (2008: 1).

To these threats to civil liberties one might add the repressive policing tactics at a number of anti-globalization demonstrations in the 1990s and early 2000s, conduct that continued in the context of protests at various G-8 and G-20 meetings, culminating in Toronto in June 2010.

According to the Economist Intelligence Unit, Canada is ensconced in the top third of what it designates as "full democracies", but problems are noted with respect to some countries in this category. For example, the U.K. and U.S. have both experienced erosion of civil liberties as a result of anti-terrorist actions, U.K. political participation is very low, and in several western countries support for extremist political parties and anti-immigrant groups has risen.

Canada is, of course, not without its share of scandals relating to recent civil liberties violations. Since 2001 there have been a number of high profile cases including allowing the U.S. to transfer Maher Arar to Syria, where he was tortured; not attempting to repatriate Canadian juvenile Omar Khadr, who has been held in Guantanamo Bay for a number of years; and the Afghan detainees debacle in which Canadian soldiers and government officials are accused of handing over prisoners to Afghan officials despite knowing that they would likely be tortured. In the Arar case, an enquiry established that Canadian security officials passed inaccurate information to the United States, linking him to Al-Qaeda, with the result that he was deported from the U.S. to Syria, where he underwent months of torture. Moreover, the officials likely knew that this would be his fate (CBC 2007a). Arrested on the battlefield in 2002 as a fifteen-year-old, Omar Khadr was accused of killing a U.S. soldier in Afghanistan and imprisoned in the Guantanamo Bay base. Successive Canadian court verdicts have concluded that Canadian officials breached Khadr's right to life, liberty, and security of the person under the Charter of Rights and Freedoms. However, the government has refused to intercede on his behalf or authorize his return to Canada to face trial there (CBC 2010c). Eventually Khadr was put on trial by a U.S. military court. The trial concluded in October 2010. The *Globe and Mail* (2010: A16) editorialized: "The jury's sentence of 40 years — on top of the eight Mr. Khadr already served [reduced by a prior plea bargain to eight years]… takes the breath away…. Mr. Khadr had every reason to fear what might happen if he did not plead guilty in return for a lighter sentence of eight years, of which one will be served in the U.S., before he can apply for transfer to Canadian custody." The newspaper referred to the trial as a "bizarre spectacle" and went on to note that

> evidence that had been coerced from Mr. Khadr after he was drugged after surgery at (age) 15, or after he was threatened with gang rape by an interrogator at around that same age, was permitted to be heard in court; a plea bargain that was coerced with the very real threat of a life sentence hanging over his head…. And what role did Canada play? Shamefully, it sent its officials to bully him into giving out incriminating information that it then handed to his prosecutors, an act the Supreme Court unanimously condemned. The Canadian government then declared, "Let the process work." Some process.

While all of these incidents drew harsh public criticism and earned sustained media attention, there is also a significant proportion of the public who are either indifferent or even supportive of the government's security-related policies. For instance, with respect to the Afghan detainees scandal, despite a majority of Canadians believing that the detainees handed over by the Canadian military were tortured (and 83 percent of this group also believing that the government was aware of the likelihood that they would be tortured), 24 percent of those polled also said they are nonetheless satisfied with the government's handling of the affair and 35 percent have no opinion whatsoever (CBC 2009c). Similarly, 40 percent believe that preserving national security is more important than protecting civil liberties (*Ottawa Citizen* 2006). At the very least, one can say that a significant minority of Canadians have become inured to the use of torture when this is applied to individuals who are depicted, accurately or not, as security threats.

The Economist Intelligence Unit's report also expressed another concern about the impact of the economic crisis: that it has the potential to undermine the legitimacy of free market capitalism (2008: 12–14). Here its focus is on the danger of a reversal of privatization and deregulation, and of increased recourse to the state, including nationalization measures. Clearly these concerns reveal a certain ideological position on behalf the Unit. The references to civil liberties erosion may display worry about basic democratic and liberal political values. But the report is alert to the need to defend property rights and to the inegalitarian social structure that capitalism has spawned and which may trigger social unrest in times of crisis, as it has already done in the current crisis in countries like France, Portugal, and Ireland. At bottom, the Unit argues that: "Political and economic freedom are often closely associated. Our democracy index is negatively correlated with levels of government regulation in various fields, including the degree of financial sector regulation. While the causality is unclear, a rise in economic nationalism may be associated with less democracy" (Economist Intelligence Unit 2008: 14). The focus of the Economist Intelligence Unit is on how property rights will fare under conditions of crisis-induced social unrest. From this perspective, as is traditional in liberal thought, the threat to democracy emanates from an excessive state role, particularly regulation of the economy that infringes property rights. Thus, the threat to democracy is essentially equated with the threat to neoliberal privileging of markets that could emerge in dealing with the crisis.

However, a more sophisticated understanding of the history of neoliberalism (as both policy practice and mode of accumulation) would point to the ways in which democratic decline is instead related to the exacerbation of inequalities already present in a market economy. Attitudes such as trust are often cited as being important for the health of democratic governance. In a systematic synthesis of what is known about the social effects of inequality, Richard Wilkinson and Kate Pickett use international comparisons (OECD countries) and data from the states of the United States to show that trust levels are higher in more equal jurisdictions. Other data indicate that trust levels in the U.S. have fallen as inequality has increased (Wilkinson and Pickett 2010: Ch. 4). Citing research by other authors (Putnam 2000; Uslaner 2002; Rothstein and Uslaner 2005) Wilkinson and Pickett go on to show that the causal arrow runs from inequality to lack of trust. Notable inequalities generated by neoliberalism include a concentration of wealth at the top amid stagnating wages for the majority of the working class, longer working hours, more precarious working conditions, and a deterioration of the welfare state leading to a decline in the health and well-being of the less affluent. In the U.K., Dorling (2010) has documented the extent of inequality produced by both Conservative and (new) Labour parties in the neoliberal era. Dorling is quoted as saying that: "In countries like Britain, people last lived lives as unequal as today, as measured by wage inequality, in 1854, when Charles

Dickens was writing 'Hard Times'" (*The Guardian* 2010: S1). Dorling identifies five sets of beliefs — elitism, exclusion, prejudice, greed, and despair — which serve as bulwarks of the systemic inequality, and it can be argued that all contribute to what we designate here as "democratic malaise."

In Canada, as is the case elsewhere, we see an increase in democratic malaise during the neoliberal era. We use the term to refer to a growing condition of generalized cynicism and apathy leading to democratic decline, along with lowered expectations with respect to the extent and nature of support offered by the state. To date, therefore, heightened economic insecurity and inequality do not appear to be regenerating engagement with the political sphere but instead causing a retreat from it. While there are certainly other potential explanations for the rise of democratic malaise, we are interested in how the influence of neoliberalism, and the inequalities it generates, promotes democratic decline.

The Democratic Deficit

Discussions of a democratic deficit and apathetic citizenry are a feature of public discussion in many countries. Commentators have highlighted the implications for democracy of low participation, negative opinions about politicians and institutions, and lack of interest in and knowledge about politics. Here we seek to explore the argument (Hay 2007; McBride 2005) that neoliberal policies of privatization, deregulation, an enhanced role for markets and a diminished one for the state, and lack of respect for basic constitutional principles by government have been bad for democracy. In other words, rather than focusing on individuals and seeking to find an attitudinal explanation for their apparent lack of interest and participation in politics, we focus on those aspects of the political system itself which repel democratic involvement.

Colin Hay (2007) notes a consistent, long-term trend of falling voter turnout across the OECD area. Although there are significant national variations the overall average decline is 8 percent between 1970 and 2005 (Hay 2007: 13–16).[1] The decline in party membership is even more dramatic than in voter turnout (Hay 2007: 20–23), and the lower propensity of younger cohorts to be involved in formal politics in any way is reflected in party membership. Poll data reveal levels of political trust and trust in public institutions and officials generally tend to be low. Hay reviews existing explanations and finds them focused on citizens' attitudes and characteristics, rather than on the nature of the political system (2007: 40–42). The following feature prominently: diminished social capital and a lower sense of citizenship (Putnam 2000); less deference to officialdom and institutions because of higher educational levels (Norris 1999); and the lowering of the voting age to eighteen, which means that an age cohort which is more atomized and has less social capital than its elders is now included (Franklin 2004). Like Hay, we find these facts compelling but the explanations unsatisfactory and instead ascribe declining citizens' knowledge and involvement, what we term here democratic malaise, to factors characteristic of the political system under neoliberal hegemony, such as growing inequality.

Rise of Democratic Malaise

A 2009 poll found that 40 percent of Canadians believe that democracy is in poorer health in this country than it was two decades ago (Travers 2009). One good indicator is voter participation. Despite historically having had very high levels of voter participation in Canadian federal elections, it has been in decline since 1988. Between 1988 and 2008, turnout in federal elections fell from 75.3 percent to 58.8 percent. The decline was continuous, except for the 2006 election, when turnout increased to 64.7 percent (Elections Canada 2009). Provincial election turnouts were no more impressive. Voter turnout in the 2009 B.C. provincial election was at an all time low, with only 50 percent of eligible voters casting a ballot, down from an already dismal 58 percent in 2005 (CBC 2009b). This is a serious decline from the 1990 level of 75 percent (CCSD 1996). Similarly, record low turnouts have been recently recorded elsewhere across Canada: Ontario, 52.6 percent in 2007 (CBC 2007b); Alberta, 41 percent in 2008 (CBC 2008a), and Quebec, 56.5 percent in 2008 — although this is not a record low, it is, however, the lowest voter turnout rate since 1927 (CBC 2008b).

Canada is now ranked 110th out of 152 countries in terms of its registered voter turnout count (Nation Master 2010). Low turnouts are problematic in a number of ways. We reject the notion that lack of participation equals satisfaction with the political system. Yet active dissent would be far healthier for the body politic than abstention and withdrawal. Moreover, the ranks of the non-participants are hardly random in terms of social attributes. They typically comprise those who are poorer, those who come from visible minorities, young people, and less-educated citizens. Arguably these groups are the most needful of government intervention to moderate market outcomes. But as long as they fail to participate in politics they can be safely ignored by the powerful, who have opposite social attributes (John Kenneth Galbraith cited by Turcotte 2005).

Most analyses of low participation have focused on the failure of the young to participate in elections, a phenomenon which has led some to conclude that the young are "tuned out" of politics altogether (Gidengil et al. 2005). The participation rate is lowest among young voters aged eighteen to twenty-four, with roughly two-thirds choosing not to cast a ballot in the 2004 federal election (O'Neill 2007: 7). This is only slightly less alarming than the 75 percent who did not vote in the 2000 election and is serious cause for concern as young people today are less likely to vote than they were in previous generations and "it is unlikely that this gap in turnout will shrink as they age" (ibid.: 8).

As today's youth age, it is possible that they will participate more. But it is also hypothesized that their general pattern of political participation will carry forward into the future, thus ensuring that the low turnout problem will persist as a permanent and probably growing feature of the political landscape. As Pammett and LeDuc (2003) note, although life cycle effects do increase participation over time, the electoral participation levels of cohorts entering the electorate over the last two decades are significantly lower than those of earlier cohorts and will likely remain lower over time.

When it comes to explanation of low turnouts, most accounts, as noted by Hay, focus on the individual characteristics of the non-voters rather than on those of the political system that may discourage them from voting. Factors which reduce involvement are often identified in terms of self-identified inefficacy, lack of civil duty, and lack of interest in politics (Pammett and LeDuc 2003) — a cultural shift in that young people pay less attention to politics and are less likely to feel that it is a moral duty (Blais et al. 2004). Some argue that disengagement of the young is confined to electoral politics and is associated with a move to more activist forms of political expression. However, notwithstanding periodic visible displays of citizen protest and activism, in general this has no strong empirical foundation (Gidengil et al. 2003). It is informative to examine the reasons offered by non-voters as to why they are not showing up at the polls on election day. A 2003 Elections Canada report dealing with the 2000 federal election sheds some light on the matter. For instance, one important explanation might be that non-voters are "just not interested," and this is affirmed by roughly half of those surveyed (Elections Canada 2003). However, it is not only apathy that is to blame. Nearly half also reported that a very or fairly important reason for not voting was that they "didn't like the parties/candidates" and nearly 40 percent also said they felt their "vote wouldn't matter" (Elections Canada 2003). However, the reasons behind these results are not really probed by this type of analysis. Few observers locate the explanation in what seems to us the far more fruitful territory of the impact of neoliberalism in delegitimizing and discrediting politics by favouring markets as decision making institutions.

Another indicator of malaise with formal political democracy is the low level of trust that exists. Like voter turnout, trust in political institutions has declined dramatically in Canada over the years. As shown in Roese (2002: 152), in 1965, 58 percent of Canadians reported that they had trust in government, and only 36 percent said that government wasted taxpayers' money. By 1993, those figures had reversed dramatically to 33 percent and 79 percent respectively. This is politically significant. Trust matters for two important reasons: the belief that government is untrustworthy can contribute to "excessive self-interest and behaviours that are deleterious at the group level" (Roese 2002: 150); and compounding the effects of neoliberal individualization and reduced trust can lead to lower political involvement and exacerbate the disenfranchisement of already marginalized members of society (Nevitte 2002: 151).

Thus it ought to be no surprise that voter turnout is so dismally low in Canada. Delli Carpini suggests that engagement in the democratic process may be low because "young adults do not believe that their participation is likely to be either effective or satisfying" and that this lack of motivation is the result of "the systemic devaluing of the public sector over the past 30 years" (2000: 344). Neoliberal reforms have certainly encouraged this devaluing, promoting the notion that the public sector is inefficient, bloated, wasteful, and inferior to the private sector (which is characterized as rational, efficient, and innovative). For Colin Hay (2007: ch. 3) the roots of this lie in public choice theory, which presents neoliberalism's preference for market solutions rather than political ones as the only feasible economic paradigm. An absence of any alternative, combined with public choice theory's pessimism and cynicism about the motives of public officials, is deeply depoliticizing.

This high level of apathy, disconnect from politics, low turnout, and feelings of mistrust toward the government thus have a number of possible root causes and have triggered a variety of reform proposals to encourage greater re-engagement of the population. However, in the mainstream literature, neither cause nor solution is typically linked to neoliberalism or the state of the political economy more generally (Crete et al. 2006: 6). Thus proposals centre on technical details that, it is anticipated by the proponents, will increase participation. Suggestions include switching to a proportional representation electoral system, the introduction of electronic voting, greater youth political education, and "get out the vote" campaigns aimed at youth (Parkinson 2007; O'Neill 2007).

However, given the pressures of austerity and the tendency for neoliberalism to shift decision making away from popular-democratic fora, consideration of their interconnection would be more appropriate. Quite simply, the political system provides, or is perceived to provide, less reason for people to bother participating in its formal mechanisms.

Erosion of Civil Liberties

Canadians pride themselves on the degree to which rights and freedoms receive constitutional protection through the Charter of Rights and Freedoms. Yet there is evidence that such protections are not deeply entrenched either within public opinion or within the practices of state officials. To go back to an earlier era, the implementation of the *War Measures Act* during the

October Crisis of 1970 was accompanied by widespread abuses of civil liberties without major public opposition, at least until the crisis was over (Clément 2008). Similarly, in the immediate aftermath of the September 11, 2001, events, the Canadian government moved quickly to demonstrate its solidarity with Washington's new security imperatives. In the United States the so-called *Patriot Act* (an acronym for the last part of the act's official title: Uniting and Strengthening America by Providing Appropriate Tools Required to Intercept and Obstruct Terrorism) contained, in Gary Teeple's words, "all the fundamentals of a police state" (Teeple 2004: 203). Canada also moved swiftly to change its own legislation to reflect the new priorities (Roach 2003: ch. 2). Two pieces of legislation were central to this, the *Anti-terrorism Act* and the *Public Safety Act*. Like its American counterpart the *Anti-terrorism Act* was passed with impressive speed. It adopted a broad definition of terrorism, subsequently amended to respond to concerns that illegal political or industrial protests or expressions of political or religious belief could be defined as terrorism. It enabled the Cabinet to designate groups as "terrorist" with only a limited possibility of judicial review of the decision (Roach 2003: 37), created a range of new offences (Roach 2003: 38–46), expanded police powers, and provided for preventative arrest. A range of civil society groups and some critics inside government did produce some changes to the legislation (Roach 2003: ch. 3). The second major piece of legislation was the *Public Safety Act*. Initial reaction to this legislation focused on the power it gave to the minister of defence to designate certain areas as military security zones, thus preventing demonstrations or protests from occurring. This provision was withdrawn and a second version of the act concentrated on airline security measures and the manufacture and transport of biological, chemical, and hazardous materials. While some concerns about civil liberties remained, many had been addressed as the legislation was progressively modified (Roach 2003: 174; Smith 2005).

Despite the legislative modifications, significant concerns continue to be expressed about the legislation and its use in a climate where security priorities typically outweigh those attached to civil liberties. The International Civil Liberties Monitoring Group (ICLMG 2009) provided a useful summary of these in its submission to the Office of the High Commissioner for Human Rights. They pointed to increased racial and religious profiling directed particularly against Arab and Muslim Canadians, information sharing between governments at the expense of individual privacy, the creation of "no fly lists," the use of security certificates or certificates of inadmissibility to detain or deport permanent residents or foreign nationals under an extremely broad definition of inadmissibility, the Arar and Khadr cases, and the fact that the O'Connor enquiry into the Arar case had discovered other examples of Arab-Canadians having been tortured in Syria and the unwillingness of the

Canadian government to intervene on behalf of other Canadians arrested or stranded abroad for security-related reasons.

The nature of policing at anti-globalization protests also reveals a disturbing pattern in that it indicates considerable willingness on the part of states to use coercion in support of globalization. The Vancouver summit of the Asia-Pacific Economic Cooperation (APEC) initially highlighted for Canadians the civil liberties issues surrounding the aggressive policing of these events. Police have a two-fold duty at such events: to protect the participants and protect the right of legal protest enjoyed by citizens in democratic societies. Richard Ericson and Aaron Doyle (1999) describe the blatantly undemocratic practices followed by the Canadian government and police involving, among other things, the censorship of protest messages, pepper-spraying of demonstrators who were already dispersing, and the arrest of forty-nine protestors, only one of whom was eventually charged with a criminal offence, with that charge being subsequently dropped. Ericson and Doyle consider that the police tactics far exceeded what was necessary to achieve security. While a measure of incompetence was involved, they lean to explanations of police behaviour based on political influence, with the Canadian government acting both at its own behest and at the behest of foreign governments. Public and media reaction was overwhelmingly negative (Ericson and Doyle 1999: 601) but this does not appear to have influenced security preparations for subsequent meetings of global negotiators.

The April 2001 Quebec City Summit of the Americas was also accompanied by violent confrontations between police and demonstrators. The summit took place behind a four kilometre concrete and steel fence "wall." Entry into "Fortress Quebec" was strictly controlled, and the perimeter was protected by the use of tear gas, rubber and plastic bullets, water cannons, and arrests and detention. In a *Globe and Mail* article (April 24, 2001), "A Police State in the Making," Sinclair Stevens, a former Conservative Cabinet minister under Brian Mulroney, reported incidents he had witnessed of police firing tear gas and rubber bullets at peaceful protestors. He concluded: "Some will say that a handful of demonstrators got out of hand and forced the police to take collective action. I can't agree. The police action in Quebec City, under orders from our government, was a provocation itself — an assault on all our freedoms."

The Toronto G-20 summit meeting in 2010 provides further evidence of this tendency. The costs of providing security for the meeting (and the preceding G-8 sessions in Huntsville, Ontario) exceeded $1 billion. Following the summit the Canadian Civil Liberties Association filed five complaints with the Office of the Independent Police Review Director. The Association alleged illegal mass arrests of 1,105 persons, illegal detentions and searches, unlawful dispersals of peaceful protests, unlawful use of excessive force on peaceful demonstrators and passersby, and unlawful and inadequate conditions of detention, The Association believed these acts contravened the Criminal Code, the Charter of Rights and Freedoms, and Canadian and international standards of policing (CCLA 2010a). Following significant civil disorder initiated by a small minority of black-clad "anarchists," aggressive policing effectively denied broad sectors of society the right to protest the summit events. The Canadian Civil Liberties Association deployed fifty human rights monitors to observe police conduct at the G-20 demonstrations and concluded that it "was, at times, disproportionate, arbitrary, and excessive... despite instances of commendable and professional conduct, the policing and security efforts... failed to demonstrate commitment to Canada's constitutional values" (CCLA 2010b: 3). Monitors reported police charging peaceful crowds without adequate warning and shooting projectiles towards the demonstrators, boxing in groups of protestors, and conducting mass arrests without allowing detainees to speak to a lawyer or their families. Elsewhere the CCLA noted arbitrary searches across the city and excessive use of force leading to the conclusion that in an effort to apprehend perhaps 100–150 vandals, "the police disregarded the constitutional rights of thousands" (CCLA 2010b: 3).

The fifteen-year pattern of policing reinforces Sinclair Stevens' observations about police state tactics to deal with dissenters on these issues. Writing from a different location on the political spectrum, social activist Murray Dobbin commented:

> Police states don't appear full blown, overnight. They are, like any other social phenomenon, part of social and political process — the end result of long term corruption of the political culture and the incremental diminishing of democracy. This is a process that has been taking place for at least twenty years in Canada and it should come as no surprise that the police in Canada are now willing to take actions — at the direction of the politicians — that escalate the threats to democratic expression and the intimidation of ordinary citizens. (Dobbin 2010)

Lack of Knowledge about the Political System

Another key feature of Canada's democratic malaise is a profound lack of knowledge about the country's constitutional system. Polls regularly reveal that the most basic aspects of the country's constitutional system are misunderstood. For example, an Ipsos Reid poll conducted for the Dominion Institute in 2008 found that half of Canadians believe the prime minister is directly elected by voters and 75 percent don't know who Canada's head of state is (Ipsos Reid 2008). Similarly, although Canadians in several provinces have voted down the chance to replace the "first past the post" electoral system by some variant of proportional representation, it does not seem that that this is based on a sound appreciation of how this system actually operates. Bricker and Redfern (2001) found that Canadians were not well informed about the nature of their electoral system. Half believed that MPs needed more than half the votes cast in their constituencies to be elected and that governments must win a majority of the seats in the House of Commons. Nor, as we have seen, do Canadians demonstrate their support for the existing electoral system by high voter participation. Comparative evidence suggests that turnout is higher in systems using some form of proportional representation (Blais and Carty 1990).

The knowledge deficit permeating the Canadian public became quite apparent during the crisis about the proposed formation of a coalition government in Canada in late 2008. And for the most part, the media, either through ignorance or design, gave the Harper government's misrepresentations of the constitutional system free rein. This allowed it to stampede public opinion with wild rhetoric of a coup being attempted by separatists and socialists.

Thus, the mini-constitutional crisis in Canada in December 2008 reveals much about public ignorance of, and elite indifference to, basic constitutional principles. We first review the timelines and main events of this episode. The Conservative Party emerged from the October 14, 2008, election with 143 out of 308 seats and 38 percent of votes cast. The party formed a minority government, as it had prior to the election, and presented a throne speech on November 18, followed on November 27 by the release of an economic statement in Parliament. All three leaders of opposition parties immediately said they would vote against the economic statement, and the prospect of the newly elected government losing the confidence of the House of Commons loomed as early as December 1, the date when a confidence motion on the economic statement was scheduled.

On November 29 the government announced the postponement of the confidence vote until December 8. On November 30 the opposition parties announced formal agreement to form a Liberal-NDP coalition government to replace the Conservative one, with a minimum term of eighteen months and guaranteed support from the Bloc Québécois. On December 3 the governor general returned to Canada from an overseas trip and on December 4 the three opposition leaders sent identical messages to the governor general signed by 161 MPs (that is by a majority of the members of the House of Commons) stating their intention to vote against government on the confidence motion scheduled for December 8 and their intention to form and support in Parliament an alternative government. On December 4 Prime Minister Harper met with the governor general and she agreed to prorogue

Parliament until January 26, thus denying Parliament the opportunity to vote no confidence in the Harper government and giving that government time to launch a campaign against the coalition proposal outside Parliament, rather than being held responsible to Parliament.

It is argued here that in agreeing to the prime minister's request to prorogue Parliament the governor general failed to defend basic principles of Canada's parliamentary democracy, enhancing the power of the prime minister in the Canadian system, even of one who was on notice that he lacked the confidence of the House of Commons and that an alternative government, enjoying such a majority, was waiting in the wings to assume office.

According to Andrew Heard (2009: 19) there are several constitutional principles that the governor general violated during this crisis. The governor general has an obligation to let normal political processes resolve political problems. By agreeing to prorogue Parliament she prevented this from happening in a timely manner. Similarly the governor general is duty-bound to act on any constitutional advice by a prime minister who enjoys the confidence of the House of Commons. However, the advice to prorogue was unconstitutional because it was intended to evade defeat in the House and because a signed agreement by a majority of MPs indicated that an alternative government would have the support or confidence of the House.

Precedent suggests that issues of confidence in a government should be settled in a timely manner (a week to ten days according to Heard; not two months). There was an alternative government in place. Therefore the governor general was free to refuse the advice of an incumbent. It is clear that the effort to avoid certain defeat by the incumbent government is a serious abuse of power: "By granting a prorogation, the governor general not only allowed the current Prime Minister to escape almost certain defeat in a confidence motion, but she also set the stage for every future prime minister to follow suit" (Heard 2009: 20).

Since the constitution only requires that Parliament meet once annually, the period of future prorogations could be much longer than the two months covered by this one. Heard concludes (2009: 21) that: "On balance, it appears that the governor general failed to defend Canadian parliamentary democracy and opened the door to repeated abuses of power by future prime ministers.... We elect Parliaments not governments in Canada, and Parliament must be free to determine who governs after an election.... Future prime ministers now know they can shut down Parliament whenever they are threatened with defeat."

Far from the governor general's actions arousing major criticism in the media, it was complicit in the entirely false constitutional notions advanced by the government and, with a few honourable exceptions, failed to provide accurate information. The public demonstrated itself largely ignorant of the constitutional principles on which its system of government is based and was all too ready to be influenced by a demagogic campaign that claimed the opposition parties, whose ranks included "socialists" and disloyal "separatists" (albeit ones elected to Parliament), were engaged in a coup d'état to overturn the results of the previous election which, it was said, had established the right of the minority government to stay in office or, if defeated in the House, to trigger another election within a few weeks of the previous one.

Winnipeg journalist Frances Russell (2009: 32) described the public relations campaign: "The Conservatives' campaign to keep power through fear, loathing and demagoguery deliberately re-opened all the old wounds and divisions between French and English and East and West. They labeled the coalition as 'treasonous' and opposition MPs as 'traitors.'" Even more troubling for the health of democracy in Canada, Russell noted that the campaign was effective. By December 5, Ipsos Reid (2008) reported that 68 percent of Canadians supported the governor general's decision to prorogue Parliament. The pollster reported that "Fear and anger grips the nation as almost three quarters (72%) of Canadians say they are truly scared for the future of the country with what is going on in Ottawa" (cited in Russell 2009: 33). Russell concluded her survey by noting that: "The deliberate destruction and discord wreaked by the Harperites leaves Canadians angry, hostile, misinformed and politically alienated" and noted particularly the degree of divisions between different regions and provinces.

The combination of a complicit media, an ill-informed public swayed by anti-Quebec rhetoric, a determined executive determined to stay in power at any cost, and a weak and incompetent head of state figure indicates a country at risk of an authoritarian turn in crisis conditions. Public and media reaction in other crisis contexts suggests that this be may a well established part of Canadian political culture (McBride 2005b).

It is clear that the operation of Canada's parliamentary system is largely governed by conventions of the constitution — institutions, principles, and practices that are known and considered binding — but which are not written into law or the constitution acts. The latter contain, for example, no mention of the prime minister, the key official within our government system. Yet these institutions, principles, and practices are fundamental to the operation of our system of government, and its claim to be democratic rests on abiding by them. The fact that the system is imperfectly democratic is well known, as in, for example, the notorious imbalance between votes cast and seats received that result from our electoral system and an appointed upper chamber. The system is called a parliamentary one because it is the result of elections as they are reflected in Parliament, effectively in the elected House of Commons, that determine whether a party has sufficient support to form a government. A party will form the government if it enjoys the confidence of the House of Commons; if it loses that confidence it should resign and the governor general must either find another government that does or will enjoy the confidence (i.e., majority support) of the House, or call an election to see if one will emerge. According to Heard (2009: 6), this is the fundamental feature of parliamentary systems: people elect legislatures not governments. It is what happens inside the legislature that determines who will form the government and how long it will last: "Without the confidence of the House of Commons, the prime minister and the Cabinet have no right to govern at all" (Heard 2009: 7). This confidence is something that must be won at the outset of a government's life and retained throughout it, a situation that is masked under majority governments by the well-founded belief that government MPs will always sustain the government on issues of confidence.

Given that the operation of Parliament is defined by conventions and not by statute, the head of state, or in Canada the governor general as a functional equivalent, assumes potential significance as enforcer of the constitutional rules in those very rare cases where a government loses the confidence of the House and, even more rare, where it seeks to avoid the consequences of doing so. It, short of outraged public opinion expressed in extra-parliamentary fora, is all that stands between the phenomena of executive dominance of our political system within a parliamentary context, which is the norm, and authoritarian rule by that executive without the sanction of the elected Parliament.

Having established a dangerous principle that might encourage governments to avoid meeting the House of Commons for lengthy periods, even if their sole purpose in doing so is to avoid defeat, it was not long in being followed. A year after the original constitutional crisis, on December 30, 2009, Parliament was prorogued for a second time, from a projected start date of January 25 until March 3, 2010. On this occasion there *was* considerable national and international media criticism (see *The Economist* January 7, 2010), and public opposition in the form of well-attended rallies in major centres against the decision to prorogue Parliament. The government was seen to be avoiding parliamentary scrutiny of its record on Afghan detainees who were believed to have been handed over to Afghan authorities with the knowledge that they faced torture and/or execution. In addition, the government would have two months before it faced discussion of its budget priorities, global warming record, and future plans for the deployment of Canadian troops in Afghanistan (Ibbitson 2009). Public opinion polls revealed significant opposition to the move. For example, CBC reported that of the 67 percent of Canadians who were at least somewhat aware of Harper's decision to prorogue, 58 percent were opposed, and only 31 percent of all those polled were in favour (CBC 2010d). On the other hand, looking at this through the lens of continuing democratic malaise, these figures mean that just under 40 percent of Canadians opposed the measure and that 60 percent were either in favour, didn't know, or were ignorant of the fact that the event had happened — hardly a recipe for a healthy democracy.

Inequalities Generated by Neoliberalism

Democratic malaise has developed in tandem with the growth of inequality. In the neoliberal era, liberal democracies generally have experienced increased disparities of income and wealth: on the one side, private affluence and excess; on the other, if not public squalor,[2] then at least public austerity. Between 1981 and 2008 real GDP per capita grew by a total of 52.6 percent (IOW 2009: 15) and by 33 percent between 1996 and 2007 alone (Baragar 2009: 77). The neoliberal claim to have conducted a successful experiment in political economy rests on statistics such as these, together with arguments that inflation has been tamed, government deficits are reduced (until the financial crisis), and trade surpluses are now the norm. Downturns are conceded to have occurred in this period, yet the Canadian economy has always rebounded: the 2008 unemployment rate was 1.5 percent lower than it had been in 1981, declining from 7.6 percent to 6.1 percent (IOW 2009: 19). Many Canadians even made more money as after-tax personal income per capita rose by 28.8 percent between 1981 and 2008 (ibid.: 16). Thus, on the surface it would appear as though most Canadians would be better off now as a result of neoliberalism than they had been before.

Unfortunately the reality is that the gains produced by restructuring, re-regulating, privatizing, and liberalizing the economy and labour market have not been shared equally. In fact serious inequalities have been produced along the way, generating greater insecurity amid concentrated wealth and prosperity.

When we scratch the surface we see that despite growth in GDP and labour productivity, real hourly wages have been stagnant for decades, increasingly by only 0.8 percent from 1981 to 2008 (IOW 2009: 15). Gains made are also unequal: the after-tax income of the top income quintile in the country rose by nearly 39 percent between 1981 and 2007, while the increase for all other quintiles was only 25 percent over that same period (Sharpe and Arsenault 2009: 50–51). Thus the distribution of economic gains made during the neoliberal period was disproportionately concentrated among the top 20 percent of Canadian families. In addition, greater household after-tax earnings are in part the result of an increase in the hours worked, with the average annual hours worked per person rising by 2.9 percent over the same period (ibid.: 16). Furthermore, despite declining unemployment rates, long-term unemployment of more than fifty-two weeks was higher in 2008, at 6.7 percent, than it was in 1981, when it was 5.7 percent (ibid.: 19). Job quality, measured in terms of relative stability, relative compensation, and the full-/part-time distribution, also declined by 11.3 percent from 1988 to 2008 (ibid.).

In summary, fewer Canadians are now reaping the rewards of economic growth and many people are now working longer with little real wage gain and performing lower-quality tasks, all while facing the very real possibility that losing their job could translate into long-term unemployment. With far less generous unemployment benefits to fall back on (see NCW 2008), this can mean a serious deterioration in standard of living.

The implications of these labour market and income trends are serious and can be wide ranging. For instance, Canadians are now more isolated than they were in the past, perhaps as a result of working longer hours. Social networks are shrinking such that between 1994 and 2003 the number of people reporting six or more close friends fell from 40 percent to 30 percent (IOW 2009: 29). Furthermore, Canadians are reporting that they feel less healthy than before. After the peak year of 1998, those reporting that they felt they were in very good or excellent health dropped from 65.2 percent to 58.4 percent just five years later (Labonte et al. 2009: 2). This is almost certainly related to the dispersion of wealth and income, as it has been shown that money matters when it comes to health. Higher incomes are associated with longer lives in Canada; males born in the upper third of earning households in 2001 could expect to live three years longer than those in the bottom third, while for women it was one year (Labonte et al. 2009: 15). Mental health is also positively related to income, as middle-aged and older Canadians earning under $15,000 annually are four times more likely to have depression than those earning over $80,000 annually (ibid.: 56).

The Relationship between Neoliberal Inequalities and Democratic Malaise

With the Keynesian-style welfare state demonized for its inefficiencies and bureaucratic red tape, the neoliberal alternative sought to actively undo decades of reform and institution building aimed at creating greater social equity and job security. Accomplishing this goal has relied not only on program restructuring but also on ideological and psychological techniques. As Ferge puts it, the neoliberal project "is about the withdrawal from social commitments and hence... about the rejection of the importance of an integrated society or even of society: the individualization of the social" (1997: 23). How this individualization is promoted can take many forms. Derogatory inferences relying on negative stereotypes and social stigma directed toward those most marginalized in a market society are one popular way of accomplishing this transition. For instance, during the mid-1990s neoliberal restructuring campaign in Ontario, the provincial government actively "fostered discourses about dependency and fraud to criminalize those receiving social assistance" (Bezanson 2006: 57). Negative stereotypes of "welfare mothers" and undeserving immigrants were also exploited, and welfare fraud hotlines were set up to allow anonymous callers to report suspected cheaters (ibid.).

Another technique has been to minimize public expectations of government. Years of neoliberal balanced budget fixation, public program retrenchment, and celebration of the reduced role of the state means that citizens can no longer expect government to provide much in the way of a social wage. The state can also no longer be relied on to provide key services or redistribution; thus benefits derived from labour market prevail. The fraying of the Keynesian social safety net, which tied citizenship rights to receipt of public services and support regardless of ability to pay, is necessarily accompanied by a narrowing of the sphere of democratic influence. This is reflected in a narrowing of consultation practices. In Ontario, for example, key pieces of neoliberal policy, such as the 1996 *Savings and Restructuring Act*, included no provision for public consultation, which, at that time, constituted a "departure from established democratic and parliamentary practice" (Bezanson 2006: 48).

Considered together, it ought to be no surprise that the derogatory discourse and lowered expectations associated with neoliberal reforms have helped to create a generalized mood of apathy, mistrust in government, and overall democratic decline. Public choice theory, a key ingredient in the neoliberal mix, breeds cynicism about the motives of political actors and casts doubt on the possibility of a collective or community interest. In fact it would be hard to imagine why the "insulation of key aspects of the economy from the influence of politicians or the mass of citizens" would not invoke malaise with the formal political process (Gill 1995: 412).

International Priorities

In the neoliberal period Canada's international priorities have become focused on economic issues in which the bilateral relationship with the United States has loomed increasingly more important. Impressionistic evidence of a diminished global role, which needs more investigation than is provided here, would include the low levels of Canadian overseas development assistance: 0.32 percent of gross national income, compared to a U.N. target of 0.7 percent, and to an actual average of 0.47 percent achieved among the twenty-two member countries of the OECD Development Assistance Committee (Paul and Pistor 2009). Similarly, the U.N.'s 2009 ranking of military and police contributions to U.N. peacekeeping operations shows Canada's 179 personnel in forty-ninth place out of 120 contributors, slightly ahead of Cote d'Ivoire and Yemen.

One of the hallmarks of neoliberalism was the conclusion first of a bilateral free trade agreement with the U.S., and later the trilateral NAFTA agreement. In a cogent summary of the provisions of NAFTA, Richard Stubbs and Austina Reed characterized the agreement as one that "discourages government intervention in the economy, encourages the... operation of rule-based markets, and underwrites Anglo-American individualistic consumer economics that stresses the importance of the maximization of short-term profits and a return for shareholders" (2006: 292). And Tony Porter emphasized the terms of the agreement in his observation that NAFTA "is striking in its blending of an unprecedented level of legal detail on international trade obligations with very weak collaborative institutions" (2006: 320).

In a 2002 report issued by the Standing Committee on Foreign Affairs, Professor Gordon Mace, director of Inter-American Studies at the Institut Québécois des Hautes Etudes Internationals, told the committee that "the FTA and NAFTA trade deals have fundamentally and inescapably altered the foreign policy landscape. Canada's increased economic vulnerability within the 'new Economic management framework'... has 'greatly decreased' Canada's leeway in bilateral relations with the United States" (House of Commons 2002: 14). In order to mitigate the effect of this asymmetrical relationship, Mace argued that Canada needed to pursue an expanded relationship with Mexico and other states in the Americas (ibid.: 14–15).

But this has not been the Canadian priority. In considering Canada's role in NAFTA Stephanie Golob (2008) has made the argument that just as Canada entered NAFTA to protect its already existing bilateral free trade agreement with the U.S., its conduct inside the agreement has continued to exhibit bilateralism rather than trilateralism — pursuing a more traditional approach based on attempting to become an "insider" in Washington while seeking to privilege Canadian over Mexican interests. Recent crises have highlighted the narrowing of Canada's international focus. Post 9/11 Canadian priorities focused on the bilateral relationship driven by trade dependence and the intense pressure from Canadian business to move to greater integration. Canada's response to the 2008 financial crisis can be analyzed using a number of descriptors, some of which highlight its government's lack of speed and urgency, a feature that could be ascribed to the country's avoidance of the worst impact of the crisis and/or to its government's innate neoliberalism and disinclination to interfere with the operation of market forces. Other categories focus attention on the importance of the bilateral relationship with the United States and the government's determination to fit Canada's response to emerging priorities in Washington.

From time to time other initiatives are pursued. An example is the Canada-E.U. trade treaty, the Comprehensive Economic and Trade Agreement (CETA). Critics detect an apparent desire to further limit government capacity where, especially at the sub-national level, government procurement policies have been important development tools. As well, the proposed treaty would push the privatization agenda to new heights by enhancing the use of public-private partnerships (P3s) as well as other forms of privatization (Sinclair 2010). The negotiations and contents of a leaked, early version of the draft treaty provide an indicator of the resilience of neoliberalism in Canada. Despite lacking transparency and public debate, the CETA involves both the federal and provincial governments in Canada and could hold significant implications for future government procurement practices, public service contracts, national marketing and price setting institutions, such as the Canadian Wheat Board, and economic development programs, such as Ontario's *Green Energy Act* (Lewenza 2010; Beltrame 2010). The negotiations began in Brussels in May 2005 and are expected to wrap up in 2011. If government procurement protections are weakened substantially this could turn out to have serious consequences for future industrial policy including green energy initiatives. For example, Japan has launched a WTO complaint against Ontario's green energy plan, alleging that its local content provisions are in breach of the agreement. Canada's defence is likely to feature the argument that these local content provisions are permissible as they involve government procurement (Blackwell 2010). Any sacrifice of that exclusion could therefore be costly in the future.

Canada seems to have played a limited role in handling the global economic crisis although Prime Minister Stephen Harper did win media kudos for achieving two of his goals at the G20 summit: successful resistance to the idea of a G-20-wide bank tax, and setting targets for reduction of budget deficits, to be halved by 2013, to be followed by reductions in debt-to-GDP ratios by 2016 (Geddes 2010). The Canadian agenda strategy revealed the government to be among the most resistant to reconsideration of, let alone deviation from, the neoliberal norms established in previous decades.

Conclusion

In political terms, neoliberalism has been profoundly disempowering for most citizens, at the same time as it has concentrated power in the hands of the economically powerful. Notwithstanding other tendencies in the theory of democracy, practical democratic politics has always been focused on the state. Its relevance, internationally and domestically, has been denied or rejected by the dominant neoliberal ideology. The claimed irrelevance or ineptitude of the state has little empirical substance, but it is a mantra that has become widely believed. And it is true that neoliberal governments in office have reduced the state's role, not from necessity but from choice, as they have referred its functions to private actors in many fields and reduced its role in social provision. In other respects they have changed the state's role in ways that made it less accountable than formerly. In short, neoliberals have made the state seem less relevant than it once was as an act of policy, and politicians and public servants of all political stripes have seemingly internalized the neoliberal view on this issue. In these conditions democratic malaise of the kinds noted above seems logical. It has little to do with individual attitudes or cultural shifts except as these are responses to the devaluation of democratic politics that is central to neoliberalism.

CONCLUSIONS

Some thirty-five years after neoliberalism developed as a project to counter the Keynesian hegemony of the day, an ample track record exists to assess its legacy. And being in the midst of a financial and economic crisis, frequently described as the most serious since the Great Depression of the 1930s, it seems a good time to raise the question of what the future holds for this ideology, policy paradigm, and accumulation strategy. In this chapter, therefore, we address the questions: what is the legacy of neoliberalism? What is its future? Much of the book has been about the first of these questions. Although the first task is not uncontroversial, it seems much less daunting than the second. It is tempting to say that the only thing that can be said with certainty about neoliberalism's future is that it is uncertain. However, there are at least signs of the way existing elite are trying to construct that future, and we will address that issue. As we have done throughout the book we retain a focus on Canada but discuss Canadian developments within a theoretical and international or comparative context. That gives rise to a third question: what role is Canada playing in shaping the response to the impact of the financial crisis and in charting a course for the future of neoliberalism?

The Legacy of Neoliberalism

In previous chapters we have argued that neoliberalism has produced unequally distributed private affluence and public austerity as the state's role in social and equalizing redistributive activities has been reduced. Chapter 4 provided a detailed account of the policies and programs that have achieved this result in Canada. Like all hegemonic ideologies neoliberalism makes claims of positive sum effects resulting from its priorities. But for us the picture is one of the interests of the powerful being met as a matter of priority, and the fate of the many being consigned to their success in the market place, decreasingly backed by an adequate system of social supports. We are unconvinced that the same rules apply to the affluent. It could be said that their success, too, depends on their ability to prosper in the market. However, recurrent episodes of financial excess followed by the state socializing resulting debts and bailing out institutions and organizations deemed too big to fail suggest a different picture.

Two other elements complete neoliberalism's legacy. The first of these is a sense of democratic malaise, a growing feeling that democratic governance is in difficulty, that civil liberties have been eroded, political institutions and leaders are not accountable, and that in any case they lack power in the face of powerful private actors associated with globalization and are thus of diminishing relevance. This amounts to a widespread concern that is often expressed in terms of a democratic deficit. Finally, the period of neoliberalism has been one of recurrent crises. It is an unstable policy package and accumulation strategy, and the instability with which it is associated results in widespread insecurity for many people. Of course, this is felt most strongly at the bottom of the social ladder among the most vulnerable, and overseas in less developed countries afflicted by economic crises, and which have had to rely on conditional financial assistance from international agencies like the World Bank and the IMF. The 2007 financial crisis was the most severe of neoliberalism's crises to date and, unlike the other strictly financial ones, had major effects in the neoliberal heartlands of the developed world. This crisis, so far, has migrated from housing markets to financial markets, to the banking sector, found expression in the real economy through global recession, triggered corporate bankruptcies and bailouts, and has also released the spectre of sovereign debt default.

In view of this track record, for the first time in thirty years the future of neoliberalism was seriously called into question. Measures such as stimulus spending that looked like Keynesianism revived, except that they were not embedded in a coherent paradigm addressing the broader economic conditions, were widely utilized in order to avoid a generalized economic depression. Paradoxically, to the extent that these measures were successful, they may have impeded a paradigm shift away from neoliberalism by preventing a much worse recession or depression from developing. Since the reforms were temporary and shallow, they did not move beyond neoliberalism but did dampen the worst of the crisis. With collapse seemingly averted, decision makers in many countries, including Canada, have now reverted to the neoliberal roadmap and are pursuing policies of austerity, particularly as these affect remaining government programs. Such measures are needed to pay off the costs incurred in socializing the private sector debts that triggered the crisis. The costs of the crisis thus are to be born largely by people who had no hand in creating it.

The Future of Neoliberalism

Given this interpretation, what are the prospects for neoliberalism? Understandably, accounts of what will likely happen to the neoliberal project as a result of the recent global crisis vary. Some suggest that the heyday of neoliberalism appears to be over. David McNally, for example, argued in 2009 that there was "a profound systemic crisis of neoliberal capitalism" (McNally 2009: 56). French President Nicholas Sarkozy suggested that "a certain idea of globalization is dying with the end of a financial capitalism"

(Erlanger 2009: C9). Two years later, these views may appear to have been premature. Even if that proves to be the case, however, they probably contain at least this element of truth: the conviction that market solutions are always preferable to public ones has become a harder sell. The days of easy assurance that neoliberal advocates have enjoyed, with little danger of their views being seriously challenged, are probably over.

However, David Harvey has argued that neoliberalism, considered as a class project aimed at restoring the power of the capitalist class, is far from finished (Harvey 2009). Thus whether neoliberalism has run its course might depend largely on how one defines the term. For Harvey neoliberalism entails a "breaking down of every possible barrier to profitability" and has proven unique in "its capacity to organize and orchestrate gigantic devaluations of capital world-wide without, up until now, crashing the whole system" (Harvey 2006: xxv–xxvi). This ability to lurch from crisis to crisis over the course of three decades is astonishing indeed. Whether the recent crisis episode will end up crashing the whole system or not remains unclear. However, at this point it does not appear likely since the state, via its unique power of general taxation, has once more played the indispensable role of bailing out capital by socializing private sector debt.

Given neoliberalism's record, the recent crisis ought to be understood as only the latest among many, and thus the astute observation by Peck, Theodore, and Brenner (2009: 112) that its dynamics may paradoxically lead to an intensification of neoliberal "logics, forces, and relations such that some modalities of neoliberal rule are reconstituted by default" is one that deserves serious attention. Not only could this create roadblocks to post-neoliberal projects, but it also indicates that some of its more draconian elements may be poised for return. A clear indication of this is the about-face made over the course of 2009–10 with respect to domestic and international policy harmonization. Whereas in 2009 demand stimulus and pro-growth and pro-employment policies were still in fashion, by 2010 the search for exit strategies from stimulus spending was answered through a return to austerity beginning in 2010–11.

A Return to Austerity

In contrast to 2008 claims that "we're all Keynesians now," 2010 marked the beginning of a planned period of spending retrenchment through a wide-spread return to fiscal austerity. Thus with stimulus packages less than two years old, and real recovery far from certain, the search for exit strategies has begun in earnest.

A 2009 IMF report gave one of the first indications that austerity was on the horizon (IMF 2009a). Despite dire warnings issued by the IMF one year earlier of the threat of a looming Great Recession, the institution had quickly returned to its familiar neoliberal policy stance in a report on the state of public finances which warned of the evils of rising government debt among the advanced capitalist countries of the G-20. In order to correct this, it was suggested that members of the G-20 should avoid renewing the stimulus measures of 2008–09 and freeze real per capita spending (IMF 2009c: 26). Similar sentiments were present in a May 2010 OECD editorial, which instructed that an "exit from exceptional fiscal support must start now, or by 2011 at the latest" (OECD 2010a: 6), and in its 2010 Economic Outlook the OECD proclaimed that "in those countries that have not yet begun the consolidation process, public finances need to start being brought credibly onto a sound footing by next year at the latest" (OECD 2010c: 9). Closer to home, as early as 2009 the TD Bank Financial Group was counseling that Canada should return to an aggregate budget balance of zero, achieved through fiscal restraint and structural reforms to social programs (TD Bank Financial Group 2009).

These types of reports helped initiate a change in policy focus, from stimulating economic growth and assisting with job recovery to the development of so-called exit strategies that could be put in place in order to unravel earlier economic stimulus commitments. However, in 2009 it remained unclear how soon a return to neoliberal austerity would take place. Indeed, whether the termination of stimulus spending would take place was still up for debate at that time, given that a continuation of government stimulus was championed by the likes of U.S. President Obama and the British Chamber of Commerce — both warning that recovery was weak and the threat of a "double dip" recession was a real possibility (MSNBC 2010; Reuters 2010b). Furthermore, despite the IMF proclaiming in July 2009 that the worst of the recession was over (*Sydney Morning Herald* 2009), the G-8 issued a more cautious and less optimistic communiqué later that month proclaiming that the world economy still faced "serious risks" and that pro-growth spending policies should only end once world recovery had clearly begun (Elliott and Wintour 2009).

However, despite the lack of significant economic recovery, by 2010 it had become apparent that for most of the G-20 countries experimentation with economic stimulus through government spending would soon come to an end. Furthermore, the 2008–10 spending levels would be replaced with a draconian return to austerity, placing the onus on labour to pay for the follies of capital. Germany has been particularly notable in this regard, pledging in mid-2010 to eliminate $100 billion (U.S.) of public spending between 2011 and 2014, and to reduce public sector employment by 15,000 over that same period (Reguly 2010). Similarly, in its emergency budget of June 2010, Britain committed to slashing $145 billion worth of public spending by 2015–16, freezing all public sector salaries above $31,000 a year, and reducing most public sector departments' budgets by 25 percent over five years (Omonira-

Oyekanmi 2010). Spain similarly passed austerity measures in May 2010, as did Italy and New Zealand, in order to reassure markets that government deficits would be brought under control. France imposed a freeze on all spending between 2011 and 2013, and will cut operating costs (but not state budgets) by 10 percent over the same period (Reguly 2010). In November 2010, the Irish government, which had already cut its budget by 15 billion euros, announced a further round of cuts: "By 2014 the Irish will cut €10bn from public spending and raise an extra €5bn in taxes. These measures will also include a new property tax, water charges, cuts to the minimum wage and rises in student fees. The austere economic programme is aimed at winning back the confidence of global markets and securing the €85bn bailout offered by the International Monetary Fund and the European Central Bank. The bulk of that aid package will go to save the debt-ridden Irish bank system" (McDonald 2010). Speculation in the days after the announcement centred on whether the government would survive long enough to enact the cuts, decided upon after intense pressure from the E.U., which feared an Irish collapse could trigger the end of the euro zone.

Recent provincial and federal budgets in Canada indicate that austerity will soon be making a comeback. A return to balanced budgets will be sought in the short term, though Canada did extend its stimulus program timeline. Originally scheduled to expire in March 2011, in November 2010 the federal government announced that it will now be extended through to October 2011. No further money will be spent on stimulus-related support beyond that point. Government deficits run up by a crisis induced by capital will therefore not be paid through increased corporate tax, but through spending restraint and program cuts. For example, the Ontario government seeks to balance the budget through expenditure restraint, and by imposing a pay freeze on government workers and implementing several tax breaks for business (*Daily Commercial News* 2010). Likewise, the 2010 federal budget concerned itself with tax cuts for business, spending cuts to federal departments, and further freezes placed on operating budgets (CUPE 2010).

So popular is the return to austerity that economist Paul Krugman wrote in May 2010 that "the idea that what depressed economies really need is even more suffering seems to be the new conventional wisdom" (Krugman 2010). In part this return to austerity among the advanced capitalist countries is related to the most recent phase of the crisis: the emergence of a sovereign debt crisis in 2010, experienced most profoundly in Greece and Ireland, yet with the potential to impact other vulnerable economies in Europe (especially Italy, Portugal, and Spain). This latest form of the crisis also foreshadows turbulence for the euro and the global economy, prompting familiar calls for prudence and thrift.

The Sovereign Debt Crisis of 2010

One of the initial crisis events in the history of global neoliberalism was the international debt crisis of the early 1980s. The repercussions were so severe that the 1980s have been dubbed the "lost decade" of development for the south.[1] Upon examination of how recovery from this crisis was managed, Loxley suggested that a key strategy involved the socializing of debt through official intervention so as to avoid bank collapse (1998: 29). This strategy has been repeated time and time again through state and international financial institution interventions. Peter Gowan argued that the process of neoliberal globalization itself had been driven forward through official intervention following debt and financial crises. He argued that the entire regime relies on crises as "the IMF covers the risks and ensures that the U.S. banks don't lose," meaning that countries pay up, for example, through structural adjustments (1999: ch. 4). These sentiments were echoed by Wade and Veneroso with regard to the Asian Financial Crisis of 1997–98, when they wrote that "the combination of massive devaluations, IMF-pushed financial liberalization, and IMF-facilitated recovery may even precipitate the biggest peacetime transfer of assets from domestic to foreign owners in the past fifty years anywhere in the world" (1998: 3–23). This process of devaluation that accompanies financial crises is also a way of providing a fix for overaccumulated capital, and thus is central to creating new types of spatio-temporal fixes under the neoliberal regime (see our discussion of David Harvey in chapter 2). However, as is evident from the social dislocation and hardships that are inevitably produced by fairly regular crisis intervals followed by publicly funded bailouts, the neoliberal fix cannot be considered to be a successful social structure of accumulation, since this would necessitate the creation of widespread stability, prosperity, and growth (see chapter 2 on SSA theory).

To date, the sovereign debt crisis has been experienced most visibly by Greece in its efforts to ward off bankruptcy in May 2010 by securing euro zone and IMF rescue loans to repay $10.43 billion worth of ten-year state bonds (Becatoros 2010). In keeping with the dictates of the IMF and other international lending institutions, and championed especially vigorously by German Chancellor Merkel, these loans were secured upon agreement that austerity measures would be imposed by the Greek government. The measures that were enacted promise a serious retrenchment of the Greek state in an effort to slash its budget by 30 billion euros over three years (BBC 2010b). This will be achieved through pay freezes for all public sector workers, pay cuts, the elimination of annual bonuses, an increase in the retirement age, a reduction in pensions, an increase in the Value Added Tax and indirect taxes, and privatization for some industries (ibid.). This means that the debt incurred by the state will be paid for largely by labour rather than capital. Popular dissatisfaction with this prospect was made apparent as the May 5 Greek austerity law touched off a series of general strikes and episodes of violence in the streets. These involved large demonstrations throughout the country including one on May 20, 2010, in which more than 20,000 people marched in the streets of Athens in a twenty-four-hour general strike (Becatoros 2010).

In other vulnerable countries in Europe a similar trend toward public austerity has emerged. Yet violence, demonstrations, and strikes have thus far done little to halt the wave of austerity that is being implemented. For instance, in an effort to assuage concerns over Portugal's creditworthiness and fight contagion from Greece, the Portuguese government also enacted a plan to cut its budget in May 2010 (Laxmidas 2010). As in Greece, this has led to widespread popular dissatisfaction. In one day alone, May 30, 2010, tens of thousands of working people took to the streets of Lisbon to indicate their rejection of the government's austerity plan (Laxmidas 2010).

It is interesting to note that while both the Greek and Portuguese governments could be considered to be left-leaning, the austerity imperative remains firm given that state policy must still concern itself with conforming to dictates of credit rating agencies (despite their failure to predict any of the major financial market crises that have occurred over the past decade) since this component of the international financial architecture remains essentially unchanged. Not only have credit rating agencies maintained their privileged position in the Basel banking sector agreements and within American and other leading bond markets (in order to be sold, all bonds must first be rated by a handful of approved rating agencies), but they are also in large part responsible for sparking off the 2010 Greek debt crisis. In December 2009 Standard & Poors (S&P), one of the world's leading rating agencies, downgraded Greek debt to "junk" status, essentially cutting it off from financing earned through global financial markets. As is a familiar pattern, this downgrade then acted as a self-fulfilling prophesy, whereby fund managers began selling bonds they were holding and stopped buying newly issued bonds (BBC 2010a). Michel Barnier of the E.U.'s European Commission did announce in December 2009 that a new regime for credit rating agencies is being examined, but this has yet to be put in place. The regime, if implemented, aims to have rating agencies explain how downgrade decisions are made, and a new agency to rate government creditworthiness may even be created (ibid.). While these changes are certainly needed, internal E.U. reforms offer no reprieve for non-members like Canada, where painful downgrades were handed out. Ontario's creditworthiness was downgraded as a result of the GM bailout that had increased the provincial deficit by 32 percent (Ferguson 2009). In October 2009 S&P downgraded the province one category, from AA to AA-, and one category by DBRS, from AA to AA low (Abma 2009). These downgrades lead to higher borrowing costs for the province and its citizens and therefore serve to justify the implementation of spending austerity by all governments reliant on financing through international bond and other credit markets.

Of course, the sovereign debt crisis that is threatening vulnerable economies in Europe, and the stability of the euro itself, cannot be blamed on the credit rating agencies alone. It is founded in the larger crisis that was touched off in 2007 and in the economic disequilibrium that exists within Europe. As a condition of entry into the European Monetary Union, trade liberalization and monetary policy harmonization must be agreed upon. This means that the option of currency devaluation is removed from a country's policy toolkit since the same currency is used among trading partners within the monetary union. Within this context it must be understood that when there is a trading partner that is experiencing a deficit (for example, Greece) then there is likely one who is experiencing a surplus (for example, Germany). Currently the international trade system is structured such that the burden of adjustment falls on the deficit country. However, it has long been recognized that surplus countries are equally part of the problem (for instance, Keynes's position at the Bretton Woods conference, and more recently discussions at the June 2010 G-20 summit with regards to countries such as Germany and China). Without the option of currency devaluation, internal disequilibrium remained present within the E.U., yet adjustment was avoided during the 1990s and 2000s given that cheap credit and neoliberal financialization allowed for consumption and borrowing without real growth. Once confidence was lost, housing and financial markets crashed, liquidity dried up, and banks began to collapse. All countries faced debt and deficit problems, yet for the weakest it exposed these larger structural problems, taking the form of a sovereign debt crisis.

Thus the question now becomes: who will pay for the excesses and contradictions of the neoliberal age? So far the austerity measures implemented across Europe (and elsewhere) are proving once again that labour and the most vulnerable will bear the burden of adjustment. However, as Schmidt argues, this latest form of debt socialization is potentially far more dangerous than similar efforts in the past have been as it is now leading to public debt bubbles much like the internet, housing, and resource bubbles we have seen in the past decade (2010). What makes a public debt bubble qualitatively different from previous bubbles is that now "the bubble and the bailout are both expected to come from the same public purse" (ibid.). This not only holds potentially disastrous implications for those most reliant on support from what is left of the tattered welfare state, but may also be the death knell of any incipient post-neoliberal project, at least in the short term.

Canada, the G-20, and the Search for Exit Strategies

While there were several items on the agenda, it could be argued that the central aim of the June 2010 G-20 meeting was to resolve some of the policy differences that had emerged among the core capitalist countries. These related to the lack of agreement over whether stimulus or austerity should be prioritized in the future, and thus to the ways in which economic growth in the global economy will be encouraged; and to what types of reforms should be undertaken to avoid some of the problems, especially in the financial sector, that led to the crisis in the first place.

As representatives of the host country, and given that Canada emerged relatively unscathed from the financial crisis, the Harper Conservatives were afforded a degree of influence at this meeting not typically experienced internationally. This position was utilized by Prime Minister Harper and Finance Minister Flaherty in the months leading up to the meeting, as they widely promoted a return to neoliberalism and a marginalization of calls for significant reform. At the top of their agenda was to scuttle a bank tax proposed by the IMF and backed by France and Germany. This proposal recommended the creation of two new bank taxes: a financial stability contribution, which would be levied at various rates to discourage risky banking practices and would provide a fund which could be used to bail out banks in the event of a future crisis; and a financial activities tax, which would be a tax imposed on bank profits, salaries, and bonuses (Curry and Torobin 2010). The IMF recommended that in order to be truly effective, these reforms would need to be implemented by all G-20 countries, yet Finance Minister Flaherty maintained that "Canada will not go down the path of excessive, arbitrary or punitive regulation of its financial sector" (Scoffield 2010). Canada's stance on the matter galvanized opposition to the bank tax as countries with relatively stronger banking systems, such as Australia, ultimately failed to lend their support, effectively squashing the proposal and ensuring it did not make its way onto the agenda of the G-20 meeting.[2] Duncan Cameron (2010) called this move "a new low for Canadian internationalism" given that the Harper Conservatives used their influence to avoid the serious reforms needed by most countries linked to the global banking system.

Rather than any significant innovations, the reforms that emerged from the June 2010 meeting were much closer to a business as usual, neoliberal-style regulatory regime. The measures agreed to were thus limited in their creativity, with the official communiqué featuring commitments such as increases to capital requirements decided through the Basel Committee on Banking Supervision and measures to strengthen liquidity standards (G-20 2010).

In addition, on the contentious issue of austerity versus stimulus, Harper's May 2010 announcement that he would "push G20 leaders next month to commit themselves to some benchmarks on the fiscal health of their national governments" (Akin 2010) later proved persuasive.[3] This is somewhat surprising since, while it was no secret that the Harper Conservatives desired for the G-20 to "send a clear message that as our stimulus plans expire, we will focus on getting our fiscal houses in order" (MSNBC 2010b), this position clearly contradicted that of U.S. President Obama; prior to the meeting, Obama had been urging the G-20 countries to "avoid the costly mistakes made during the 1930s when countries reduced government support too quickly and ended up prolonging the Great Depression" (ibid.). Ultimately, it appears as though the schism among the G-20 was resolved by adopting a cautious position in the final communiqué. There the leaders agree to halve deficits by 2013 and stabilize or reduce debt-to-GDP ratios by 2016, as well as to follow through on delivering existing stimulus plans, recognizing that serious economic challenges remain.

It is worth considering what this cautious position means for the global order more generally. Although both the austerity and stimulus positions are reflected in the outcome of the talks, the loss of U.S. hegemonic influence is notable. Furthermore, the fact that recovery from the ongoing crisis lacks a hegemon that is either capable or willing to take the reins and forge new institutions and regimes that are more encouraging of growth and stability for the global economy may very well exacerbate the problems experienced.

The Conditions for Change

There are a number of general factors involved in changes to the dominant or hegemonic paradigm (McBride 2005: ch. 9). One is a crisis that undermines confidence in the dominant approach; another, the existence of an alternative paradigm within which the problem can be framed differently and alternative solutions developed; and a third, a period of political struggle and the emergence of a bloc of social and political actors committed to the alternative paradigm. Looking at these three conditions with today's situation in mind, the first is amply met and the second is hardly in place, though it is possible to discern what its main lines might be. But it exists, to the extent it does, merely as programs on paper. It lacks the social and political base that would be necessary to launch a challenge to the prevailing paradigm.

As early as 1999 Neil Bradford (1999: 53) argued that already "the economic failures of neoliberalism and the continued political opportunism of governing parties are creating space for questioning Canada's authoritative policy ideas." He noted that neoliberalism lacks the solid base of "cross-class or inter-regional accommodation that underpinned Keynesianism." This shortcoming renders it vulnerable to other forces and may well account for the power-holders' project of institutionalizing it through incorporation in international agreements. As we have noted several times in this book, the neoliberal globalization paradigm has delivered a more volatile economic environment than its Keynesian predecessor. The 1990s saw deep recessions and several financial crises. The crisis that began in 2007 is the most serious to date.

It is very clear to us that the neoliberal paradigm is impoverished and threadbare when considered as a set of ideas. It has no convincing explanation of any of the crises that occurred in its period of primacy, and for solutions it prescribes more of the same policies that led to these situations in the first place. But this alone will not lead to its replacement.

The space for an alternative has long been present. It is possible to provide a general sketch of what a viable alternative based on social justice and environmental sustainability might look like, and numerous writers and civil society organizations have made contributions to defining it. But the awkward fact is that no serious political force has occupied that space. And the alternative paradigm itself remains undeveloped, though this point is not fatal to its development. Paradigms do not spring to life fully formed; they develop in given contexts and in a process of contention with opposing ideas. But for that to happen they need to be championed by political and social forces strong enough to force them onto the agenda and force, too, a response from the defenders of the currently hegemonic paradigm. It is difficult to see evidence this is happening in Canada or any of the other states where neoliberalism has been adopted. Until that happens the political economy of Canada and similar countries will likely exhibit the features it does today and which we have depicted as a combination of unevenly distributed private affluence, public austerity, and malaise surrounding the operation of democracy. Such a situation seems sustainable in the short run, if hardly so in the long run. Moreover, were a change to occur there are no guarantees about what kind of change it would be; malaise and crisis are at least as susceptible to authoritarian responses as progressive ones.

The neoliberal project is, of course, more than a policy paradigm. It is also a capital accumulation strategy designed to fix problems encountered by capital. Labour and its social movement allies have proven capable of considerable resistance and sometimes successful defence of the pre-neoliberal order, albeit while being on the defensive and fighting a rearguard action. It is, of course, possible that successive rounds of austerity and coercion will galvanize these social forces, but presently they seem too weak to displace capital from its dominant position in contemporary society, and it is many years since any hint surfaced that this was their goal. Nor, since the demise of Keynesianism, has anyone demonstrated a way in which capital's self-defined accumulation needs could be reconciled with a more just and secure social order, even though the numerous benefits of the attributes of such a society, such as equality, have been amply proven (Wilkinson and Pickett 2010). Thus matters stand at an impasse: the old neoliberal order has little to offer except more austerity and less democracy, while the new order has not yet taken shape or become a factor in the thinking of the majority of the population.

Possible opposition to the existing global order is emerging in the global south and from leading developing states which recognize a system constructed to defend the already powerful and are acquiring sufficient strength to challenge it. Whether the global power structure can be reconstructed to be sufficiently inclusive for the economic and political interests and elite of these states remains to be seen. If not, a significant change in the global order might ensue.

So far, business interests in most countries have remained remarkably united around the neoliberal strategy. However, the defection of important fractions of capital at the international, regional, national, or sectoral levels would open up opportunities that might shake the social base of neoliberalism. One would expect that if that were to occur, resulting political struggles would be fought out primarily at the national level, if for no other reason than that global political institutions with entrance points for democratic input are feebly developed. In that context, overcoming the political and democratic malaise which neoliberalism has produced would be a major priority of advocates of change. Indeed, the struggle for more accountability, respect for democratic principles and civil liberties, democratic decision making at all levels, and increasing the scope within which democratic governance can be practised, could usefully begin now.

NOTES

Chapter 1

1. Subprime markets are those that are involved with making the most risky consumer loans. Borrowers tend to have the lowest credit rating scores, least amount of credit history, excessive debt, and/or a history of missing payments, defaulting on loans, or declaring bankruptcy. Subprime lending markets typically involve a variety of credit types, such as mortgages, auto loans, and credit cards.
2. See the following for a sample of the types of reform recommendations issued in response to the 2008 crisis: U.K. Treasury 2009; U.S. Treasury 2009; European Commission 2009; de Larosiere 2009; G-30 2009; U.K. Financial Services Authority 2009; Committee on Capital Market Regulation 2009; FSB 2008; G-20 2009; Issing Committee 2009; IMF 2009b.
3. Jobcentre Plus is an executive agency of the Department for Work and Pensions. It provides services that support people of working age from welfare into work, and it helps employers to fill their vacancies. (U.K. Department of Work and Pensions <dwp.gov.uk/about-dwp/customer-delivery/jobcentre-plus/>.
4. Harris (2010: 69) puts greater weight on the conservative management practices of Canada's leading banks than on the efficacy of regulation.

Chapter 2

1. It should be understood that the perspectives and theorists examined here do not constitute an exhaustive list of all heterodox approaches to capitalist crises.
2. Analyses of the recent crisis abound. Notable sources include Albo, Gindin, and Panitch 2010; Guard and Antony 2009; Gamble 2009; Callinicos 2010; Peck, Theodore, and Brenner 2010; Harvey 2010; Gowan 2009; *Socialist Register* 2011 (see, for example, Leo Panitch and Sam Gindin, "Capitalist Crises and the Crisis This Time"; Hugo Radice, "Confronting the Crisis"; Alfredo Saad-Filho, "Crisis in Neoliberalism or Crisis of Neoliberalism").
3. For SSA theory, the institutions that promote sustained economic growth and stability are often extra-economic in nature, an insight which recognizes that capitalist developments are affected greatly by the social and institutional environment in which they take place. To the usual list of institutions that form an SSA, O'Hara adds the notion of a family-community social structure of accumulation (FCSSA). Notable facets of the FCSSA are stability within families, trust and association in the community, and the degree of relative equality. O'Hara suggests that the FCSSA does not currently operate in the U.S. because "the emerging family type is not promoting sufficient stability, trust has diminished to low levels, and structural inequality has continued to rise" (see O'Hara 2006: ch. 9). Factors such as these feature in our own discussion of political malaise in chapter 6.

4. During the neoliberal era that followed, the accord would be replaced by increased use of coercion against labour (see Panitch and Swartz 1988) and the dull compulsion of unemployment (McBride 1992).
5. While there is certainly some merit to this critique, it is also somewhat outdated now as Harvey's more recent work (for example 2003b; 2010) incorporates to a greater extent a variety of social and political factors in his analysis of crises and fixes.

Chapter 3

1. Much of the text in Chapters 3 and 4 is drawn from McBride 2005. For present purposes, however, it has been updated, revised, and reorganized.
2. For an outline of Canadian development in terms of successive "national policies" see Eden and Molot 1993.
3. For a fuller account see McBride and Shields 1997: ch. 2.

Chapter 4

1. See McBride 1996 for an analysis of the NDP government in Ontario.
2. For a fuller, though still incomplete account of neoliberal policy measures, see the contributions to Burke, Mooers and Shields 2000; and McBride 2005: ch. 5. Some of the material in this chapter is drawn from McBride 2005.
3. As Gamble (1988) pointed out in his analysis of Thatcherism, the neoliberal state was far from uniformly weak.
4. For an overview of monetarism, see McBride 1992: ch. 3.
5. BOOT projects refer to arrangements where the private partner is responsible for the design, construction, finance, and operation of an asset, and feature long-term contracts (typically twenty-five to thirty years). The DBFO model is similar to BOOT projects except that at the end of the contract ownership reverts back to the public sector for a fee. DBO does not involve private financing, but instead integrates design, construction, and maintenance into one contract, which the public partner purchases once the commission period is over (Hodge and Greve 2005: 64).
6. Medicare in Canada has meant the reduction of costs for companies such as the Big Three automakers (Ford, GM, and Chrysler). In 2006 they were spending more than $10 billion on health care benefits in the U.S. that they did not need to pay in Canada (Caron 2008: 9). This, and similar examples from other industries, has led many commentators in the private sector (including Richard Nesbitt, CEO Toronto Stock Exchange Group, and A. Charles Baillie, former Chairman and CEO, TD Bank, and honorary chair of the Canadian Council of Chief Executives) to advocate for maintaining a system of public health care in Canada.
7. This does not imply that Canada adopted its policies as a result of the Jobs Study; it means merely that its policies are consistent with the neoliberal ethos of that program, and, consequently, the OECD has comparatively few recommendations to make for improvement.
8. For a review and rebuttal of literature suggesting that the unemployment insur-

ance system acted as a disincentive to work and hence raised the unemployment rate, see Jackson 1995: 3–9; see also McBride 1992: ch. 6.

9.   The CLC's figures refer only to women who were laid-off and do not include those on maternity leave.

10.   Savoie (1999: ch. 4), playing with the old concept of the prime minister as first among equals or *primus inter pares,* heads his chapter on prime ministerial power "*Primus:* There Is No Longer Any *Inter* or *Pares.*"

Chapter 5

1.   Given the recent government stimulus packages introduced around the world, especially among the OECD, it remains to be seen whether this indicates the initiation of a fourth phase of the neoliberal project, perhaps one which is more accommodating and less austere. Recent provincial and federal budgets in Canada suggest that austerity will be making a comeback as a return to balanced budgets will be sought in the short term and stimulus spending will run out in 2010 without renewal. Government debt burdens will not be paid through increased corporate tax, but through spending restraint and program cuts. Thus, as is consistent with neoliberalism generally, capitalist crisis will be met with debt socialization and corporate bailouts at the taxpayers' expense.

Chapter 6

1.   Linking this analysis to institutional factors, rather than to cultural or attitudinal ones, as is so often done, Hay uses the "varieties of capitalism" literature to show that turnouts are lower in the liberal market economies than in the coordinated market economies.

2.   As John Kenneth Galbraith once depicted the lack of public investment in the U.S. (Galbraith 1958).

Conclusion

1.   Although it should be mentioned that this was largely a current account crisis, not a capital account crisis like we see in later phases of neoliberal rule.

2.   Although at the time of writing it was uncertain whether countries such as the U.S. and U.K. might impose their own type of bank tax domestically.

3.   Interestingly, there was no talk of fiscal austerity when it came to financing security at the June 2010 G-20 and G-8 summits in Ontario. The price tag amounted to $1 billion, an amount that dwarfs the cost of previous summits. The "fake lake" at the G-8 pavilion alone cost more than the annual earnings brought in by 40 percent of Canadian families (CBC 2010b).

BIBLIOGRAPHY

Abma, Derek. 2009. "Ontario Credit Downgraded by S&P After Record Deficit Projection." *Financial Post* October 29.

Aglietta, Michael. 1998. "Capitalism at the Turn of the Century: Regulation Theory and the Challenge of Social Change." *New Left Review* 1, 232.

Akin, David. 2010. "Harper Urges G20 Leaders to Get Fiscal Health in Shape." *Financial Post.* May 17. <financialpost.com/story.html?id=3039137>

Akintoye, Akintola, Matthias Beck, and Cliff Hardcastle (eds.). 2003. *Public-Private Partnerships: Managing Risks and Opportunities.* Oxford: Blackwell.

Akyuz, Yilmaz. 2000. "The Debate on the International Financial Architecture: Reforming the Reformers." United Nations Conference on Trade and Development 148, April.

Albo, Greg, Sam Gindin, and Leo Panitch. 2010. *In and out of Crisis.* Oakland: PM Press.

Altman, Roger C. 2009. "The Great Crash, 2008." *Foreign Affairs* January/February. <foreignaffairs.com/articles/63714/roger-c-altman/the-great-crash-2008>

Andersen, Camilla. 2009. "Germany Faces Extended Downturn Despite Stimulus." *IMF Survey Magazine: Countries & Regions.* Global Financial Crisis. January 22. <imf.org/external/pubs/ft/survey/so/2009/car012209a.htm>

Anderson, John. 2004. "Paul Martin and the Liberal Social Policy Record." In Todd Scarth (ed.), *Hell and High Water: An Assessment of Paul Martin's Record and Implications for the Future.* Ottawa: Canadian Centre for Policy Alternatives.

Andre, Christine. 1995. "The Welfare State and Institutional Compromises." In Robert Boyer and Yves Saillard (eds.), *Regulation Theory.* New York: Routledge.

Appleton, Barry. 1994. *Navigating NAFTA: A Concise User's Guide to the North American Free Trade Agreement.* Scarborough: Carswell.

Applied Research Branch, Strategic Policy. 1998. *An Analysis of Employment Insurance Benefit Coverage.* Ottawa: Human Resources Development Canada.

Armstrong, Pat, and Hugh Armstrong. 2008. *Health Care.* Halifax: Fernwood.

Ashman, Sam, and Alex Callinicos. 2006. "Capital Accumulation and the State System: Assessing David Harvey's The New Imperialism." *Historical Materialism* 14, 4.

Aucoin, Peter. 1996. "Political Science and Democratic Governance." *Canadian Journal of Political Science* December.

_____. 1995. *The New Public Management: Canada in Comparative Perspective.* Montreal: Institute for Research on Public Policy.

Bajaj, Vikas. 2008. "Whiplash Ends a Roller Coaster Week." *New York Times.* October 10. <nytimes.com/2008/10/11/business/11markets.html?hp>

Bakker, Isabella. 1990. "The Size and Scope of Government: Robin Hood Sent Packing?" In Michael Whittington and Glen Williams (eds.), *Canadian Politics in the 1990s*, third edition. Toronto: Nelson Canada.

Balakrishnan, Ravi, and Helge Berger. 2009. "Comparing Recessions in Germany,

Spain, and United Kingdom." *imf Survey Magazine: Regional Economic Outlook.* November 18. <imf.org/external/pubs/ft/survey/so/2009/num111809a.htm>

Bansal, Paritosh. 2010. "U.S. Bailout Cost Seen Lower at $89 Billion: Report." April 12. <reuters.com/article/idU.S.TRE63B05N20100412/>

Banting, Keith G. 1987. *The Welfare State and Canadian Federalism,* second edition. Montreal: McGill-Queen's University Press.

_____ (ed.). 1986. *The State and Economic Interests.* Toronto: Royal Commission on the Economic Union and Development Prospects for Canada and University of Toronto Press.

Baragar, Fletcher. 2009. "Canada and the Crisis." In Julie Guard and Wayne Antony (eds.), *Bankruptcies and Bailouts.* Halifax and Winnipeg: Fernwood Publishing.

bbc. 2010a. "EU warns credit rating agencies." *bbc News.* May 4.

_____. 2010b. "Greece's Austerity Measures." *bbc News* May 5. <bbc.co.uk/news/10099143>

_____. 2009 "G20: Economic Summit Snapshot." *bbc News* September 24. <news.bbc.co.uk/2/hi/in_depth/business/2009/g20/7897719.stm#uk>

_____. 2008. "Lehman Bros Files for Bankruptcy." *bbc News* September 15. <news.bbc.co.uk/2/hi/7616068.stm>

bea (Bureau of Economic Analysis). 2010. "National Income and Product Accounts Table." U.S. Department of Commerce. <bea.gov/national/nipaweb/index.asp>

Becatoros, Elena. 2010. "20,000 People in Greek Protest March to Parliament." *Nashua Telegraph* May 21. <nashuatelegraph.com/news/worldnation/744695-227/20000-people-in-greek-protest-march-to.html>

Beltrame, Julian. 2010. "Big Stakes in Canada-Europe Trade Talks, But Little Attention." *The Canadian Press* April 26.

Bernanke, Ben S. 2008. "Fostering Sustainable Home Ownership." March 14. <federalreserve.gov/newsevents/speech/bernanke20080314a.htm>

Bezanson, Kate. 2006. *Gender, the State, and Social Reproduction.* Toronto: University of Toronto Press.

Black, Errol, and Paula Mallea. 1997. "The Privatisation of the Manitoba Telephone System." *Canadian Dimension* 31: 2 (March/April).

Blackwell, Richard. 2010. "Japan Takes Issue with Ontario's Green Energy Plan." *Globe and Mail* September 13. <heglobeandmail.com/report-on-business/japan-takes-issue-with-ontarios-green-energy-plan/article1705239/>

_____. 2008. "No Further Stimulus in the Works, Flaherty Says." *Globe and Mail* November 28. <theglobeandmail.com/report-on-business/no-further-stimulus-in-the-works-flaherty-says/article725174/>

Blais, A., and K. Carty. 1990. "Does Proportional Representation Foster Voter Turnout?" *European Journal of Political Research* 18, 2: 167–81.

Blais, Andre, Elisabeth Gidengil, Neil Nevitte and Richard Nadeau. 2004. "Where Does Turnout Decline Come From?" *European Journal of Political Research* 43: 221–36.

Bluestone, Barry, and Bennett Harrison. 1982. *The Deindustrialization of America.* New York: Basic Books.

Boychuck, Gerard W. 2002. "The Changing Political and Economic Environment of Health Care in Canada." Discussion paper no. 1. Ottawa: Commission on the Future of Health Care in Canada.

Boyer, Robert, and Yves Saillard (eds.), 1995. *Regulation Theory.* New York: Routledge.

Bradford, Neil. 1999. "The Policy Influence of Economic Ideas: Interests, Institutions and Innovation in Canada." *Studies in Political Economy* Summer.

_____. 1998. *Commissioning Ideas: Canadian National Policy Innovation in Comparative Perspective.* Toronto: Oxford University Press.

Brenner, Robert. 2006. *Economics of Global Turbulence: The Advanced Capitalist Economies from Long Boom to Long Downturn, 1945–2005.* London: Verso.

Bricker, D., and M. Redfern. 2001. "Canadian Perspectives on the Voting System." *Policy Options* 22: 6.

Brodie, Janine, and Jane Jenson. 1988. "The 'Free Trade' Election." *Studies in Political Economy* 28, Spring.

Brown, Gordon. 2007. "Speech to Mansion House." June 20. <hm-treasury.gov. uk/2014.htm>

Buchanan, James M., and Richard E. Wagner. 1977. *Democracy in Deficit: The Political Legacy of Lord Keynes.* New York: Academic Press.

Burke, Mike. 2000. "Efficiency and the Erosion of Health Care in Canada." In Mike Burke, Colin Moores, and John Shields (eds.), *Restructuring and Resistance: Canadian Public Policy in an Age of Global Capitalism.* Halifax: Fernwood.

Burke, Mike, Colin Moores, and John Shields (eds.). 2000. *Restructuring and Resistance: Canadian Public Policy in an Age of Global Capitalism.* Halifax: Fernwood.

Callan, Eoin. 2008. "G20 Nears Deal for Global Oversight of Banks." *Financial Post* November 15. <financialpost.com/story.html?id=961828>

Callinicos, Alex. 2010. *Bonfire of Illusions.* UK: Polity.

Cameron, Duncan. 2010. "Harper's Bank Tax Rejection Harms International Relations." May 25. <rabble.ca/columnists/2010/05/harpers-bank-tax-rejection-harms-international-relations>

Campbell, Bruce. 2009. "The Global Economic Crisis and its Canadian Dimension." Canadian Centre for Policy Alternatives, National Office. July 1. <policyalternatives.ca/publications/monitor/global-economic-crisis-and-its-canadian-dimension>

Campbell, Robert M. 1991. *The Full Employment Objective in Canada, 1945–85: Historical, Conceptual and Comparative Perspectives.* Ottawa: Council of Canada.

_____. 1987. *Grand Illusions: The Politics of the Keynesian Experience in Canada, 1945–75.* Peterborough: Broadview.

Canada. 2009. *Canada's Economic Action Plan: Budget 2009.* Ottawa: Department of Finance.

Canada. 1991. *Canadian Federalism and Economic Union: Partnership for Prosperity.* Ottawa: Minister of Supply and Services.

Canada. 1985. *Report: Royal Commission on the Economic Union and Development Prospects for Canada* (three volumes). Ottawa: Minister of Supply and Services.

Canada. 1979. *A Future Together.* Task Force on Canadian Unity. Ottawa: Minister of Supply and Services.

Canada. 1945. *Employment and Income with Special Reference to the Initial Period of Reconstruction.* Department of Reconstruction. Ottawa: Queen's Printer.

CCSD (Canadian Council on Social Development). 1996. "Voter Turnout in 1988 and 1993 Federal Elections and in Provincial Elections circa 1990." Progress of Canada's Children. <ccsd.ca/factsheets/fs_vote.htm>

Canadian Institutes for Health Information. 2004. "The Cost of Health Care." *Health Care in Canada*. <secure.cihi.ca/cihiweb/dispPage.jsp?cw_page=PG_263_E&cw_topic=263&cw_rel=AR_43_E>

_____. 2008. "Research About – Health Systems." <cihr-irsc.gc.ca/e/38485.html>

CanWest News Service. 2008. "Harper Criticizes US Economic Policy While Unveiling Help for Apprentices." October 3. <canada.com/topics/news/features/decision-canada/story.html?id=bc22b1f3-a93c-41b0-a97a-d05d4f3409eb>

Caron, Guy. 2008. *Best Kept Secret: Canada's Health Care Competitive Advantage*. Ottawa: The Council of Canadians.

Carroll, William K. 2004. *Corporate Power in a Globalizing World*. Toronto: Oxford University Press.

_____. 1989. "Neoliberalism and the Recomposition of Finance Capital in Canada." *Capital and Class* 38.

_____. 1986. *Corporate Power and Canadian Capitalism*. Vancouver: UBC Press.

CBC. 2010a. "'Buy American' Deal Exempts Canadian firms." February 5. <cbc.ca/canada/story/2010/02/05/ott-buy-american-deal.html>

_____. 2010b. "PM Defends G8 Fake Lake Pavilion." June 8. <cbc.ca/politics/story/2010/06/08/g20-fakelake-costs.html>

_____. 2010c. "Khadr Repatriation Overturned by Top Court." January 29. <cbc.ca/canada/story/2010/01/29/omar-khadr-supreme-court.html>

_____. 2010d. "Little Support for Proroguing Parliament: Poll." <cbc.ca/politics/story/2010/01/07/ekos-poll-prorogue.html>

_____. 2009a. "Buy American Exemption Deal in the Works." September 30. <cbc.ca/canada/story/2009/09/29/buy-american.html>

_____. 2009b. "Record Low Voter Turnout in BC Election." May 13. <bc.ca/canada/british-columbia/story/2009/05/13/bc-low-voter-turnout.html>

_____. 2009c. "Most Canadians Believe Afghan Detainees Tortured: Poll." December 10. <cbc.ca/canada/story/2009/12/09/ekos-poll009.html>

_____. 2009d. "BC's Amended Balanced Budget Law to Allow for 2 Years of Deficits." February 9. <cbc.ca/canada/british-columbia/story/2009/02/09/bc-legislature-budget-deficit-vote.html>

_____. 2008a. "Low Voter Turnout in Alberta Election Being Questioned." March 5. <cbc.ca/canada/edmonton/story/2008/03/05/edm-turnout.html>

_____. 2008b. "Almost Half of Quebec Voters Shunned Polls." December 9. <cbc.ca/news/quebecvotes2008/story/2008/12/09/qv-voterturnout1209.html>

_____. 2007a. "CSIS Suspected U.S. Would Deport Arar to Be Tortured: Documents." August 9. <cbc.ca/canada/story/2007/08/09/arar-report.html>

_____. 2007b. "Ontario Voter Turnout a Record Low." October 11. <cbc.ca/canada/ontariovotes2007/story/2007/10/11/ov-turnout-071010.html>

CCPA (Canadian Centre for Policy Alternatives). 2009. *Federal Budget 2009: CCPA Analysis*. Ottawa: CCPA.

_____. 1995a. *Monitor*. July/August.

_____. 1995b. *Monitor*. March.

CCLA (Canadian Civil Liberties Association). 2010a. "CCLA Files Five Policing Complaints with OIPRD." Press release. July 15.

_____. 2010b. "A Breach of the Peace: A Preliminary Report of Observations During the 2010 G20 Summit." Toronto: CCLA. June 29.

Cerny, Philip G. 1997. "Paradoxes of the Competition State: The Dynamics of Globalization." *Government and Opposition* 32, 2 (March).

Chorney, Harold. 1988. *Sound Finance and Other Delusions: Deficit and Debt Management in the Age of Neo-Liberal Economics.* Montreal: Concordia University.

Clark, Campbell, and Barrie McKenna. 2009. "'Buy American' Bill Puts Canada on Edge." *Globe and Mail* January 30. <theglobeandmail.com/news/national/article969132.ece>

Clark, David. 2002. "Neoliberalism and Public Service Reform: Canada in a Comparative Perspective." *Canadian Journal of Political Science* 35, 4 (December).

CLC (Canadian Labour Congress). 2003. *Falling Unemployment Insurance Protection for Canada's Unemployed.* Ottawa.

_____. 1999. *Left Out in the Cold: The End of UI for Canadian Workers.* Ottawa.

Clément, Dominique. 2008. "The October Crisis of 1970: Human Rights Abuses Under the War Measures Act." *Journal of Canadian Studies* 42, 2 (Spring).

CNBC. 2008. "JP Morgan Buys Failed WaMu Assets for $1.9 Billion." September 25. <cnbc.com/id/26893741/JPMorgan_Buys_Failed_WaMu_Assets_for_1_9_Billion>

Cohn, Daniel. 2004. "The Public-Private Partnership 'Fetish': Moving Beyond the Rhetoric." *Revue Gouvernance* 1, 2 (Fall).

_____. 1997. "Creating Crises and Avoiding Blame: The Politics of Public Service Reform and the New Public Management in Great Britain and the United States." *Administration and Society* 29, 5 (November).

Committee on Capital Markets Regulation. 2009. *The Global Financial Crisis: A Plan for Regulatory Reform.* May.

Conference Board of Canada. n.d. <conferenceboard.ca/HCP/Details/society/income-inequality.aspx#evidence>

Courchene, Thomas J. 1986. *Economic Management and the Division of Powers. Studies of the Royal Commission on the Economic Union and Development Prospects for Canada* volume 67. Toronto: University of Toronto Press.

Crete, Jean, Rejean Pelletier, and Jerome Couture. "Political Trust in Canada: What Matters: Politics or Economics?" Paper presented at the Canadian Political Science Association. June. <cpsa-acsp.ca/papers-2006/Crete.pdf>

CUPE (Canadian Union of Public Employees). 2010. "Budget 2010: Overview and Summary." March 4. <cupe.ca/budget/budget-2010-overview-analysis-summary>

Curry, Bill, and Jeremy Torobin. 2010. "Canada, EU at Loggerheads over Bank Tax." *Globe and Mail* May 5.

Daily Commercial News. 2010. "Ontario Budget: Austerity for Workers, Tax Cuts for Bay Street." March 25. <www.dailycommercialnews.com/nw/17681/en>

De Larosiere, Jacques. 2009. "Report of the High-Level Group on Financial Supervision in the EU." February 25. <ec.europa.eu/internal_market/finances/docs/de_larosiere_report_en.pdf>

Deen, Mark. 2010. "OECD Reduces Outlook, Predicts 2011 'Soft Spot.'" November 18. <businessweek.com/news/2010-11-18/oecd-reduces-growth-outlook-predicts-2011-soft-spot-.html>

Delli Carpini, Michael X. 2000. "Gen.com: Youth, Civic Engagement, and the New

Information Environment." *Political Communication* 17: 341–49.

Di Matteo, Livio. 2000. "The Determinants of the Public-Private Mix in Canadian Health Care Expenditures, 1975–1996." *Health Policy* 52, 2.

Dobbin, Murray. 2010. "Is This What a Police State Looks Like?" June 29. <rabble.ca/blogs/bloggers/murray-dobbin/2010/06/what-police-state-looks>

Doern, G. Bruce, and Mark MacDonald. 1998. *Free Trade Federalism: Negotiating the Canadian Agreement on Internal Trade.* Toronto: University of Toronto Press.

Doern, G. Bruce, Allan M. Maslove, and Michael J. Prince. 1988. *Public Budgeting in Canada: Politics, Economics, and Management.* Ottawa: Carleton University Press.

Doern, G. Bruce, Leslie A. Pal, and Brian W. Tomlin. 1996. "The Internationalization of Canadian Public Policy." In G. Bruce Doern, Leslie A. Pal, and Brian W. Tomlin. *Border Crossings: The Internationalization of Canadian Public Policy.* Toronto: Oxford University Press.

Doern, G. Bruce, and Bryne B. Purchase. 1991. *Canada at Risk? Canadian Public Policy in the 1990s.* Toronto: CD Howe Institute.

Doern, G. Bruce, and Brian W. Tomlin. 1992. *Faith and Fear: The Free Trade Story.* Toronto: Stoddart.

DOF (Department of Finance). 2009. "Update of Economic and Fiscal Projections." September.

Dorling, Danny. 2010. *Injustice: Why Social Inequality Persists.* Bristol: Policy Press.

Duhigg, Charles. 2008. "Loan-Agency Woes Swell From a Trickle to a Torrent." *New York Times* July 11. <nytimes.com/2008/07/11/business/11ripple.html>

Economic Council of Canada. 1984a. *Western Transition.* Ottawa: Minister of Supply and Services.

_____. 1984b. *Steering the Course.* 21st Annual Review. Ottawa: Minister of Supply and Services.

The Economist. 2010. "Canada's Parliament: Harper Goes Prorogue." January 7. <economist.com/node/15213212>

_____. 2010. "Canada Without Parliament: Halted in Mid-debate." January 7. <economist.com/node/15211862>

Economist Intelligence Unit. 2008. "Index of Democracy 2008." *The Economist.* <http://graphics.eiu.com/PDF/Democracy%20Index%202008.pdf>

Eden, Lorraine, and Maureen A. Molot. 1993. "Canada's National Policies: Reflections on 125 Years." *Canadian Public Policy* 19, 3 (September).

Edwards, Pamela, and Jean Shaoul. 2003. "Partnerships: For Better Or Worse?" *Accounting, Auditing & Accountability Journal* 16, 3 (January).

Elections Canada. 2009. "Voter Turnout at Federal Elections and Referendums, 1867–2008. <elections.ca/content.asp?section=pas&document=turnout&lang=e>

_____. 2003. "Explaining the Turnout Decline in Canadian Federal Elections." March. <elections.ca/content.asp?section=loi&document=index&dir=tur/tud&lang=e&textonly=false>

Elliott, Larry, and Patrick Wintour. 2009. "We're Not Out of the Woods — G8 Leaders Fear Double Dip Slump." *The Guardian* July 8. <guardian.co.uk/world/2009/jul/08/g8-recession-plan-global-economy>

Ericson, Richard, and Aaron Doyle. 1999. "Globalization and the Policing of Protest: The Case of APEC 1997." *British Journal of Sociology* 50, 4 (December): 589–608.

Erlanger, S. 2008. "Sarkozy Stresses Global Financial Overhaul." *New York Times.*

September 25.

European Commission. 2009. *The Presidency Conclusions of the Council of the European Union*. June 19.

Evans, Brian. 2004. "Conquering the 'Traditional' Public Service: The Transformation of Managerial Culture Within the Ontario Public Service." Paper presented at the Canadian Political Science Association. Winnipeg, June.

Evans, Peter. 2010. "Steady Budget Offers Few Surprises." cbc News. March 5. <http://www.cbc.ca/money/story/2010/03/04/budget-flaherty-parliament-ottawa.html>

Evans, Robert G. 2002. "Raising the Money: Options, Consequences and Objectives for Financing Health Care in Canada." Discussion Paper No. 27. Ottawa: Commission on the Future of Health Care in Canada.

Federal Reserve. n.d. <federalreserve.gov/fomc/fundsrate.htm>

Feldstein, M. 1974. "Social Security, Induced Retirement and Aggregate Capital Accumulation." *Journal of Political Economy* 82, 5 (September–October).

Ferge, Z. 1997. "The Changed Welfare Paradigm: The Individualization of the Social." *Social Policy and Administration* 31, 1 (March).

Ferguson, Rob. 2009."Ontario's credit outlook taking a GM-bailout hit." Toronto Star. June 3. http://www.thestar.com/news/ontario/article/644596

Fineman, Josh and Bradley Keoun. 2008. "Merrill Lynch Posts Fourth Straight Quarterly Loss." <bloomberg.com/apps/news?pid=20601087&sid=atGti_UmcPnM&refer=home>

Franklin, Mark N. 2004. *Voter Turnout and the Dynamics of Electoral Competition in Established Democracies since 1945*. Cambridge: Cambridge University Press.

fsb (Financial Stability Board). 2008. "Report of the Financial Stability Forum on Enhancing Market and Institutional Resilience." April 7. <financialstabilityboard.org/publications/r_0904d.pdf >

Fuller, Colleen. 1996. "Doctoring to nafta." *Canadian Forum* June.

G-20. 2010. "Toronto Summit Declaration." June 27. <canadainternational.gc.ca/g20/summit-sommet/2010/toronto-declaration-toronto.aspx?lang=eng>

G-30 (Group of Thirty). 2009. *Financial Reform: A Framework for Financial Stability*. January.

Galbraith, John Kenneth.1958. *The Affluent Society*. Boston: Houghton Mifflin.

Gamble, Andrew. 2009. *The Spectre at the Feast*. Hampshire: Palgrave Macmillan.

_____. 1988. *The Free Economy and the Strong State*. London: Macmillan.

Geddes, John. 2010. "It's Harper's World Now." *Macleans* July 2. <2.macleans.ca/2010/07/02/its-harpers-world-now/2/>

Gidengil, Elisabeth, André Blais, Joanna Everitt, Patrick Fournier, and Neil Nevitte. 2005. "Missing the Message: Young Adults and Election Issues." *Electoral Insight* 7, 1 (January). <elections.ca/eca/eim/article_search/article.asp?id=122&lang=e&frmPageSize=&textonly=false>

Gidengil, Elisabeth, André Blais, Neil Nevitte, and Richard Nadeau. 2003. "Turned Off or Tuned Out? Youth Participation in Politics." *Electoral Insight* 5, 2 (July)

Gill, Stephen. 1995. "Globalisation, Market Civilisation, and Disciplinary Neoliberalism." *Millennium Journal of International Studies* 24, 3 (December).

Globe and Mail. 2010. "The Wrongful Prosecution of Omar Khadr." Editorial. October 31.

_____. 2010. "A Police State in the Making." April 24.

Goldman, David. n.d. "Bailout Scorecard." *CNN Money.* <money.cnn.com/news/storysupplement/economy/bailouttracker/index.html>

Golob, Stephanie R. 2008. "The Return of the Quiet Canadian: Canada's Approach to Regional Integration after 9/11." In Brian Bow and Patrick Lennox (eds.), *An Independent Foreign Policy for Canada?: Challenges and Choices for the Future.* Toronto: University of Toronto Press.

Gonick, Cy. 1987. *The Great Economic Debate.* Toronto: Lorimer.

Gordon, David M., Richard Edwards, and Michael Reich. 1994. "Long Swings and Stages of Capitalism." In David M. Kotz, Terrence McDonough, and Michael Reich (eds.), *Social Structure of Accumulation.* Cambridge: Cambridge University Press.

Gordon, Marsha. 1981. *Government In Business.* Montreal: C.D. Howe Institute.

Gough, Ian. 1981. *The Political Economy of the Welfare State.* London: Macmillan.

Gourevitch, Peter. 1986. *Politics in Hard Times: Comparative Responses to International Economic Crises.* Ithaca: Cornell University Press.

Gowan, Peter. 2009. "In the Heartland." *New Left Review* 55 (January–February).

_____. 1999. *The Global Gamble: Washington's Faustian Bid for World Dominance.* London: Verso.

Graefe, Peter. 2006. "The Social Economy and the American Model." *Global Social Policy* 6, 2 (August).

Grinspun, Ricardo, and Robert Kreklewich. 1994. "Consolidating Neoliberal Reforms: 'Free Trade' as a Conditioning Framework." *Studies in Political Economy* 43.

Guard, Julie, and Wayne Antony (eds.). 2009. *Bankruptcies and Bailouts.* Winnipeg and Halifax: Fernwood.

The Guardian. 2010. "Why Inequality Persists: Get the Full Data." *The Guardian Data Blog.* April 21. <guardian.co.uk/news/datablog/2010/apr/21/inequality-dorling-data>

Guest, Dennis. 1987. "World War II and the Welfare State in Canada." In Allan Moscovitch and Jim Albert (eds.), *The "Benevolent" State: The Growth of Welfare in Canada.* Toronto: Garamond.

_____. 1985. *The Emergence of Social Security in Canada,* second edition. Vancouver: UBC Press.

Guillen, Mauro F. n.d. "The Global Economic and Financial Crisis: A Timeline." The Lauder Institute, University of Pennsylvania. <lauder.wharton.upenn.edu/pdf/Chronology%20Economic%20%20Financial%20Crisis.pdf>

Guttmann, Robert. 1995. "Money and Credit in Regulation." In Robert Boyer and Yves Saillard (eds.), *Regulation Theory.* New York: Routledge.

Haddow, Rodney. 2003. "Canadian Federalism and Active Labour Market Policy." In F. Rocher and M.J. Smith (eds.), *New Trends in Canadian Federalism,* second edition. Peterborough: Broadview.

Hall, Peter A. 1993. "Policy Paradigms, Social Learning, and the State: The Case of Economic Policymaking in Britain." *Comparative Politics* 25, 3 (April).

Hankivsky, Olena, and Marina Morrow (with Pat Armstrong, Lindsey Galvin, and Holly Grinvalds). 2004. *Trade Agreements, Home Care and Women's Health.* Ottawa: Status of Women Canada.

Harris, Stephen L. 2010. "The Global Financial Meltdown and Financial Regulation: Shirking and Learning — Canada in International Context." In G. Bruce Doern and Christopher Stoney (eds.), *How Ottawa Spends 2010–2011: Recession, Realignment, and the New Deficit Era.* Montreal: McGill-Queen's University Press.

Harvey, David. 2010. *The Enigma of Capital and the Crises of Capitalism.* New York: Oxford University Press.

_____. 2009. "Their Crisis, Our Challenge." Interview with *Red Pepper.* March 15. <www.redpepper.org.uk/Their-crisis-our-challenge>

_____. 2006. *Limits to Capital.* London: Verso.

_____. 2005. *A Brief History of Neoliberalism.* Oxford: Oxford University Press.

_____. 2003a. "The 'New' Imperialism: Accumulation by Dispossession." In Leo Panitch and Colin Leys (eds.), *The New Imperial Challenge: Socialist Register 2004.* London: Merlin Press.

_____. 2003b. *The New Imperialism.* Oxford: Oxford University Press.

_____. 2001. *Spaces of Capital.* Edinburgh: Edinburgh University.

Hay, Colin. 2007. *Why We Hate Politics.* Cambridge: Polity Press.

Heap, Sean Hargreaves. 1980. "World Profitability Crisis in the 1970s: Some Empirical Evidence." *Capital and Class* 12 (Winter).

Heard, Andrew. 2009. *The Governor General's Desire to Prorogue Parliament: Parliamentary Democracy Defended or Endangered?* Edmonton: University of Alberta Centre for Constitutional Studies.

Hodge, Graeme and Carsten Greve (eds.). 2005. *The Challenge of Public-Private Partnerships: Learning from International Experience.* UK: Edward Elgar.

Holland, Stuart. 1975. *The Socialist Challenge.* London: Quartet.

Houle, Francois. 1990. "Economic Renewal and Social Policy." In Alain G. Gagnon and James Bickerton (eds.), *Canadian Politics: An Introduction to the Discipline.* Peterborough: Broadview.

House of Commons. 2002. "Chapter 1: Towards a Strategic North American Dimension of Canadian Foreign Policy." Standing Committee on Foreign Affairs. December. <cmte.parl.gc.ca/Content/HOC/committee/372/fait/reports/rp1032319/faitrp03/10-ch1-e.htm>

Howse, Robert. 1996. *Securing the Canadian Economic Union — Legal and Constitutional Options for the Federal Government.* Toronto: C.D. Howe Institute.

HRDC (Human Resources Development Canada). 1998. *1997 Employment Insurance: Monitoring and Assessment Report.* Ottawa.

_____. 1996. *Getting Canadians Back to Work.* May 30. Ottawa.

_____. 1995. "News Release." December 1. Ottawa.

Iakova, Dora. 2009. "United Kingdom: From Rescue to Recovery." *IMF Survey Magazine: Countries & Regions*: Economic Health Check. July 16. <imf.org/external/pubs/ft/survey/so/2009/CAR071609A.htm>

Ibbitson, John. 2009. "When it Comes to the Canadian Economy, Obama May as Well Be PM." *Globe and Mail,* May 20.

ICLMG (International Civil Liberties Monitoring Group). 2009. *Canada's Anti-Terrorism Laws in Violation of International Human Rights Standards.* Submission of Information by the ICLMG to the Office of the High Commissioner for Human Rights, in relation to the Human Rights Council's Universal Periodic Review (UPR) of Canada, February.

IMF (International Monetary Fund). 2009a. "Cross Cutting Themes in Major Article

IV Consultations." August 14. <imf.org/external/np/pp/eng/2009/081409.pdf>
_____. 2009b. "Lessons of the Financial Crisis for Future Regulation of Financial
   Institutions and Markets for Liquidity Management." February 4. <imf.org/
   external/np/pp/eng/2009/020409.pdf>
IMF. 2009c. "The State of Public Finances Cross-Country Fiscal Monitor: November
   2009." Washington: International Monetary Fund.
IOW (Institute of Wellbeing). 2009. "How Are Canadians Really Doing?" June 10.
   <ciw.ca/en/TheCanadianIndexofWellBeing.aspx>
Ipsos Reid. 2008. "In Wake of Constitutional Crisis, New Survey Demonstrates that
   Canadians Lack Basic Understanding of our Country's Parliamentary System."
   December 15. <dominion.ca/DominionInstituteDecember15Factum.pdf>
Ireland, Derek, and Kernaghan Webb. 2010. "The Canadian Escape from Subprime
   Crisis? Comparing the US and Canadian Approaches." In G. Bruce Doern
   and Christopher Stoney (eds.), How Ottawa Spends 2010–2011: Recession,
   Realignment, and the New Deficit Era. Montreal: McGill-Queen's University
   Press.
Issing Committee. 2009. New Financial Order. February. <bundesregierung.de/
   nsc_true/Content/DE/StatischeSeiten/Breg/G8G20/Anlagen/bericht-issing-
   london,property=publicationFile.pdf/bericht-issing-london>
Ivanova, Iglika. 2009. "Spending Cuts Would Kill Thousands of Jobs and Deepen
   Recession." Canadian Centre for Policy Alternatives, BC Office. News release.
   August 27. <policyalternatives.ca/newsroom/news-releases/spending-cuts-
   would-kill-thousands-jobs-and-deepen-recession>
Jackson, Andrew. 1995. The Liberals' Labour Strategy (and its Consequences for
   Workers). Ottawa: Canadian Centre for Policy Alternatives.
Jackson, Andrew, and Erin Weir. 2008. "The Conservative Tax Record." In Teresa
   Healy (ed.), The Harper Record. Ottawa: Canadian Centre for Policy Alternatives.
Jenson, Jane, and Denis Saint-Martin. 2003. "New Routes to Social Cohesion?
   Citizenship and the Social Investment State." Canadian Journal of Sociology.
   28, 1 (Winter).
Jessop, Bob. 2006. "Spatial Fixes, Temporal Fixes and Spatio-Temporal Fixes." In Noel
   Castree and Derek Gregory (eds.), David Harvey: A Critical Reader. Molden:
   Blackwell.
_____. 2004. "From Localities via the Spatial Turn to Spatio-Temporal Fixes: A
   Strategic-Relational Odyssey." SECONS Discussion Forum. April. <http://eprints.
   lancs.ac.uk/235/1/E-2004d_Secons6.pdf>
_____. 2002. The Future of the Capitalist State. UK: Polity.
Jessop, Bob, and Ngai-Ling Sum. 2006. Beyond the Regulation Approach. UK: Edward
   Elgar.
Juillard, Michael. 1995. "Accumulation Regimes." In Robert Boyer and Yves Saillard
   (eds.), Regulation Theory. New York: Routledge.
Kalecki, Michael. 1943. "Political Aspects of Full Employment." Political Quarterly
   14 (October–December).
Kenen, Peter B. 2001. The International Financial Architecture: What's New? What's
   Missing? Washington, DC: Institute for International Economics.
Kerstetter, Steve. 2002. Rags and Riches: Wealth Inequality in Canada. Ottawa:
   Canadian Centre for Policy Alternatives.

Keynes, John M. 1936. *The General Theory of Employment, Interest and Money.* London: Macmillan.

Kim, Soyoung, and David Lawder. 2010. "GM Repays US Loan, Government Loss on Bailout Falls." Reuters. April 21. <reuters.com/article/idU.S.TRE63K56920100421>

Kirby, J.L. 2002. *Study on the State of the Health Care System in Canada.* Ottawa: The Standing Senate Committee on Social Affairs.

Kirchhoff, Sue. 2005. "Subprime Lending a Worry for Fed." *U.S.A Today* January 12. <usatoday.com/money/economy/fed/2005-01-12-gramlich_x.htm>

Klein, Seth. 1996. "Good Sense Versus Common Sense: Canada's Debt Debate and Competing Hegemonic Projects." MA thesis, Department of Political Science, Simon Fraser University, Vancouver.

Kotz, David M. 1994. "Interpreting the Social Structure of Accumulation." In David M. Kotz, Terrence McDonough, and Michael Reich (eds.), *Social Structure of Accumulation.* Cambridge: Cambridge University Press.

Krasner, Stephen. 1999. *Sovereignty: Organized Hypocrisy.* Princeton: Princeton University Press.

Kroeger, Arthur. 1996. "Changing Course: The Federal Government's Program Review of 1994–95." In Amelita Armit and Jacques Bourgault (eds.), *Hard Choices or No Choices: Assessing Program Review.* Toronto: Institute of Public Administration of Canada.

Krugman, Paul. 2010. "The Pain Caucus." *New York Times.* Op-ed. May 30. <nytimes.com/2010/05/31/opinion/31krugman.html?_r=1>

Kudrle, Robert T., and Theodore Marmor. 1981. "The Development of Welfare States in North America." In Peter Flora and Arnold Heidenheimer (eds.), *The Development of Welfare States in Europe and America.* New Brunswick, NJ: Transaction Books.

Kuhn, P. 1997. "Canada and the 'OECD Hypothesis': Does Labour Market Inflexibility Explain Canada's High Level of Unemployment?" Canadian International Labour Network Working Paper No. 10. April. <labour.ciln.mcmaster.ca/papers/cilnwp10.html>

Kukucha, Christopher J. 2010. "Provincial Pitfalls: Canadian Provinces and the Canada-EU Trade Negotiations." Paper presented at the Annual Meeting of the Canadian Political Science Association, Montreal, June.

_____. 2008. *The Provinces and Canadian Foreign Trade Policy.* Vancouver: UBC Press

Kusch, Larry. 2010. "Manitoba to Revise Budget Law to Allow for Four Years of Deficits." *Winnipeg Free Press.* March 23. <financialpost.com/news-sectors/economy/story.html?id=2717899>

Labaton, Stephen. 2008. "Agency's '04 Rule Let Banks Pile Up New Debt." *New York Times.* October 2. <nytimes.com/2008/10/03/business/03sec.html>

Labonte, Ronald, Nazeem Muhajarine, Brandace Winquist, and Jacqueline Quail. 2009. "Healthy Populations." Institute of Wellbeing. June 10. <ciw.ca/en/TheCanadianIndexOfWellbeing/DomainsOfWellbeing/HealthyPopulations/FullReport.aspx>

Laghi, Brian, Daniel Leblanc, and Campbell Clark. 2008. "Harper Unfazed by Market Crisis." *Globe and Mail* September 15. <theglobeandmail.com/news/politics/article709599.ece>

Laghi, Brian, and Kevin Carmichael. 2009. "Canada Takes Battle Over 'Buy American' to US Senate." *Globe and Mail* February 3: A1.

Laird, Sam. 1999. "The WTO's Trade Policy Review Mechanism — From Through the Looking Glass." *The World Economy* 22, 6 (August).

Laxmidas, Shrikesh. 2010. "Thousands in Lisbon Protest Against Austerity Cuts." Reuters. May 29. <reuters.com/article/idU.S.TRE64R3L620100529>

Lemieux, Denis, and Ana Stuhec. 1999. *Review of Administrative Action under NAFTA.* Scarborough: Carswell.

Lewenza, Ken. 2010. "Canada-EU Deal Will Affect More than Trade." *Toronto Star* May 10.

Lewis, Timothy. 2003. *In the Long Run We're All Dead: The Canadian Turn to Fiscal Restraint.* Vancouver: UBC Press.

Leys, Collin. 1980. "Neo-Conservatism and the Organic Crisis in Britain." *Studies in Political Economy: A Socialist Review* 4 (Autumn).

Liu, Henry C.K. 2007. "Economics of Denial." *Asia Times Online.* June 13. <atimes.com/atimes/Global_Economy/IF13Dj01.html>

Loxley, John. 2009. "Financial Dimensions: Origins and State Responses." In Julie Guard and Wayne Antony (eds.), *Bankruptcies and Bailouts.* Winnipeg and Halifax: Fernwood.

_____. 1998. *Interdependence, Disequilibrium and Growth.* London: Macmillan.

Luz, Mark A. 2001. "NAFTA, Investment and the Constitution of Canada: Will the Watertight Compartments Spring a Leak?" *Ottawa Law Review* 32, 1.

Macaluso, Grace. 2010. "Auto Bailouts No cure for Windsor Job Losses" *Windsor Star,* July 31. <windsorstar.com/news/Auto+bailouts+cure+Windsor+losses/3347225/story.html>

Macdonald, David. 2009. *To Little Too Late.* Ottawa: Canadian Centre for Policy Alternatives.

MacDonald, Martha. 1999. "Restructuring, Gender and Social Security Reform in Canada." *Journal of Canadian Studies* 34 (Summer).

_____. 1991. "Post-Fordism and the Flexibility Debate." *Studies in Political Economy: A Socialist Review* 36 (Autumn).

Macpherson, C.B. 1972. *The Real World of Democracy.* Oxford: Oxford University Press.

Mahon, Rianne. 2008. "Babies and Bosses: Gendering the OECD's Social Policy Discourse." In Rianne Mahon and Stephen McBride (eds.), *The OECD and Transnational Governance.* Vancouver: UBC Press.

Mahon, Rianne, and Stephen McBride. 2008a. "The OECD and Transnational Governance: An Introduction." In Rianne Mahon and Stephen McBride (eds.), *The OECD and Transnational Governance.* Vancouver: UBC Press.

_____ (eds.). 2008b. *The OECD and Transnational Governance.* Vancouver: UBC Press.

Maioni, Antonia, and Miriam Smith. 2003. "Health Care and Canadian Federalism." In Francois Rocher and Miriam Smith (eds.), *New Trends in Canadian Federalism,* second edition. Peterborough: Broadview Press.

Marchak, M. Patricia. 1991. *The Integrated Circus: The New Right and the Restructuring of Global Markets.* Montreal: McGill-Queen's University Press.

Marr, William L., and Donald G. Paterson. 1980. *Canada: An Economic History.* Toronto: Gage.

Marsh, Leonard. 1943 [1975]. *Report on Social Security for Canada.* Toronto:

University of Toronto Press.

Maslove, Allan M. 1981. "Tax Expenditures, Tax Credits and Equity." In G. Bruce Doern (ed.), *How Ottawa Spends Your Tax Dollars: Federal Priorities 1981*. Toronto: Lorimer.

Maxwell, Judith. 2001. *Towards a Common Citizenship: Canada's Social and Economic Choices*. Ottawa: Canadian Policy Research Network.

McBride, Stephen. 2011. "The Global Economic Crisis." In Christopher Kukucha and Duane Bratt (ed.), *Readings in Canadian Foreign Policy: Classic Debates and New Ideas*, second edition. Toronto: Oxford University Press.

_____. 2005a. *Paradigm Shift*, second edition. Halifax: Fernwood.

_____. 2005b. "The Long Goodbye: Elite Nationalism in the Era of Globalization." In Alexander Netherton, Allen Seager, and Karl Froschauer (eds.), *In/Security: Canada in the Post-9/11 World*. Burnaby: Centre for Canadian Studies at Simon Fraser University.

_____. 2003. "Quiet Constitutionalism in Canada: The International Political Economy of Domestic Institutional Change." *Canadian Journal of Political Science* 36. 2.

_____. 1996. "The Continuing Crisis of Social Democracy: Ontario's Social Contract in Perspective." *Studies in Political Economy* 50 (Summer).

_____. 1993. "Renewed Federalism as an Instrument of Competitiveness: Liberal Political Economy and the Canadian Constitution." *International Journal of Canadian Studies* 7–8.

_____. 1992. *Not Working: State, Unemployment, and Neo-Conservatism in Canada*. Toronto: University of Toronto Press.

_____. 1983. "Public Policy as a Determinant of Interest Group Behaviour: The Canadian Labour Congress' Corporatist Initiative, 1976–78." *Canadian Journal of Political Science* xvi, 3 (September).

McBride, Stephen, and John Shields. 1997. *Dismantling a Nation: Canada and the New World Order*, second edition. Halifax: Fernwood.

McBride, Stephen, and Russell A. Williams. 2001. "Globalization, the Restructuring of Labour Markets and Policy Convergence." *Global Social Policy* 1, 3 (December).

McDonald, Henry. 2010. "Irish Austerity Plan to Save €15bn." *The Guardian* November 24. <guardian.co.uk/business/2010/nov/24/ireland-austerity-plans-unveiled>

McDonough, T. 1999. "Gordon's Accumulation Theory: The Highest Stage of Stadial Theory." *Review of Radical Political Economics* 31, 6 (December).

McIlveen, Murray, and Hideo Mimoto. 1990. "The Federal Government Deficit, 1975–76 to 1988–89." Mimeograph. Ottawa: Statistics Canada.

McNally, David. 2009. "From Financial Crisis to World-Slump: Accumulation, Financialisation, and the Global Slowdown." *Historical Materialism* 17, 2.

McNish, J., and G. McArthur.2008. "Special Investigation: How High Risk Mortgages Crept North." *Globe and Mail* December 12.

McQuaig, Linda. 1995. *Shooting the Hippo: Death by Deficit and Other Canadian Myths*. Toronto: Viking.

_____. 1992. *The Quick and the Dead: Brian Mulroney, Big Business and the Seduction of Canada*. Toronto: Penguin.

_____. 1987. Behind Closed Doors: How the Rich Won Control of Canada's Tax System. Markham: Viking.

Mendelsohn, Matthew, and Jon Medow. 2010. *Help Wanted: How Well Did the EI Program Respond During Recent Recessions?* Toronto: Mowat Centre for Policy Innovation.

Mishra, Ramesh. 1990. *The Welfare State in Capitalist Society: Policies of Retrenchment and Maintenance in Europe, North America and Australia.* Toronto: University of Toronto Press.

The Montreal Gazette. 2010. "Bank Tax is Dead, But What Comes Next?" April 27.

Moore, Matt. 2007. "ECB, Fed Inject Cash to Ease Fears." *USA Today* August 10. <usatoday.com/money/economy/2007-08-10-274019294_x.htm>

Morissette, Rene, and Xuelin Zhang. 2006. "Revisiting Wealth Inequality." *Perspectives on Labour and Income* 7, 12 (December).

Morissette, Rene, Xuelin Zhang, and Marie Drolet. 2002. "Wealth Inequality." *Perspectives on Labour and Income* 3, 2 (February).

Moseley, Fred. 1999. "The United States Economy at the Turn of the Century." *Capital & Class* 67 (Spring).

MSNBC. 2010a. "Citing 'Obscene' Bonuses, Obama to Tax Banks." January 14. <msnbc.msn.com/id/34833757>

_____. 2010b. "Obama Lauds G-20 Pledge to Halve Deficits." June 27. <msnbc.msn.com/id/37954067/ns/business-world_business/>

_____. 2008. "$17.4 Billion Auto Bailout Has Strings Attached." December 19. <msnbc.msn.com/id/28311743/>

Muir, Gilbert A. 1964–65. "A History of the Telephone in Manitoba." *MHS Transactions* Series 3. <mhs.mb.ca/docs/transactions/3/telephone.shtml>

Nation Master. 2010. <http://www.nationmaster.com/graph/dem_par_ele_reg_vot_tur-parliamentary-elections-registered-voter-turnout>

NCW (National Council of Welfare). 2008. "Welfare Incomes Over Time." *Welfare Incomes, 2006 and 2007.* Ottawa.

_____. 2006. "Fact Sheet: Number of People on Welfare." October. Ottawa.

Neill, Robin. 1991. *A History of Canadian Economic Thought.* London and NY: Routledge.

Nevitte, Neil. 2002. *Value Change and Governance in Canada.* Toronto: University of Toronto Press.

New York Times. 2007. "BNP Paribas Suspends Funds Because of Subprime Problems." August 9. <ytimes.com/2007/08/09/business/worldbusiness/09iht-09bnp.7054054.html?_r=1>

Newman, Rick. 2009. "The AIG: Bonuses: A Welcome Scandal." *US News & World Report* March 18. <usnews.com/money/blogs/flowchart/2009/03/18/the-aig-bonuses-a-welcome-scandal>

Norrie, Kenneth, Richard Simeon, and Mark Krasnick. 1986. *Federalism and Economic Union in Canada.* Toronto: University of Toronto Press.

Norris, P. 1999. *Critical Citizens: Global Support for Democratic Governance.* Oxford: Oxford University Press.

O'Brien, Robert, and Marc Williams. 2004. *Global Political Economy: Evolution and Dynamics.* New York: Palgrave Macmillan.

O'Connor, James. 1973. *The Fiscal Crisis of the State.* New York: St. Martin's Press.

O'Hara, Phillip Anthony. 2008. "A Social Structure of Accumulation for Long Wave Upswing in Australia?" *Journal of Australian Political Economy* 61 (June).

_____. 2006. *Growth and Development in the Global Political Economy.* London: Routledge.

_____. 2004. "A New Family-Community Social Structures of Accumulation for Long Wave Upswing in the United States." *Forum for Social Economy* 34, 2 (December).

_____. 2000. *Marx, Veblen, and Contemporary Institutional Political Economy: Principles and Unstable Dynamics of Capitalism.* UK: Edward Elgar.

O'Neill, Brenda. 2007. *Indifferent or Just Different? The Political and Civic Engagement of Young People in Canada.* Ottawa: Canadian Policy Research Networks.

OECD. 2010a. "Quarterly Unemployment Rates." <oecd.org/dataoecd/30/61/44367840. pdf>

_____. 2010b. "A Strengthening Recovery, but Also New Risks." Editorial. <oecd.org/ dataoecd/4/50/39739655.pdf>

_____. 2010c. "General Assessment of the Macroeconomic Situation." *Economic Outlook.* <oecd.org/dataoecd/36/57/43117724.pdf>

_____. 2010d. "Economic Survey of Germany 2010." <oecd.org/document/48/0,33 43,en_2649_34569_44791728_1_1_1_1,00.html>

_____. 2009a. "Policy Responses to the Economic Crisis: Stimulus Packages, Innovation, and Long-term Growth." Directorate for Science, Technology, and Industry. May 11. <olis.oecd.org/olis/2009doc.nsf/ENGDATCORPLOOK/ NT00002C4E/$FILE/JT03264323.PDF>

_____. 2009b. "Employment Outlook 2009." US. <oecd.org/dataoecd/62/37/43707050. pdf>

_____. 2009c. "Employment Outlook 2009." UK. <oecd.org/dataoecd/62/36/43707062. pdf>

_____. 2009d. "Employment Outlook 2009." Germany. <oecd.org/datao- ecd/61/54/43707146.pdf>

_____. 1994. *The Jobs Study — Facts, Analysis, Strategy.* Paris: OECD.

Omonira-Oyekanmi, Rebecca. 2010. "Britain Becomes Latest to Slash Budget, Freeze Salaries." *Washington Post* June 23. <washingtonpost.com/wp-dyn/content/ article/2010/06/22/AR2010062202306.html>

Ontario Ministry of Intergovernmental Affairs. 1991. *A Canadian Social Charter: Making Our Shared Values Stronger.* Toronto: Queen's Printer.

Ottawa Citizen. 2006. "Sacrifice Civil Liberties for Security, Canadians Say." June 24.

Pal, Leslie A. 1988. *State, Class and Bureaucracy: Canadian Unemployment Insurance and Public Policy.* Kingston and Montreal: McGill-Queen's University Press.

Pammett, Jon H., and Lawrence LeDuc. 2003. "Explaining the Turnout Decline in Canadian Federal Elections: A New Survey of Non-voters." Ottawa: Elections Canada. March. <elections.ca/res/rec/part/tud/TurnoutDecline.pdf>.

Panitch, Leo, and Sam Gindin. 2011. "Capitalist Crises and the Crisis This Time." *Socialist Register* 47.

Panitch, Leo, and Donald Swartz. 2003. *From Consent to Coercion: The Assault on Trade Union Freedoms,* third edition. Aurora, ON: Garamond Press.

_____. 1988. *The Assault on Trade Union Freedoms: From Consent to Coercion Revisited.* Toronto: Garamond Press.

Parkinson, Rhonda. 2007. "Voter Turnout in Canada." March 1. <mapleleafweb.com/ features/voter-turnout-canada>

Paul, Jennifer, and Marcus Pistor. 2009. "Official Development Assistance Spending."

International Affairs, Trade and Finance Division. May 13. <2.parl.gc.ca/content/LOP/ResearchPublications/prb0710-e.pdf>

Peck, J., N. Theodore, and N. Brenner. 2009. "Postneoliberalism and its Malcontents." *Antipode* 41s1 (January).

Peck, Jamie, and Adam Tickell. 2002. "Neoliberalizing Space." *Antipode* 34, 3 (July).

Pelaez, Carlos M., and Carlos A. Pelaez. *International Financial Architecture.* Hampshire: Macmillan.

Petras, James, and Henry Veltmeyer. 2001. *Globalization Unmasked: Imperialism in the 21st Century.* London: Zed Books.

Petrou, Michael. 2009. "The End of Democracy?" *Macleans* March 3. <2.macleans.ca/2009/03/03/the-end-of-democracy/>

Phillips, Stephen. 2000. "The Demise of University: The Politics of Federal Income Security in Canada, 1978–1993." Paper presented at the Annual Meeting of the Canadian Political Science Association, Montreal. May.

Pierre, Jon. 1995. "The Marketization of the State." In B. Guy Peters and Donald J. Savoie (eds.), 1995. *Governance in a Changing Environment.* Montreal: McGill-Queen's University Press.

Pitelis, Christos. 1992. "Toward a Neo-classical Theory of Institutional Failure." *Journal of Economic Studies* 19, 1

Porter, Tony. 2006. "The North American Free Trade Agreement." In Richard Stubbs and Geoffrey R.D. Underwood (eds.), *Political Economy and the Changing Global Order,* third edition. Toronto: Oxford University Press.

Porter, Tony, and Michael Webb. 2008. "Role of the OECD in the Orchestration of Global Knowledge Networks." In Riane Mahon and Stephen McBride (eds.), *The OECD and Transnational Governance.* Vancouver: UBC Press.

Prince, Michael J. 1999. "From Health and Welfare to Stealth and Welfare: Federal Social Policy, 1980–2000. In Leslie A. Pal (ed.), *How Ottawa Spends 1999–2000.* Toronto: Oxford University Press.

Putnam, Robert D. 2000. *Bowling Alone: The Collapse and Revival of American Community.* New York: Simon and Schuster.

Rachlis, Michael. 2004. *Prescription for Excellence.* Toronto: Harper Collins.

Rachlis, M., R. Evans, and P. Lewis. 2001. *Revitalizing Medicare.* Vancouver: Tommy Douglas Research Institute.

RBC (Royal Bank of Canada). 2010. "U.S. Daily Economic Update." RBC Economics Research. <rbc.com/economics/market/daily_us.html>

Reguly, Eric. 2010. "France Balks at Austerity." *Globe and Mail.* June 10. <heglobeandmail.com/report-on-business/economy/france-balks-at-austerity/article1599810/>

Resnick, Phillip. 1989. "The Ideology of Neo-Conservatism." In H.B. McCullough (ed.), *Political Ideologies and Political Philosophies.* Toronto: Thompson Educational Publishing.

Reuters. 2010. "UK at Risk of Double-Dip, Fiscal Cuts Should Wait — BCC." May 30. <in.reuters.com/article/idINIndia-48908920100530>

_____. 2009. "Factbox: Fiscal Stimulus in G20 Countries." March 27, 2009. <reuters.com/article/idU.S.TRE52Q53A20090327>

Richardson, Jack. 1992. "Free Trade: Why Did it Happen?" *Canadian Review of Sociology and Anthropology* 29, 3 (August).

Roach, Kent. 2003. *September 11: Consequences for Canada*. Montreal: McGill-Queen's University Press.

Robinson, Ian. 1995. "Trade Policy, Globalization and the Future of Canadian Federalism." In Francois Rocher and Miriam Smith (eds.), *New Trends in Canadian Federalism*. Peterborough: Broadview Press.

Roese, Neal J. 2002. "Canadians' Shrinking Trust in Government: Causes and Consequences." In Neil Nevitte, (ed.), *Value Change and Governance in Canada*. Toronto: University of Toronto Press.

Romanow, Roy J. 2002. *Building on Values: The Future of Health Care in Canada*. Saskatoon: Privy Council, Commission on the Future of Health Care in Canada.

Rothstein, B., and E. Uslaner.2005. "All for All: Equality, Corruption and Social Trust." *World Politics* 58, 1 (October)

Ruggeri, G.C. 1987. *The Canadian Economy: Problems and Policies*, third edition. Toronto: Gage.

Russell, Bob. 2000. "From the Workhouse to Workfare: The Welfare State and Shifting Policy Terrains." In Mike Burke, Colin Moores, and John Shields (eds.), *Restructuring and Resistance: Canadian Public Policy in an Age of Global Capitalism*. Halifax: Fernwood.

_____. 1991. "The Welfare State and the Politics of Constraint." In B. Singh Bolaria (ed.), *Social Issues and Contradictions in Canadian Society*. Toronto: Harcourt Brace Jovanovich.

Russell, Frances. 2009. "'You Can Fool Some of the People...' Conservatives Exploit Canadians' Political Misconceptions." ccpa *Monitor* (March).

Russell, Peter, and Lorne Sossin (eds.). 2009. *Parliamentary Democracy in Crisis*. Toronto: University of Toronto Press.

Safarian, A.E. 1974. *Canadian Federalism and Economic Integration*. Ottawa: Privy Council Office.

Samuelson, Paul. 1983. "Sympathy from the Other Cambridge." *The Economist* June 25.

Sauvé, Roger. 2001. "The Current State of Canadian Family Finances — 2000 Report." Ottawa: Vanier Institute of the Family.

Savage, Stephen P., and Lynton Robins (eds.). 1990. Public Policy Under Thatcher. London: Macmillan.

Savoie, Donald J. 1999. *Governing from the Centre: The Concentration of Power in Canadian Politics*. Toronto: University of Toronto Press.

_____. 1995. "Globalization, Nation States and the Civil Service." In B. Guy Peters and Donald J. Savoie (eds.), *Governance in a Changing Environment*. Montreal: McGill-Queen's University Press.

Sawyer, Malcom. 2004. "The nairu, Labour Market 'Flexibility', and Full-Employment." In Jim Stanford and Leah Vosko (eds.), *Challenging the Market: The Struggle to Regulate Work and Income*. Montreal: McGill-Queen's University Press.

_____ (ed.). 1985. *The Legacy of Michal Kalecki*. Basingstoke: Macmillan.

Schmidt, Ingo. 2010. "Greece: Driven into Crisis." *The Bullet* 345 (April 27). <social-istproject.ca/bullet/345.php>

Schwanen, Daniel. 2000. "Happy Birthday, ait!" *Policy Options* (July–August).

Scoffield, Heather. 2010. "Ottawa Rejects imf Bank Tax Recommendations, Shows Flavour of Summit to Come." *The Canadian Press* April 21. <http://thetyee.ca/CanadianPress/2010/04/21/G20-Flaherty/>

Sears, Allan. 1999. "The 'Lean' State and Restructuring: Towards a Theoretical Account." *Studies in Political Economy* 59 (Summer).

Seidenstat, Paul (ed.). 1999. *Contracting Out Government Services*. Westport: Praeger.

Shalal-Esa, Andrea. 2008. "Factbox: Top Ten U.S. Bank Failures." Reuters. September 25. <reuters.com/article/idU.S.TRE48P0YC20080926>

Sharpe, Andrew, and Jean-Francois Arsenault. 2009. "Living Standards." Institute of Wellbeing. June 10. <ciw.ca/en/TheCanadianIndexOfWellbeing/DomainsOfWellbeing/LivingStandards/FullReport.aspx>

Shields, John. 1990. "Democracy Versus Leviathon: The State, Democracy and Neoconservatism." *Journal of History and Politics* 9.

Shields, John, and B. Mitchell Evans. 1998. *Shrinking the State*. Halifax: Fernwood.

Simeon, Richard. 1991. "Globalization and the Canadian Nation-State." In G. Bruce Doern and Bryne B. Purchase (eds.), *Canada at Risk? Canadian Public Policy in the 1990s*. Toronto: CD Howe Institute.

Simeon, Richard, and Mary Janigan (eds.). 1991. *Toolkits and Building Blocks: Constructing a New Canada*. Toronto: CD Howe Institute.

Simeon, Richard, and Ian Robinson. 1990. *State, Society, and the Development of Canadian Federalism*. Toronto: University of Toronto Press.

Sinclair, Scott. 2010. *Negotiating from Weakness: Canada-EU Trade Treaty Threatens Canadian Purchasing Policies and Public Services*. Ottawa: Canadian Centre for Policy Alternatives.

Smiley, Donald. 1975. "Canada and the Quest for a National Policy." *Canadian Journal of Political Science* 8, 1 (March).

Smith, Patrick J. 2005. "Anti-Terrorism and Rights in Canada: Policy Discourse on the 'Delicate Balance'." In Alexander Netherton, Allen Seager, and Karl Froschauer (eds.), *In/Security: Canada in the Post-9/11 World*. Burnaby: Centre for Canadian Studies at Simon Fraser University.

Socialist Register. 2011. "The Crisis This Time." 47.

Sorkin, Andrew Ross. 2008. "JP Morgan Pays $2 a Share for Bears Stearns." *New York Times* March 17. <nytimes.com/2008/03/17/business/17bear.html>

Stanford, Jim. 2004. "Paul Martin, the Deficit, and the Debt: Taking Another Look." In Todd Scarth (ed.), *Hell and High Water: An Assessment of Paul Martin's Record and Implications for the Future*. Ottawa: Canadian Centre for Policy Alternatives.

_____. 1999. "Waiting for 'It': The Mechanics of Financial Boom and Bust." In Brian K. Maclean (ed.), *Out of Control: Canada in an Unstable Financial World*. Toronto and Ottawa: Lorimer and the Canadian Centre for Policy Alternatives.

Statistics Canada. 2005. "Study: Trends in Income Inequality in Canada from an International Perspective." *The Daily*. February 10. <statcan.gc.ca/daily-quotidien/050210/dq050210c-eng.htm>

_____. 2003. "Sources of Workplace Stress." *The Daily*. June 25. <statcan.gc.ca/daily-quotidien/030625/dq030625c-eng.htm>

_____. 2000. "The Non-Profit Sector: Publicly Available Data Resources." *The Daily*. June 12. <statcan.gc.ca/daily-quotidien/000612/dq000612e-eng.htm>

Stewart, Heather. 2008. "IMF Says US Crisis Is 'Largest Financial Shock Since Great Depression'." *The Guardian*. April 9. <guardian.co.uk/business/2008/apr/09/useconomy.subprimecrisis>

Stewart, Ian A. 1991. "How Much Government Is Good Government?" In G. Bruce

Doern and Bryne B. Purchase (eds.), *Canada at Risk? Canadian Public Policy in the 1990s*. Toronto: CD Howe Institute.

Struthers, James. 1983. *No Fault of Their Own: Unemployment and the Canadian Welfare State, 1914–1941*. Toronto: University of Toronto Press.

Stubbs, Richard, and Austina Reed.2006. "Introduction: Regionalization and Globalization." In Richard Stubbs and Geoffrey R.D. Underwood (eds.), *Political Economy and the Changing Global Order*, third edition. Toronto: Oxford University Press.

Sydney Morning Herald. 2009. "IMF Head Says Worst of Recession Over." September 17. <smh.com.au/business/world-business/imf-head-says-worst-of-recession-over-20090917-fs06.html>

Tabb, William K. 1999. *Reconstructing Political Economy*. London: Routledge.

TD Bank Financial Group. 2009. "The Coming Era of Fiscal Restraint." October 20. <d.com/economics/special/db1009_fiscal.pdf>

Teeple, Gary. 2004. *The Riddle of Human Rights*. Aurora: Garamond Press.

Ternowetsky, Gordon W. 1987. "Controlling the Deficit and a Private Sector Led Recovery: Contemporary Themes of the Welfare State." In Jacqueline Ismael (ed.), *The Canadian Welfare State: Evolution and Transition*. Edmonton: University of Alberta Press.

Tett, Gillian, David Wighton, and Krishna Guha. 2007. "'Super Fund' Helps Ease Markets." *Financial Times*. October 15.

Toronto Star. 2009. "$9.5B for GM 'Regrettable but Necessary,' Says PM." June 1. <thestar.com/Business/article/643639>

Travers, James. 2009. "Witnessing a Democracy's Decline." *Toronto Star* April 21. <thestar.com/article/621607>

Turcotte, Andre. 2005. "Different Strokes: Why Young Canadian Don't Vote." *Electoral Insight* 7, 1 (January).

UK Financial Services Authority. 2009. *The Turner Review: A Regulatory Response to the Global Banking Crisis*. March. <http://www.fsa.gov.uk/pubs/other/turner_review.pdf>

UK Treasury. 2009. "UK White Paper on Reforming Financial Markets." July 9. <http://www.mofo.com/files/uploads/Images/090709UK_White_Paper.pdf>

US Treasury. 2009. *Financial Regulatory Reform: A New Foundation*. <http://www.treasury.gov/initiatives/wsr/Documents/FinalReport_web.pdf>

Uslaner, E. 2002. *The Moral Foundations of Trust*. Cambridge: Cambridge University Press.

Valpy, Michael. 2009. "The 'Crisis': A Narrative." In Peter Russell and Lorne Sossin (eds.), *Parliamentary Democracy in Crisis*. Toronto: University of Toronto Press.

Van Alphen, Tony, and Rob Ferguson. 2010. "Canadian Government to Sell Part of GM Stake." *Toronto Star*, November 4.

Van Praet, Nicolas, and Paul Vieira. 2008. "GM Shares Drop to 60-Year Low." *Financial Post*. November 10. <financialpost.com/story.html?id=947652>

Vancouver Sun. 2010. "Canada Extends Stimulus Program Timeline to October 2011." December 2. <vancouversun.com/news/Canada+extends+stimulus+program+timeline+October+2011/3918124/story.html>

Vieira, Paul, and Eoin Callan. 2008. "Canada Set to Fight Europe over Financial Cure." *Financial Post* November 5.

Waddell, Christopher. 2010. "The Auto Industry Bailout: Industrial Policy or Job-Saving Social Policy?" In G. Bruce Doern and Christopher Stoney (eds.), *How Ottawa Spends 2010–2011: Recession, Realignment, and the New Deficit Era*. Montreal: McGill-Queen's University Press.

Wade, R., and F. Veneroso. 1998. "The Asian Crisis: The High Debt Model versus the Wall Street-Treasury-IMF Complex." *New Left Review* 228 (March–April).

Wallace, Bruce, Seth Klein, and Marge Reitsma-Street. 2006. *Denied Assistance: Closing the Front Door on Welfare in BC*. Vancouver: Canadian Centre for Policy Alternatives.

Weiss, Linda. 1997. "Globalization and the Myth of the Powerless State." *New Left Review* 225 (September–October).

Whiteside, Heather. 2009. "Canada's Health Care 'Crisis': Accumulation by Dispossession and the Neoliberal Fix." *Studies in Political Economy* 84 (Autumn).

Whittington, Les. 2009. "Deal Close on 'Buy USA' — with Strings." *Toronto Star* December 4. <thestar.com/mobile/news/canada/article/734439--deal-close-on-buy-usa-with-strings-attached>

Wilkinson, Richard, and Kate Pickett. 2010. *The Spirit Level: Why Equality Is Better for Everyone*. London: Penguin.

Wilson, Michael H. 1984. *Economic and Fiscal Restraint*. Ottawa: Department of Finance.

Wolfe, David. 1985. "The Politics of the Deficit." In G. Bruce Doern (Research Coordinator), *The Politics of Economic Policy: Royal Commission on the Economic Union and Development Prospects for Canada* Volume 40. Toronto: University of Toronto Press.

_____. 1984. "The Rise and Demise of the Keynesian Era in Canada: Economic Policy, 1930–1982." In M. Cross and G. Kealey (eds.), *Readings in Canadian Social History*. Toronto: McClelland and Stewart.

Woods, H.D. 1973. *Labour Policy in Canada*, second edition. Toronto: Macmillan.

Yalnizyan, Armine. 1998. *The Growing Gap: A Report on Growing Inequality Between the Rich and the Poor in Canada*. Toronto: Centre for Social Justice.

INDEX

A

accumulation by dispossession, 30, 31, 61–63, 91
Afghan detainees, 92–93, 105
aggregate demand, 20, 25, 35–39, 45, 81, 85
Agreement on Internal Trade (AIT), 72, 77–78
anti-globalization protests, 92, 100
Anti-terrorism Act, 99
anti-terrorism and civil liberties, 92, 99
APEC (Asia-Pacific Economic Cooperation), 100
Arab oil embargo, 47
Arar, Maher, 92–93, 99
Argentina, 2, 18
Asia-Pacific Economic Cooperation (APEC), 100
austerity, neoliberal, 7, 17, 83, 88–91, 98, 106, 112–123, 126n
    and social malaise, 122–123
    expenditure restraint, 59–60, 83, 116

B

bailouts
    automotive industry, 1, 7, 14–16, 118
    Canadian Mortgage and Housing Corporation, 10, 11, 13
    financial institutions, 1, 6–7
    repayment, 90
    social structure of accumulation, 117
    socialization of private debts, 114
    sovereign debt, 116
    taxpayer funded, 126n
balanced budget policy, 12, 52, 54, 59, 69, 87–88, 90, 108, 116, 126n
Bank for International Settlements (BIS), 2
Bank of Canada
    financial crisis in the 1970s, 84
    financial crisis in the 1990s, 86
    financial crisis of 2007, 6, 13

price stability, 87
Bank of England, 6
Bank of Japan, 4
bank tax, 7, 13, 17, 110, 120, 126n
Basel Committee on Banking Supervision, 120
bilateralism with the United States, 10, 14–16, 86, 108–109
Brenner, Robert, 25–27, 30, 85
Bretton Woods system, 22, 53, 54, 82
British North American Act, 46
bubble economies, 27, 31, 119
Business Council on National Issues (BCNI), 48, 58, 77, 85, 87

C

Canada Assistance Plan (CAP), 43, 46, 64
Canada Health Act, 43, 67, 69
Canada Health and Social Transfer (CHST), 64, 68
Canada Pension Plan, 46
Canada-U.S. Free Trade Agreement (FTA), 17, 77, 86, 109
Canada-U.S. Government Procurement Agreement, 86
Canadian financial crises
    in the 1980s, 83–86
    in the 1990s, 86–90
    in 2007, 10–17, 90–91, 120
    in the postwar era, 47–50, 80–83
capital accumulation
    Keynesian welfare state, 33, 37, 39
    under neoliberal thought, 83, 85, 122
    theories of capitalist crises, 19, 21, 22, 26, 28, 29, 30, 33
civil liberties, erosion of, 92–93, 94, 98–101, 112
class compromise, 21, 39, 50
coalition crisis, 2008
    constitutional crisis, 11, 102, 105
    governor general, violation of constitutional principles, 103–104

Liberal-NDP coalition government, 102
parliamentary democracy violated, 102
prorogue, use of in Harper government, 102–106
collective bargaining rights, 22, 25, 37, 39, 40, 44–45
Commission on the Economic Union and Development Prospects for Canada. *see* Macdonald Commission
Comprehensive Economic and Trade Agreement (CETA), 109
consensus
    Keynesian, 47, 49, 50, 52
    neoliberal, 58, 76
Conservative federal governments
    Harper government, 11, 13, 15, 52, 59, 102–106, 110, 120
    Mulroney government, 52
constitutional changes, impact on provincial autonomy, 87
contracting out, 61, 62–63, 66, 69, 76
courts, impact of free trade on, 73, 79, 89
credit rating agencies and sovereign debt, 118
Criminal Code, 101
crisis prone, capitalism as inherently, 18–19, 29, 31, 33, 79–80, 90–91

D
deficit reduction policy
    in Canada, 53, 59–60, 64, 82, 84, 86, 88, 91, 110
    cause of more debt, 55, 60, 83–84
    international context of, 117–121
deregulation, 3, 11, 19, 22, 54, 82, 89–90, 91, 94, 95
democratic deficit, 95–98
democratic malaise
    apathetic citizenry, 95, 97, 98, 108
    electoral system, knowledge deficit of the, 97–98, 101–106
    erosion of civil liberties, 92–93, 94, 98–101, 112
    knowledge deficit, 101–106
    lack of national autonomy, 108–111
    media and knowledge deficit, 102–105, 110

neoliberal inequalities as a cause of, 94–95, 106–108
    political causes of democratic malaise, 98, 111
    symptoms of, 96–98
    voter turnout low, 92, 95–98, 102, 126n

E
East Asia
    as an emerging market economy, 23, 26, 27, 31
    financial crisis in, 2, 18
Economic Outlook, 2010, 114–121
Economist Intelligence Unit, 92, 93–94
    Index of Democracy, 92
education, 8, 40, 46, 47, 64, 81
EI (employment insurance), 70–71, 72
Emergency Financing Framework, 10, 13
employment insurance, 70–71, 72
employment policy
    employment insurance, 70–71, 72
    full employment, 25, 36–38, 38, 39, 40–43, 48, 50, 53
    neoliberal dismantling of full employment, 48, 50, 53, 79–83
    training, 8, 9, 10, 42, 43, 70
    workfare, 65, 124n
equilibrium model of economics, 18–19, 36, 39, 82
erosion of civil liberties, 92–93, 94, 98–101, 112
European Central Bank, 4, 116
European Commission, European Union, 118
European Monetary Union, 119
European Union (EU), 14, 21, 77, 109, 116, 118, 119

F
family-community social structure of accumulation (FCSSA), 124n
Federal Deposit Insurance Corporation, 5
federal system, impact of free trade on, 76–77, 87, 89
financial crises in Canada
    in the 1980s, 83–86
    in the 1990s, 86–90
    in 2007, 10–17, 90–91, 120

postwar era, 47–50, 80–83
financial crisis (2007-10)
    auto, 7, 15, 118
    banks and financial institutions, 1-7
    bailouts, 1–2, 6–7, 11, 13–16, 90, 114,
        116–118, 120, 126n
    Canadian minimalism, 10–17, 90–91,
        120
    exit strategies from stimulus spend-
        ing, 114–121, 126n
    Germany, 5, 6, 9–10, 115, 119, 120
    international financial architecture,
        2–4, 5–6, 13, 17, 18
    Ireland, 7, 94, 116
    Greece, 116, 117–118, 119
    France, 5, 94, 104, 116, 120
    Portugal, 94, 116, 118
    Russia, 2, 18
    Turkey, 2
    United Kingdom, 1, 2, 6, 8, 92, 94
    monetary policy, 6, 119
    return to austerity, 7, 17, 90–91,
        112–121, 126n
    subprime lending markets, 1, 3–5, 9,
        10–11, 16, 124n
Financial Stability Board (FSB), 6
financialization, 27, 31, 83, 91, 119
fiscal policy, 37, 41, 58, 60, 82, 84, 86, 88
Flaherty, Jim, Minister of Finance, 11–12,
    13, 120
Fordist regime, 24, 25, 40
free trade, 22, 52–58, 81, 85–89, 108–109
    see also specific trade agreements
frictional unemployment, 36
Friedman, Milton, 19
full employment
    and Keynesianism, 25, 36, 38, 39,
        40–43, 48, 50, 53
    labour market policy, 36–38, 48
    neoliberal dismantling of, 48, 50, 53,
        79–83

G
G-7, 2, 3, 5, 7, 91
G-8, 91, 92, 100, 115
G-20
    erosion of civil liberties, 92, 100–101
    exit from stimulus strategies, 115,
        120–121

international finance architecture, 5,
    7, 13, 17, 90
G-30, 124n
General Agreement on Tariffs and Trade
    (GATT), 77, 85
General Agreement on Trade in Services
    (GATS), 67, 75
global recession, 1, 9, 90, 113
    see also neoliberal financial crises in
        Canada
globalization
    health care, 66–69
    national political institutions, 72–79
    neoliberalism and, 17, 39, 52–53,
        55–57, 81, 82, 117
    as a paradigm, 122
    recession in the 1980s, 85
    recession in the 1990s, 86, 89
    social malaise, 113
    see also individual trade agreements
government procurement and free trade,
    14, 77, 78, 86, 91, 109–110
Gramlich, Edward, Federal Reserve
    Governor, 4
Great Depression, 121
    Keynesian responses to, 36, 54, 121
    neoclassical interpretation of, 19
    as part of historical pattern of crisis,
        18, 80
Great Recession, 7, 14, 16, 33, 114
Green Energy Act, 110
Greenspan, Alan, Federal Reserve Chair, 3
Guantanamo Bay, 92–93

H
Harvey, David, 28–31, 34, 50, 114
health care
    under the Keynesian welfare state, 40,
        43
    under neoliberal government, 8, 52,
        66–69, 79, 125n

I
IFA. see international financial architec-
    ture
IMF. see International Monetary Fund
income distribution
    and Keynesian policy, 24–25, 38–43,
        46–47

and neoliberal policy, 54, 56, 64–69,
71, 84, 105–108
incrementalism and policy implementation
Keynesian policy, 32, 34, 41–43
neoliberal policy, 52, 54, 63, 79, 82,
84, 86
inequality, neoliberal, 65–66, 83, 94–96,
106–108, 124n
inequality and lack of trust, 94–95
inflation
Keynesian crisis and, 20, 25, 38, 48
neoliberal responses to, 52–55, 69,
80, 81–84, 86, 88, 106
institutions, and theories of capitalist
crisis, 21–24, 26, 28, 29–30
institutions, neoliberal political
courts, 73, 79, 89
federal system, 76–77, 87, 89
parliamentary system, 73–75, 79
public administration, 63, 75–76
interest rates, 37
Keynesian critique, 36, 36–37, 37
neoliberal economic policy, 1, 3, 5,
53, 55, 60, 84, 86
neoliberal inflationary control, 55,
60, 84, 86
and subprime markets, 1, 3, 5
International Accounting Standards
Board, 2
International Civil Liberties Monitoring
Group (ICLMG), 99
international economic agreements and
national autonomy, 55, 57, 72–79,
86, 121
see also specific trade agreements
international financial architecture, 2–4,
5, 13, 17, 18, 120
International Monetary Fund, 5, 114, 115
assistance for sovereign debt, 113,
117
international financial architecture
reform, 2, 13, 120

K
Keynes, John Maynard, 36
Keynesian policy paradigm, 32–33, 36–38,
41, 45
Keynesian postwar era, 20–26, 32–35,

38–39, 40–46, 52–53, 66, 80–81
Keynesian theory of crisis, 36–39, 40–47
Keynesian welfare state, development of
crisis in the, 47–50, 80–83
Keynesian-style stimulus, 1, 2, 6
Canada, 11–12
exit strategies from, 114–121, 126n
Germany, 9–10
as insufficient, 16, 19, 113
United Kingdom, 7
United States, 7, 14
Khadr, Omar, 92, 93, 99
knowledge deficit, 101–106
Kondratieff cycle, 20

L
labour market policy
in Germany, 9
Keynesianism theory and, 36–38
neoliberal policies in Canada, 15,
69–72
neoliberal theory and, 82
OECD Jobs Study (1994), 69
in U.K., 8–9
see also employment policy; unemployment policy
labour-capital relations, 19, 22, 25, 34, 39,
40, 44–45, 79
legitimization and capitalism, 38, 50, 81,
83, 97
Liberal federal governments
Chrétien government, 52, 59
Martin government, 59, 64
long downturn, 19, 25–27
long wave theories of capitalist crises
long downturn, 19, 25–27
regulation theory, 19, 20, 23–25, 27,
30, 31, 33
see also social structure of accumulation

M
Macdonald Commission, 49, 50, 58, 85,
87
Marx, Karl, 19, 30, 61
Marxist overaccumulation, 19, 30
see also social structure of accumula-
tion approach
McNally, David, 30–31

Medical Care Act, 46
Mexico
    international trade agreements, 15,
        86, 109
    neoliberal financial crises, 2, 18
Minister of Reconstruction's White Paper
    on Employment Income, end of era,
    64
monetary policy, 37, 39, 55, 60, 81–82, 84,
    86, 119
mortgage-backed securities. *see* subprime
    lending markets

N
NAFTA. *see* North American Free Trade
    Agreement
national autonomy, lack of
    democratic malaise, 108–111
    international economic agreements,
        55, 57, 72–79, 86, 121
National Council of Welfare (NCW), 65
neoclassical economic theory, 18–19, 33,
    36, 54, 62, 70
neoliberal financial crises
    in Canada, 83–91
    conditions for change, 121–123
    International Financial Architecture,
        2–4, 5, 13, 17, 18, 120
    overaccumulation and spatio-tempo-
        ral fixes, 28–31
    see also financial crisis of 2007
neoliberal policies in Canada
    economic policies, 10–17, 83–91, 120
    labour market policy, 69–72
    policy tools, 58–63
    social policy, 63–69
neoliberal policy paradigm, 48–55, 76, 79,
    81, 83, 89, 98
neoliberalism, conditions for change, 121,
    122, 123
neoliberalism, future of, 112–114,
    121–123
neoliberalism as a political project, 52, 81
non-accelerating inflation rate of unem-
    ployment (NAIRU), 69, 82
North American Free Trade Agreement
    (NAFTA), 17, 55, 58, 78, 86, 87,
    108–109
    Canadian institutions, 66–67, 73,

74–75, 77
    procurement provisions, 14, 91

O
OECD Jobs Study (1994), 70, 71, 125n
Organisation for Economic Cooperation
    and Development (OECD), role of
    the, 74
Organization of Petroleum Exporting
    Countries (OPEC), 47
overaccumulation and spatio-temporal
    fixes, 28–31, 33, 34

P
parliamentary system, impact of free trade
    on, 73–75, 79
Patriot Act, 99
Pax Americana, 22
P.C. 1003, order-in- council, 44, 45
policy paradigms, 31–34, 35
    change, 112, 121–122
    Keynesianism, 32–33, 36–38, 41, 45
    neoliberalism, 48–55, 76, 79, 81, 83,
        89, 98
postwar era, 20–26, 32–35, 38–39, 40–46,
    52–53, 66, 80–81
privatization, 11, 19, 22, 30, 58, 89–90,
    91, 109
    as accumulation by dispossession,
        60–63
    as cause of social malaise, 95
    Crown corporations, 61
    in health care, 66–68
    progressive forms of, 81
    in public administration, 75
procurement liberalization, 14, 77, 78, 86,
    91, 109–110
provincial governments
    budgets of austerity, 116, 126n
    cost-shared programs, 43, 46, 65–69
    impact of constitutional change on,
        87
    impact of free trade on, 14, 58, 72–78
public administration, impact of free
    trade on, 63, 75–76
public choice theory, 62, 98, 108
public debt repayment, 15, 17, 90
Public Safety Act, 99
public-private partnerships (P3s), 61,

62–63, 69, 109–110
Build-Own Operate-Transfer
    (BOOT), 62, 125n
Design-Build-Finance-Operate
    (DBFO), 62, 125n
Design-Build-Operate (DBO), 62

Q
Quebec City Summit of the Americas, 100

R
regressive taxation, 89
    tax cuts, 8, 9, 12, 37, 69, 82, 116
    tax expenditures, 60, 84, 89
regulation theory, 19, 20, 23–25, 27, 30,
    31, 33
Report on Social Security in Canada, 42
right to strike, 11, 44–45
roll-back policies, neoliberal, 22, 53, 58,
    79, 80, 89, 99
roll-out policies, neoliberal, 8, 53, 58, 79,
    89

S
Savings and Restructuring Act, 108
Schumpeter, Joseph, 20, 23
September 11, 99
short economic cycles vs. long wave
    cycles, 23
social assistance, 43, 46, 65
social contract, 39–40, 44
social structure of accumulation approach
    (SSA), 20–23, 33, 34
    compared to Brenner's 'long down-
    turn', 26
    compared to overaccumulation
    theory, 28, 29, 30
    compared to regulation theory, 24, 25
    Keynesianism, 50, 51, 52
    neoliberalism, 83, 87, 117
    theories of capitalist crises, 19
sovereign debt crisis, 116–119
stagflation, 18, 20, 25, 48, 52, 54, 80, 89
stagnation, 19–21, 26–29, 52, 86
Standard & Poors (S&P), 1, 5, 118
stimulus spending. see Keynesian-style
    stimulus
subprime lending markets, 16, 124n
    Canada's response to the, 10–11

Germany, 9
United States, 1, 3–5

T
tax cuts, 8, 9, 12, 37, 69, 82, 116
tax expenditures, 60, 84, 89
Thatcher administration, 89
The Economics of Global Turbulence, 26
theories of capitalist crises
    long waves, 19, 20–28, 30, 31, 33
    neoclassical theory, 18–19, 36
    overaccumulation and spatio-tempo-
    ral fixes, 28–31, 33
toxic financial assets, 1, 7, 10, 16
Trade, Investment, and Labour Mobility
    Agreement (TILMA), 72, 77–78
trade panels undermining national au-
    tonomy, 73, 75, 77, 78, 79
Trade Policy Review Mechanism (TPRM),
    74
training programs, labour, 8, 9, 10, 42,
    43, 70
Troubled Asset Relief Program, 7
trust, political, 94, 95, 97–98, 108

U
U.N. peacekeeping, Canadian involve-
    ment, 108
unemployment
    2007 financial crisis, 8, 9, 10
    during the Great Depression, 35, 36
    Keynesian approach, 41, 42, 44, 46
    during Keynesian crisis, 47–48
    neoliberal approach, 63–64, 69–72,
    81–84
    statistics, 26, 86, 106
Unemployment Insurance Act, 42
Unemployment Insurance (UI)
    during 2007 financial crisis, 8
    Keynesian welfare state, 41, 42, 46,
    70, 82
    neoliberal policies, 63, 71
unions, 19, 37, 44–45, 82
United Nations
    target levels for overseas assistance,
    108
United States
    bilateralism with the, 10, 14, 14–16,
    86, 108–109

financial crisis of 2007, 1–8, 14–16,
     115, 121
Uruguay round, GATT, 73
U.S. Federal Reserve, 3, 4
U.S. Presidential Administrations
     Reagan administration, 89
     Obama administration, 7, 15, 115,
     121
U.S. Securities and Exchange
     Commission, 3–4

V
Vancouver summit, 100
voluntary unemployment, 36

W
Wagner Act, 44
War Measures Act, 98
welfare state
     Keynesian management demand and
     the, 22, 25, 35–37, 39–44, 46–49
     neoliberal dismantling of the, 63–64,
     76, 89, 94, 119
White Paper on Employment and Income,
     41
workfare programs, 65, 124n
World Bank, 2, 113
World Trade Organization (WTO)
     precludes national control, 55, 58, 67,
     73–75, 77, 87, 91
     and procurement liberalization, 14,
     110